Living with History /
Making Social Change

GERDA LERNER

Living with History /
Making Social Change

The University of North Carolina Press

CHAPEL HILL

$10 ♯$

*This volume was published
with the assistance of the
Greensboro Women's
Fund of the University
of North Carolina Press.*

*Founding Contributors:
Linda Arnold Carlisle,
Sally Schindel Cone,
Anne Faircloth,
Bonnie McElveen Hunter,
Linda Bullard Jennings,
Janice J. Kerley (in honor of
Margaret Supplee Smith),
Nancy Rouzer May, and
Betty Hughes Nichols.*

Set in Bembo
by Tseng Information Systems, Inc.
Manufactured in the United States
of America

The paper in this book meets the guidelines
for permanence and durability of the Committee
on Production Guidelines for Book Longevity
of the Council on Library Resources.

The University of North Carolina Press has been a
member of the Green Press Initiative since 2003.

Library of Congress Cataloging-in-Publication Data

Lerner, Gerda, 1920–
Living with history / making social change /
Gerda Lerner.
p. cm.
Includes bibliographical references and index.
ISBN 978-0-8078-3293-6 (cloth : alk. paper)
1. Lerner, Gerda, 1920– 2. Women—History—Study
and teaching (Higher)—United States. 3. Women
college teachers—United States. 4. Feminism and
higher education—United States. 5. Social change—
United States. I. Title.
HQ1410.L378 2009
305.4071'1073—dc22

2008043129

13 12 11 10 09   5 4 3 2 1

Contents

Note on Style

The terms of reference by which African Americans have referred to themselves have changed over the course of history. I have followed the practice of using the designation chosen by the author or by the group in question during a particular historical period (thus: "Negro women's club movement," but "Black Liberation"). According to the same principle I refer to the nineteenth-century "woman's rights movement" and to the twentieth-century "women's rights movement."

African Americans have struggled for over a hundred years to have the term used to designate them capitalized, as are the designations for other ethnic or racial groups (Italian, Spanish, Caucasian). Thus, whenever the noun "Black" is used as a substitute for "African American" or "Negro," it should be spelled with a capital "B." There is some confusion about the spelling of the adjective "black." One can reason both ways—"Black women and Italian women," both designating group adherence, or "black and white women," both designating skin color. I capitalize the noun and lowercase the adjective, but I recognize this is a term in transition.

I also capitalize "Women's History" when it is an academic field, just as I would capitalize English, Physics, Math. When it refers to a specific case ("women's history differs from that of men," or, "we study the history of women"), it is lowercased.

In English, capitalization has always been used to indicate high or honorific status. When dealing with long-neglected subject groups, the choice of spelling cannot be arbitrary or accidental. It must reflect the historical context, even if it questions traditional usage.

Living with History /
Making Social Change

Introduction

At this time, when I look back on my life and my work, I see patterns and connections that were not so clearly visible at an earlier stage of my life. The impact of outside political and social events that I experienced in childhood and as a teenager shaped my connection to history: I was a victim of terror and persecution; my life was deeply affected by historical events. As a witness to terrible events, I early learned that history matters. On the other side, a childhood in which artistic creativity and expression were cherished and in which learning was considered not only a practical means of career building, but a means of finding equilibrium and meaning in life well equipped me for survival as a refugee. The life of learning and thinking would always be connected for me with teaching others and with finding a way of applying what I knew to the problems in society.

This book combines essays written over a period of several decades that touch upon the highlights of my practical work as a teacher and as an agent of social change in and out of the academy, and others, recently written, that focus on some of my main concerns as a historian and a political thinker. In this book I want to show how thought and action have been connected in my life; how the life I had led before I became an academic affected the questions I asked as a historian; how the social struggles in which I engaged as an academic woman informed my thinking. I want to explain how a decision to change the content of historical scholarship and knowledge so as to give women just representation became a challenge to develop new teaching methods and to create alternate models of academic discourse. I want to trace how feminist teaching led to the development of "outreach" projects that influenced a large number of people, far beyond the reach of the academy.

Social change is made by strategic analysis and by consistent and continuous organizational work. An adequate strategic analysis—that is, one that can be proven successful by pragmatic application—needs to be based on deep analysis that takes many factors into consideration, and on an understanding of what can be learned from historical precedent. It relies on the building of coalitions and it encourages a lifelong commitment to social action in its participants.

Growing up under a fascist government as a young girl, I wanted to change the world. Antifascism was real to me, a ray of hope in a hopeless environment—it meant democracy, free elections, equal rights for all citizens, freedom of thought. During a short stay in a Nazi jail, from which at the time I had no hope of ever escaping, I learned from my cell mates that political action meant working with others. One could not survive alone.

Later, in America, as an unskilled immigrant worker, I learned firsthand what it meant to be poor and without a support network. I had lived my childhood and adolescence in middle-class comfort; now I was on my own in a labor market in which women were restricted to only the most undesirable jobs. I worked as a domestic, as an office worker, as a salesgirl, and, after a year of training, as a medical technician—always at minimum wages and without job security. During job searches and on the job I experienced discrimination against women—pervasive, sometimes subtle, often open. At times it was mixed with other forms of discrimination. I applied for a job as a switchboard operator at the New York Telephone company. I never made it past the first interviewer. "We don't hire Jewish girls," she informed me. "Why?" "Their arms are too short to reach the switches." That was a new one . . .

Jobs were offered in gendered listings—jobs for men, jobs for women. All required previous experience. If you did not have that, you could not get an interview. If you claimed it, you had to provide written references. If you admitted to being an immigrant, you were not considered fit for an interview. It took four months of such hopeless job searches for me to learn that lying was essential. I got my first paid job by lying about my ethnicity, my religion, and my experience and by providing fake references. My employers were Jewish refugees from Vienna, like myself, only they were rich and I was poor. I was required to wear spike-heel shoes and stand on them forty-eight hours a week (sitting down was not allowed), in order to provide an elegant and glamorous look to their 5th Avenue store. With my feet painful and damaged for life, I learned that gender mattered. After a year of working for these employers, I reported them anonymously to the Department of Labor for paying below minimum wages to their factory workers, all of whom were Jewish refugees from Europe. Anonymous or not, I immediately got fired, without a reference. Thus, I learned about class the hard way, and I have never forgotten it. When I became an academic, it was natural for me to consider class and gender as categories of analysis in all my work.

During two decades as a mother, housewife, writer, and community organizer I gained much practical wisdom that would later influence my academic practice and thought. When I organized neighborhood women for child care centers and better public schools, I learned that I could accomplish nothing by myself. It took a neighborhood organization to get a stop light in front of the public school. It took years of patient, small-scale organizational work before a corrupt and authoritarian school principal could be restrained from running his school like a private enclave, in which elementary school children were treated as recruits in an Army boot camp.

When, in the 1950s, I worked in support of United Nations' activities in a neighborhood PTA, in which it was considered "un-American" to urge that, together with candy, donations to UNICEF be collected at Halloween, I learned that I needed to make the work of UNICEF concrete and comprehensible as a neighborhood welfare effort on a larger scale. Abstractions, moral principles, and high-sounding resolutions would not convince my working-class neighbors.

In that period, with Communist witch-hunting and the blacklisting of "subversives" a national pastime, it was still possible to win support for blacklisted individuals by inviting them to present their work, their music, their films at a house-gathering. People might not be ready to fight the system of blacklisting, but they would respond to an individual in need. Also, the display of courage needed to organize such a gathering could make the invited guests question their own actions and, perhaps, serve as a model.

The women who organized peace committees in Queens, New York, during the Korean War exercised similar courage, persistence, and vision. The vision was the firm conviction that small, local organizing efforts would, in the long range, influence policy and lead to social change. In my decades as a historian I was able to confirm that vision as an actual organizing principle for several generations of women reformers.

When, living in an integrated neighborhood, I worked with black women in progressive women's organizations fighting for housing and school integration and for racial justice, I learned to appreciate their effectiveness, their leadership, and their strength. I saw mothers who combined paid work and family obligations and yet found time for neighborhood activism. Their style and culture was different from that of their white neighbors, but their long-range commitment to lifelong activism was unquestioned, grounded in self-help necessity. Having myself been victimized by racist oppression, I felt close to them and shared their long-range vision of a better future. Without these practical experiences of organizing and living with black women I would never have undertaken my research and work on black women's history.

In 1967, all the experts, white and black, assured me that trying to do a book on the history of black women in America was a useless undertaking. Unfortunately, most black women had been illiterate and thus left no records, I was told by a leading historian of African American History. Tragically, due to their oppressed condition they had not been able to make major contributions to American life and culture. And so on.

But I had worked with black women and seen what they could do. I found it inconceivable that they had not so acted in the past. And, in my researches on the antislavery movement, I had found numerous sources on black women activists. My life experience, contradicting conventional academic wisdom, convinced me to edit and publish in 1972 *Black Women in White America: A Documentary History*, the first collection of historical primary sources by and about black women.[1] I continued to do scholarly work in that field and am happy to say that the field of Black Women's History is today well established and generally recognized.

These and my experiences as a radical, the wife of a blacklisted film editor and the friend of many blacklisted people in Hollywood and in New York, shaped my mind and thought prior to my embarking on an academic career.

I trace, in rather broad strokes, my intellectual development from adolescence on in Chapter 1 of this book. I intend this chapter to serve as a framework for the rest of the book. In that chapter I deal with the development of my feminist thought only as it relates to particular books I have written. I intend, in this book, to deal more fully with the development of my historical thinking as it related to women's history and to let the various chapters illuminate certain steps along the way, steps taken either in practical or in theoretical work.

My earliest approach to dealing with women in history was, like that of most of the early practitioners, compensatory. What had women done, experienced, thought in the past? And how did their actions contribute to history? While I already questioned the male focus and male bias of traditional history, I then still thought that simply filling in the forgotten stories about women would be a large enough challenge and would of itself rectify the distortions of past historiography. About a decade after doing and teaching "complementary and contribution history," the shortcomings of this approach became clear to me and to other Women's History scholars. We understood by then that women's actions in their own right and women's work in association with other women changed the discourse and the course of history in ways not well understood previously. How did women's separate organizations affect the historical outcome? Did women have a separate culture, different from that of men? For me, these questions became urgent during the early years of teaching in the Graduate Program in Women's History at Sarah Lawrence College (see Chapter 3). Team-teaching with anthropologists and literary scholars made me aware of the complexities of defining women's status and position in society and, at the same time, be sensitive to the way women's consciousness of self and their dependency on familial interaction and demands were pulling them in different directions. How did women negotiate this complex terrain? Under what circumstances did they find the courage and necessary strength to put self-interest over familial responsibilities? How did they compromise between the two? The three-volume *Notable American Women*, a compendium of 1,359 biographies, offered one answer to these questions.[2] It showed that most women who were active in behalf of women's issues up to the 1930s chose not to have families and that those who did began their organizational work after having raised families.

In the first decade of doing Women's History I became more and more intrigued with basic questions: How to define women as a group. How did this group differ from other oppressed groups in history? What are the historical preconditions for the formation of feminist movements? My daily work in carrying graduate education in Women's History forward forced me to improvise answers or to take educated guesses and finally impelled me to focus my theoretical work on answering these basic questions. Chapters 4–8 deal with specific problems in that quest for theory.

Organizationally, the 1970s were a period of intense activity for women historians. We were preoccupied with winning equity for women in academic institutions and professions and in establishing a new field of inquiry, Women's Studies. In each of the specialized academic fields we challenged the omission of women and worked toward getting women-focused courses into the curriculum. Activity erupted spontaneously on every level of the educational establishment; advances in one area inspired and influenced struggles in another. In this work, some of what I had learned in my past as a community activist served me well.

In Chapter 2 I describe the way women historians changed the profession and the professional organizations. I trace the decades of effort by women historians to gain equal access to career ladders, to win equity in compensation and career advancement, and to raise awareness about the pervasive sexism in academic institutions. We needed to break the isolation of women in the academy and convince them that their individual grievances were not their own fault, nor were they personal matters — they were built on historic foundations of exclusion and discrimination against women. We built networks of support among graduate students, junior faculty, and women established in academic positions, many of them administrators. As we advanced concrete demands — open hiring procedures, equal pay, no sexual harassment on the job — we began to trust in each other and to experience that women could and would help each other. This simple insight was an enormous step forward for many of us, who had always assumed that we were dependent on the help of men to advance our careers.

The organizational struggles I describe in this chapter took place over four decades and involved not only the two major history societies, the American Historical Association (AHA) and the Organization of American Historians (OAH), but many smaller and regional groups. The Coordinating Committee of Women in the Historical Profession (CCWHP) was founded in 1969 by seventeen historians, but nearly a hundred attended our first public meeting. Today there are twenty-one regional or local Women's History groups affiliated with the organization. The status of women in the historical profession has certainly improved, and we have made great gains in salary equity and career development. The most visible and dramatic gains have been the institution of a democratic, open, and unbiased hiring process, which has benefited men as well as women and minorities; democratization of the electoral process for organizational leadership; and equal access to program and other committees as well as equal representation of women in all functions of the organizations. As the chapter explains, these achievements were not easily won. The goal of economic equity for women was advanced, but is, as yet, far from fully achieved.

I wrote Chapters 2 and 3 not only as part of my autobiography, but in order to set down a historical record. I used not only my memories and those of other participants, but ample documentation as well. The transformation of academic disciplines by and through the efforts of women academics was widespread and encompassed all aspects of academic life. It has proceeded at an uneven pace—for example, in the sciences, issues women historians fought for decades ago are still embattled and controversial. I believe that women's struggles for equal access and for equity in the professions profoundly altered academic institutions. They not only led to practical and institutional changes, but also profoundly affected the content of education.

The promotion of Women's History as a respected subject matter and as a core part of any curriculum has always been my central concern. The struggle for that transformation is still ongoing and incomplete.

In Chapter 3 I describe the development and growth of the Sarah Lawrence College Graduate Program in Women's History. I deal with it largely in a descriptive manner, again, in order to establish a historical record. Yet this program, the first of its kind, was a pioneering effort, whose impact was felt far beyond the small group of students we were able to train. It was here that I was challenged to answer basic theoretical questions about the nature of Women's History and here that I learned and helped to develop a feminist pedagogy. The constant organizational and theoretical outreach of this program to the general population provided our theoretical work with a solid foundation. We not only asserted and taught that women's thought could be grounded in women's own experience; we actually practiced it and constantly learned in the process.

I experienced the transformative power of women learning about their own history not only in seminars and workshops, but in the several summer institutes I organized at Sarah Lawrence College. Becoming aware that women had a history, that they had not only contributed to, but vitally shaped culture and social institutions, imbued women with new self-confidence and with a strong urge to do likewise. The political dynamic and resourcefulness of the women's movement of the '70s and '80s inspired many of our students, and many came to graduate study already committed to feminist goals. But many others neither were feminists nor wished to become such. What studying Women's History did for them was to give them a long-range perspective and to teach them how women of the past had solved their problems. They could learn about doing coalition work in the present by studying the nineteenth-century woman's suffrage movement and by analyzing its strategy and tactics. They could learn how to test theoretical formulations on the past experience of women, and in so doing, they could learn to value their own experience as a testing ground for future action.

I learned from my students that changing institutions not only meant curbing obvious abuses that led to discrimination, but that it also meant experimenting and modeling other forms of educational structures. In creating and maintaining graduate programs in Women's History at Sarah Lawrence and at the University of Wisconsin–Madison, I had to unlearn much of my previous reliance on established academic structures and conventions. Students insisted on helping to shape the programs and on taking their own initiatives to change institutional practices. Adjusting to these changes did not come easily to me, but I learned. And as I became more open to student involvement in administration, I was pleasantly surprised by the sense of responsibility and the good judgment of the students, and I came to admire their organizational skills. I became looser and less directive, both in my teaching and administrative style, which was all to the good for my personal human development.

As a writer and a historian I have learned to stand aside as an outside observer who can and must encompass more than one viewpoint, more than one consciousness. I have learned the benefits of looking at events from a long-range perspective, of seeking multicausal explanations for events and of exploring patterns and recurring themes. My fascination with recurring themes has often led me far afield, both in my research and in my teaching. In trying to understand the world my students and I live in I have sought for connections to events of the past, to long-range causes, and to the effects of decisions made centuries ago that limit the choices citizens can make in the present. It is difficult to understand the major problems in the history of women without references to the distant past. The institutions and customs that affect the lives of men have undergone many changes over the centuries. By contrast, women's primary role as unpaid providers of domestic services and as the nurturers and rearers of children has hardly changed over the centuries. The educational disadvantaging and deprivation of women spans several millennia and has changed only relatively recently. The control of women's sexuality by men and male-dominated institutions began 4,000 years ago and remains in force in much of the world, although somewhat changed in form. Why were women, of all groups oppressed in society, so slow in coming to a consciousness of their own situation and in organizing to remedy it?

The oppression of women being the oldest form of oppression, it became incorporated in the ideologies, myths, religions, and philosophies of Western civilization and thus was perceived as natural and God-given, something that could not be resisted. Since the subordination of women was assumed to be natural in all explanatory systems, a new conceptual framework was needed in order to properly understand the past of women and conceptualize an alternative future to patriarchy. I spent the next decades trying to define such a conceptual framework in personal discussions with other feminist scholars and in my writings, first in articles, then in my two major works. In *The Creation of Patriarchy* I historicized the long process of the institution of patriarchy as the dominant form of social organization and offered a multicausal explanation for its establishment.[3] I then spent nine years researching the development of women's thought about their own situation and set down my findings in *The Creation of Feminist Consciousness: From the Middle Ages to 1870*.[4] Part of the answer is that individual women did resist patriarchy for far longer than has been recognized in historical studies and that women's organized feminist efforts were often trivialized, misinterpreted, and misunderstood. And much of what women actually did and accomplished was forgotten and lost to history.

In 1994 I was invited to write an article in *Dissent* magazine about the meaning of the Seneca Falls convention. It appears in this book as Chapter 4. In it I sought to point out the neglect of women's historical agency as compared to historical turning points initiated by men, such as the foundation of Marxist theory and practice and the French Revolution.

In Chapter 5 this theme is examined based on a large oral history research project I initiated and directed at the University of Wisconsin between 1988 and 1992. It encompassed twenty-two interviews with Midwestern women who had played leading roles in organizing the modern women's movement. Their important contributions to the growth of that movement had not been recorded or recognized and might have been lost to history were it not for this project. In a like manner, the history of the first fifty years of the nineteenth-century woman's movement omitted

the significant contributions of many women, among them black abolitionists, who had differed with Elizabeth Cady Stanton in later years, and
were therefore ignored or mentioned only briefly in Stanton and Susan B.
Anthony's foundational sourcebook, *History of Woman Suffrage*.[5] These
omissions distorted later interpretations of that movement and could not
be corrected until twentieth-century Women's History scholarship offered
a corrective. Those who control the sources often control the judgment of
history.

This is an obvious, but not a trivial matter. In U.S. historiography, as
in American popular culture, historians have tended to over-emphasize
the role of the individual in history. Great men are identified as founders
and leaders; they become the virtual representatives of the movement:
William Lloyd Garrison for abolition, Eugene Debs for the socialist movement, Martin Luther King Jr. for the civil rights movement. In fact, no
mass movement of any significance is carried forward by and dependent
upon one leader, or one symbol. There are always leaders of subgroups, of
local and regional organizations, competing leaders representing differing viewpoints, and, of course, the ground troops of anonymous activists.
And, as can be shown in each of the above cases, emphasis on the "great
man" omits women, minorities, many of the actual agents of social change.
In so doing it gives a partial, an erroneous picture of how social change
was actually achieved in the past and thereby fosters apathy and confusion
about how social change can be made in the present.

As was to be expected, the same distorted historiography would be applied to the nineteenth-century woman suffrage movement. By elevating
Stanton and Anthony to the great and unique leaders of the movement;
by omitting Lucy Stone and most of the New England activists; by downplaying the role of radicals like Frances Wright, Ernestine Rose, and labor
movement activists; and by disregarding the parallel struggles of African
American women for suffrage and equal rights the movement's breadth
and depth were lost and the complexities of its tactics were obscured.

It is ironic to observe the same pattern of omission and distortion in regard to the twentieth-century feminist movement. In historical accounts,
in the media, and in popular culture the emergence of the movement is
credited to Betty Friedan's book, *The Feminine Mystique*, and her leadership
of the mainstream movement, with the more radical sections of the movement described as the product of discontented young women coming out
of the civil rights and the student movements. While these descriptions

are true, they are not sufficient. They have led to endlessly repeated stereotypes of the modern feminist as being unmarried, white, middle-class, and living in a big urban center. While I do not wish to diminish the importance of Betty Friedan's work, nor the creative energy of the young women coming out of the civil rights movement, I want to argue that up to now we have insufficiently realized the breadth and depth of the movement and the contributions to it made by other groups of women, such as those represented in the Midwestern leaders oral history project. Chapter 5 demonstrates one case of such omissions.

In Chapters 6 and 7 I deal with problems of teaching. Chapter 6 offers some general strategies by which women's history can be added to textbooks that are entirely androcentric and organized in traditional ways. I developed the analytical questions I use in this chapter in the 1970s. Textbook editors and traditional historians, wanting to add "women" to the textbooks, thought in terms of whom to add and whom to omit. I was often approached with such attitudes by publishers and teachers. I encountered the same question when I was asked to contribute a "brief entry" on the Grimké sisters to various encyclopedias. My first response usually was to ask how many women they had already included. The numbers were pitiful and did not even amount to respectable tokenism. When I declined to contribute unless there were a representative number of important U.S. women added to the work, I was challenged to say which men should be omitted to make such a new balance possible. Such discussions, over a number of years, convinced me that merely adding a few women here and there, even though this was a necessary first step, would not do justice to the major challenge women's history represented to the profession. It was necessary to question the conceptual framework whereby decisions of selection were made. As long as military and political issues were considered by historians to be more important than the lives of people and of communities, the activities of men would always emerge in the narrative as more significant than those of women. What was needed was to rethink the criteria by which encyclopedias and survey textbooks were organized, so as not to perpetuate exclusionary categories.

In the 1970s I was asked to write a pamphlet on Women's History for the AHA. I sent a questionnaire to thirty teachers of the subject and asked them to share their best strategies and approaches. I also asked for their suggestions on what to include in such a pamphlet. The answers were generous and very interesting and enabled me to base the pamphlet on a consensus of practitioners, rather than just on my own experience. Still, I concluded that the field could not be developed quickly and effectively unless teachers would challenge the traditional mode of selecting what was deemed historically important and what was deemed trivial. I developed some simple analytical questions that would accomplish this purpose. I got very positive feedback from teachers about the AHA pamphlet, which became the best-selling pamphlet published by the organization. Nearly a decade later, when I was invited to speak to historians on the topic of the inclusion of women into courses on World History, I decided to use the same analytical questions I had developed for U.S. Women's History to promote discussion and a new conceptualization of the subject. Chapter 6 is based on that lecture.

When I undertook to study the past of women I did not know that I would have to learn more than several advanced academic degrees could encompass. I would have to learn to think in opposition; to free myself from patriarchal thought and constraints; to learn to withstand ridicule, contempt, and obstinate resistance.

As a citizen I have always striven to be an agent for social change and to carry my values and intellectual insights into practical applications. I believe that there is a constant, fruitful interaction between theory and practice. The art of it is to be conscious of that interaction and flow with it, rather than resist it. Teaching is one arena for such creative exchange. The obvious danger and one of which one must constantly be aware is indoctrination. As an agent of social change one believes passionately and wants to share one's experiences with others. This must be resisted, since that would be an abuse of the privileged position and power one holds as a teacher. I believe that I should teach my students ways of obtaining information, ways of evaluating and selecting such information, and let them experiment themselves with how to use such information for practical purposes. It is not my job as a teacher to use myself as a model for imitation. It is my job to demystify knowledge and to teach students how to evaluate what they are taught in light of their own experience, not of mine. Part of demystifying knowledge is the teacher's obligation to expose her own biases and allow students fully to contradict and oppose her without fear of ridicule or intimidation.

I taught students how to do "graduate reading"—a skill designed to extract all necessary knowledge out of any book in an hour. I taught them how to take notes from lectures, articles, or books, using no more than a

4 x 6 card, which involves the skill of analyzing essentials out of a flood of detail. To teach such useful skills meant to demystify the hidden structure in all written arguments and to help students discover the hidden structure in all explanatory schemes. I taught students how to lose their fear of tests by making them practice how to create tests out of a given field or topic. They would then discover that there are only a limited number of test and essay questions that can be constructed and that, in fact, it is possible to anticipate a great number of them in preparation for a test.

I have never before summarized all these practices, but as I do it I discern a clear underlying theme: teach students to understand the structure of intellectual product and of institutions and allow them to acquire a sense of mastery in doing so.

In Chapter 7 I present in outline form a workshop I have taught to diverse groups on several continents. It represents the essence of my theoretical work on the social construction of deviant out-groups, distilled into a few simple principles. I approach the construction of deviant groups, the process of "othering" various target groups for the purpose of exploiting them and turning them into scapegoats, as a necessary aspect of maintaining hierarchical social systems. Rather than focusing on various forms of discrimination—sexism, racism, ethnic hatred, anti-Semitism, homophobia—as aberrations in otherwise well-functioning social systems, I look on them as one technique with an infinite variety of arbitrary targets designed to keep oppressive systems in power. In analyzing the ways in which the creation of deviant out-groups reinforces oppressive power, I show how such processes can be interrupted and defused.

Of necessity the format of Chapter 7 is different from that of other chapters. It consists of my outline—the analytic concept underlying the workshop. The course syllabus and an outline of psychological exercises designed to connect students emotionally to what is being discussed appear in Appendixes B and C. By representing these basic ingredients of the workshop I hope to enable other teachers to use it as it is or to adapt it to their own purposes.

The reflections in Chapter 8 were generated by a large body of my written work and by decades of teaching on the subject. I have written a scholarly biography and a short biography of my mother, two autobiographies, and a partially autobiographical novel. In several oral history projects I learned about the strengths and weaknesses of personal interviews as historical biography. I taught several graduate seminars entitled "Biography and Autobiography as History and Literature," in which I compared various genres of telling the stories of individuals in history in an effort to find out if any one of them comes closer to the historical truth than do the others. How can any of these genres be used as sources for the historian? Which of these genres best transmits a story of the past to present-day readers?

Researchers in women's history often have to depend on autobiographical writings—diaries, letters, memoirs, and fiction—to piece together the life stories of women of the past. In Chapter 8 I discuss the reliability of such sources and the problems connected with their use. Self-descriptive narratives of women abound in omissions and disguises. These are means that allow women to break out of their gender-defined roles to assert the dignity and value of their own lives. Attention to the ways in which women's autobiographical writings differ from those of men can help in the interpretation of women's sources. The answers to the questions I discuss in this chapter are not only of theoretical interest, but should also have value for the practicing historian and scholar.

A subset of autobiographies and biographies concerns women who had special friendships with other women prior to the period when lesbian relationships were publicly defined. Carroll Smith-Rosenberg's essay, "The Female World of Love and Ritual: Relations between Women in Nineteenth Century America," had long defined the discourse and also limited it.[6] Smith-Rosenberg had argued that single-sex friendships among women were accepted by society in the nineteenth century and were not considered marks of deviance. Were modern historians justified in defining such friendships as lesbian relationships? Were they reading modern interpretations into the past record? The subject was mostly discussed and written about by lesbian historians, while heterosexual historians, coming upon ample evidence of such special relationships, gingerly danced around them. Among the many prominent nineteenth-century women who had lifelong stable relationships with other women, which involved shared home-making, shared finances, and often shared organizational responsibilities, were Jane Addams, Frances Willard, and M. Carey Thomas. What kind of "evidence" did one need to define the relationship as lesbian? Were such relationships lesbian if one could not prove sexual aspects? Heterosexual authors often chose to ignore such relationships or to refer to them simply as "friendships," allowing the reader to draw her/his own conclusions.

I urged historians to report honestly on what their sources told them about these relationships, without necessarily being able to report on how the participants or their contemporaries defined such relationships. It is obvious that U.S. society regarded such female friendships differently in different historical periods and that such social definitions must have exerted an influence on the women living in the past. We must distinguish between the lived reality, the consciousness and self-definitions of participants, and the societal definitions of normalcy or deviance attached to such relationships. Late nineteenth-century social reformers, such as Henry George, Frances Willard, and Edward Bellamy, could refer to themselves as Socialists or Christian Socialists without incurring societal censure. After the political struggles and the fierce witchhunts against Socialists in the 1920s, this designation carried the connotation of deviance and even of treason. Just so did societal definitions of female friendships change over time.

I argue in my essay that the biographer must recreate the life and times of a subject from within the subject's own consciousness and from the context of her time. Homoerotic or homosexual relationship must be treated forthrightly and be given the same respectful consideration that would be given to heterosexual relationships.

Chapter 9 reproduces my acceptance speech on the occasion of my receiving the Bruce Catton Prize of the Society of American Historians in 2002. This speech allowed me to focus on the problems of history writing, a topic in which I have long been deeply interested. The way in which graduate training in history often works to train students in bad writing has long concerned me. Most historians either think it is not their job to teach students writing skills or feel unqualified to do so. Graduate training in proper documentation and footnoting, as it is usually offered, makes students anxious and induces them to overly qualify their statements and generalizations. The emphasis is on producing well-documented essays, extensively footnoted, in which opinions and conclusions are carefully separated from documentation and proof. Dissertations are treated as though they were an assemblage of separate essays. Very seldom is there any emphasis on telling a story, and even rarer is the concept that a book is a whole. The very assumption, shared by mentors and publishers, that a dissertation needs to be "reworked" in order to make a book reveals the way in which the separation of good writing and historical writing is institutionalized.

I believe proper graduate training should encourage a merging of both skills. I have tried to teach my students to think of a dissertation as a book. I stress that conceiving the work as a whole is a strategy that keeps the writer focused and inspired. I emphasize that throughout the process of working on a dissertation they should make a distinction between the historian's and the writer's work. Both need to be done; one disciplines the other. I encourage students to draft their last chapter first and state their hypothetical conclusions before they have worked out all the proof. This has the advantage of making them conscious of the book as an entirety and it energizes them, as they struggle through the more pedantic work of laying out their proof. Arguing for and displaying the proof has to be done carefully and with rigorous attention to verification. If, as the student goes through this phase, the proof in some way contradicts the previously written conclusions, these should be altered and adjusted to what can be proven.

Once a first draft of argument and proof, as laid out in successive chapters, is written, students enter a new phase, the writer's phase of the process. This consists of several successive readings of the manuscript, each focused on a separate editing problem: structure, style, grammar. Only after that prolonged editing process should they deal with checking and verifying the footnotes.

By integrating instruction in writing in my history teaching I have helped students to cut the time they spend on dissertation-writing and to produce publishable books. My Catton award speech allowed me to summarize my thinking on this subject, to reflect on my teaching practice, and to give needed emphasis to an important aspect of the historian's work.

In Chapter 10 I look at the present state of Women's History, assess its accomplishments in the past forty years, and project its possible future. As one of the founders of this field, I have often been asked in interviews and after lectures to address such questions. As director of two graduate programs in Women's History I have been challenged to justify students' investment of time, effort, and considerable expense in training in this new field. Is Women's History not simply a fad, inspired by feminist politics, and would it not vanish after a short spurt of interest? I had to take such questions seriously, especially when they came from college and university administrators who used me as a consultant, when they were considering starting or upgrading their Women's History programs. I answered those questions with as much hard evidence as I could muster, and I wrote several articles on the topic. The last of these was based on my survey of three years of scholarly work (1998–2000), 817 items in all, as cited in eight issues of the *Journal of American History* under their "Current Scholarship" bibliography.[7]

In Chapter 10 I reiterate my basic belief that the development of Women's History as a field is a serious, highly significant, and irreversible stage in intellectual history. I discuss the major contributions the field has made to historical knowledge and practice and show, on the example of several important recent books, how Women's History scholarship has led to new directions in the general field. The new interest by historians in multicausal, multiracial, and transnational historical narratives points to the emergence of a more holistic approach to telling the stories of the past. I discuss the implications of this trend and welcome it as evidence of the transformative power of Women's History scholarship.

In Chapter 11 I argue that feminism is a practical, political program for the liberation of both women and men and for the creation of a better social order. It is, in fact, the only existing such program which has a likelihood to succeed.

I argue that patriarchy—the alliance of male dominance over resources with militarism and the hierarchical ordering of society—has long outlived its usefulness. It is actually dangerous to the survival of humankind in the twenty-first century. Wars no longer solve national problems and warfare falls most heavily on civilian populations. Rampant consumerism threatens the survival of animal and plant species and the contamination of the atmosphere and the seas through global warming. The increasing gap between the rich and the poor, the power of global corporations, and the predominance of military influence over civilian control of the state, together with rampant global exploitation of labor and resources, makes reform and amelioration very difficult, if not entirely unlikely. Because patriarchal leaders in politics and the military are unable to conceive of different forms of social organization, they are, in effect, a danger to the survival of human civilization.

I do not argue that women are better than men or wiser or kinder. I simply observe that throughout the millennia of patriarchy women as a group have been kept out of major positions of power. They have therefore, like all the oppressed, had to focus on individual and group survival, and develop characteristics that would improve their chances for it. I also argue that women, because they are half of all human beings and are distributed in every group of society, are the only group strategically placed in such a way that they cannot be decimated by violence in the long run. The history of Western civilization abounds with examples of the successful destruction of rebellious or revolutionary groups, such as the Albigensian heretics in the thirteenth century, or the suppression of native peoples by colonial powers. In such cases the liberation movement was destroyed with the bodies of its adherents. But feminism as a movement cannot so be destroyed. It is obviously possible to restrict, confine, and abuse women in a given region or state, as did the Taliban in Afghanistan for a given period of time. But in the long run, women cannot be wiped out that way without bringing about the destruction of the oppressor society.

My belief in feminism as a transformative worldview has meant much to me in my work—it has been a foundation of my thought and has given me the courage and the conviction to continue my work over decades, in the face of obstacles and opposition. I have in recent years lectured frequently on the subject and found audiences surprisingly responsive to my message.

Men and women hunger for a vision, a philosophy that transcends the boundaries of hierarchical social structures, the dog-eat-dog race of unchecked competition and of the outdated polarized systems of ideas that dominate our culture. We all want and need to believe in utopian possibilities. And yet we have had it drummed into our brains that we must be realists and what we think about must be practical. Human beings have a need for something more than practical reforms and the solution of present-day problems. They want and have always wanted a dream of an ideal, a transcendent future that will make the world better for their children than it has been for themselves. The great world religions, the various world philosophies have provided that dream, even if they could not point to its realization. Since the fall of Communism and the socialist vision that sustained it, there seems to be no system of hope-giving ideas available for the future. I believe that feminism is such a system, for women and for men, and I believe that the peaceful transformation of attitudes and customs that feminism has already achieved in the past 150 years attests to its strength and realistic potential.

Chapter 12, "Reflections on Aging," marks a thematic turning point in my work. It was recently written, and it is based on an interview, conducted via email, and printed in an Austrian feminist journal. Doing an

English translation and rewriting it as an article came almost as an after-thought, as I became aware of my own life process of aging. I surprised myself by discovering that I had no need or desire to research the subject, but that I simply wanted to set down my thoughts.

I also wanted to engage intellectually with the challenging life processes that I am now experiencing. Aging is still one of the taboo subjects in our culture; people deal with it in symbols and euphemisms. Advertisements addressed to old people are inevitably illustrated with images of youthful-looking middle-aged people. Despite the fact that the vast majority of the very old are women, the media depict the aged as consisting of cheerful active couples. As I experience the eighth decade of my life, I find little has been written that speaks to my actual experience. I find few models that can help me adjust to the inevitable disturbances and disabilities of very old age.

I find this phase of my life challenging and demanding. I close my book with reflections on it because that is the last task set before me. Up to now, in my life, action was usually motivated by thought; theory led to practice. In this case, the reverse is happening. I'm living the experience and it is forcing me to reflect on it, to think about it, to meet it with awareness. It is a new stage of life that demands its own process and engagement.

Notes

1. Gerda Lerner (ed.), *Black Women in White America: A Documentary History* (New York: Pantheon Books, 1972).

2. Edward T. James, Janet Wilson James, and Paul S. Boyer (eds.), *Notable American Women, 1607–1950: A Biographical Dictionary*, 3 vols. (Cambridge, Mass.: Belknap Press of Harvard University Press, 1971). A fourth volume, with 442 additional biographies, appeared nine years later: Barbara Sicherman and Carol Hurd Green, with Ilene Kantrov and Harriette Walker (eds.), *Notable American Women, the Modern Period: A Biographical Dictionary* (Cambridge, Mass.: Belknap Press of Harvard University Press, 1980).

3. Gerda Lerner, *The Creation of Patriarchy* (New York: Oxford University Press, 1986).

4. Gerda Lerner, *The Creation of Feminist Consciousness: From the Middle Ages to 1870* (New York: Oxford University Press, 1993).

5. Elizabeth Cady Stanton, Susan B. Anthony, and Matilda J. Gage, *History of Woman Suffrage*, 6 vols. (New York: Fowler and Wells, 1881–1922).

6. Carroll Smith-Rosenberg, "The Female World of Love and Ritual: Relations

between Women in Nineteenth Century America," *SIGNS* 1, no. 1 (Autumn 1975): 1–29.

7. Gerda Lerner, "U.S. Women's History: Past, Present, and Future," *Journal of Women's History* 16, no. 4 (2004): 10–27. The items studied consisted of 150 books, 280 dissertations, and 290 articles plus the 97 additional books that were reviewed in those issues of the journal, making a total of 817.

PART I

Redefining the Profession of History

chapter one

A Life of Learning

This essay is based on my Charles Homer Haskins Lecture, presented to the American Council of Learned Societies on May 6, 2005.* Being chosen for this lectureship is a distinct honor, which comes with the obligation common to all honorees to address the assigned topic, "A Life of Learning"—in short, to present an intellectual autobiography. It is a daunting assignment. I would never have volunteered for it, especially not after having recently finished a partial autobiography that carefully avoided discussing my academic life and thought. The honor of this lectureship seduced me, and since the work was done, I think it fitting to open this book with it. It can serve as a framework and background for the essays presented in this volume. I try here to trace the evolution of my thought and the process of my learning, which has always been characterized by close interaction between analysis and application, theory and practice.

My life has been marked by breaks and discontinuities—abrupt fissures; destruction, loss, and new beginnings. I am a survivor of terror and persecution; I have changed cultures and languages, nationality and class. I'm an outsider as a woman, a Jew, an immigrant, and a radical. I have also been a successful insider, an institution-builder and a respected member of my profession. My various transformations have been driven by necessity, imposed by outside events, yet they have been counter-balanced by certain lifelong continuities: my work as a creative writer, my pervasive preoccupation with historical events and the shaping of history, my deep commitment to social action and to responsibility in the public sphere, and my lifelong focus on the condition of women in society. And always I have tried to bridge the gap between theory and practice, between action and thought. I have tried to find the right balance between the life of the mind and what people call "real" life, the life in social context.

Perhaps, what I need to explain in this lecture is how, finally, it all came together.

---

*ACLS Occasional Paper, Gerda Lerner, "A Life of Learning: Charles Haskins Lecture for 2005."

I was born a middle-class Jewish girl in Vienna in 1920. My family always lived in a nest of security surrounded by the vast insecurity of a truncated former empire, repeatedly threatened by invasion and instability. To be born and raised Jewish in a country in which Catholicism was the state religion and anti-Semitism was an honored political tradition meant, from early on, to be branded as different. Jews were set apart, we were not "normal." Fascists and anti-Semites were organized in political parties and, in the years of my growing up, became more and more powerful. Finally, it was not a question of whether they would come to power, but when.

What of the life of the mind? I received mixed messages in the family. My father, a pharmacist, exemplified the virtues of scientific inquiry, of respect for verifiable truths and replicable experiments.

My mother was a sort of feminist, heavily influenced by Ibsen, Scandinavian novelists, and French *avant garde* thinkers. She was a self-defined Bohemian, rebelling against bourgeois standards of propriety, advocating sexual freedom, and experimenting with all kinds of then novel practices, from vegetarianism to Yoga. She was unhappy in her marriage and revolted against the traditional roles of housewife and mother. She fashioned an alternate lifestyle for herself that scandalized her mother-in-law, with whom she lived in a constant state of warfare. My mother was an artist and wanted to focus on that vocation, something she was not fully able to do until the years of emigration, when she was free of familial responsibilities. She had a studio in the city, where she kept a kind of salon for young artists and writers. Despite their marital difficulties, my father helped her artistic development in every way.

The power struggle between my mother and my grandmother and the constant tensions in the home confronted me early with the need to make choices among conflicting loyalties. In my teenage years I sided with my mother and regarded her as a victim of societal restrictions. I saw the world as divided into warring fields; I felt an obligation to choose among them.

In 1934 a violent civil war raged in Austria, and in Vienna virtually at my doorstep. After a week of bloody fighting Austria's democracy was replaced by a clerical-fascist dictatorship. Parliamentary democracy and its parties were outlawed; trade unions were banned and opponents to the new regime were jailed. Supported by the German government, an underground Nazi movement carried out a war of terrorism inside Austria, with the goal of *Anschluss*, the absorption of Austria into Nazi Germany.

In this climate of totalitarianism I learned to dispel my sense of despair and helplessness by exploring the world of ideas in books I found in our library. I read Tolstoy and Maxim Gorky and B. Traven's romantic novels about South American revolutionaries. I made pictures in my mind of prisons, torture, of brave, dedicated fighters for freedom. With school friends I listened to American jazz and discovered Louis Armstrong, Bessie Smith, and Duke Ellington. These cultural impressions and the art films from Russia, France, and Italy to which my mother took me encouraged me toward a more active political involvement.

Still, it took nearly a year before I found the courage to participate, even in the smallest way, in underground activity. In my case this consisted in reading and passing on an underground newspaper and in helping through "Red Aid" a family whose father had been exiled as the result of the 1934 fighting. Even though these actions were relatively insignificant, each carried a six-month to one-year jail sentence with it, in case of discovery. I was full of fear, yet I lost the sense of defeatism that had so oppressed me; I felt myself coming closer to the antifascist movement, that unknown band of political resisters out there in the wider world.

In 1936, my parents arranged for me to spend six weeks in England as part of a student-exchange program. Unfortunately, the suburban family to which I had been assigned turned out to be British fascists and anti-Semites. I managed to leave them and join a Socialist youth encampment in Wales, which was run by J. B. S. Haldane, the eminent biochemist, and his wife, both longtime pacifists, who had recently publicly joined the Communist Party. I succumbed to their charm, their warmth, and the stimulation of their conversation, which seemed to encompass the world. I made friends with an Oxford student who made it his business to convert me to Marxism the proper way, which consisted of my reading the classics, followed by hours of his explicating the finer points to me in true Oxford fashion. I swallowed these new and to me forbidden ideas the way a thirsty person swallows a cool drink. And I got an entirely new view of myself in a community of young people who looked upon me as a bit of a heroine, for having survived youth in a fascist country and having shown some spirit of resistance. I returned from England with increased self-confidence, a stronger commitment to antifascism, and a new interest in Marxist thought.

During my years of adolescent exploration, I also came under the influence of Karl Kraus, the greatest satirist and by many accounts the greatest modern poet in the German language. In his magazine, *Die Fackel* (The

Torch), he mercilessly satirized militarism, bureaucracies, and, above all, the debasement of the German language. I attended his brilliant one-man readings of Shakespeare plays and Offenbach operettas—unforgettable performances. His powerful writing, his poetic force, his dedication to the structure of thought enraptured me. Years later, in making myself into a writer in English, my second language, his reverence for language guided me along the way. I knew I must learn more than vocabulary and syntax; I must learn the different culture expressed in the grammar and poetics of my new language before I could become a writer. I consider myself a Kraus disciple to this day.

While still in Vienna, I was fortunate in attending, for eight years, a private *Realgymnasium* for girls headed by a Jewish woman director and staffed by well-educated, highly motivated women teachers, many of whom held advanced degrees. I loved the rigorous training I received in that school and enjoyed the sense of power I got from learning easily and with enjoyment. My favorite subject, German, was taught by a small, friendly woman, who, as it turned out later, was an avid member of the underground Nazi Party. I learned High and Middle High German from her and studied the ancient ballads in their original. I choose to write an honors thesis on twelve German ballads, representative of the genre's changing styles from the Middle Ages to the present. The fact that I combined literary history and stylistic analysis in this early work foreshadowed my future interests. I managed to complete the essay just a month ahead of the Nazi takeover. That my Nazi teacher judged it excellent and felt it accrued credit to her would later lead her to support me when I was jailed.

My classical *Gymnasium* training compared favorably with the best American high school and junior college education, but the existence of the Americas was barely acknowledged in it. These continents were considered marginal in the ethnocentric definition of humanist knowledge of pre–World War II Austria. Later, when I began to critique the exclusions and omissions of traditional history, I would recall the partial and biased training in history I had received. It was possible in my day to be a European intellectual, excellently trained and credentialed, and yet to be ignorant of the history and culture of several continents.

The Nazi occupation of Austria in March 1938 affected my family directly. Within two weeks my father was informed by a "friendly Nazi" that he was on a list of people to be arrested, and he left the country the same day. He was able to do so because he had five years earlier established a pharmacy in the small principality of Liechtenstein, a tiny neighboring country, and he had regularly gone there on business. His foresight and the fact that he never returned to Vienna saved our entire family by providing us with a place of residence when all the world was closing its borders against Jews. Immediately, it led to two raids of our home by armed Nazis and, a few weeks later, to the arrest of my mother and myself. We were separated from one another, put into a regular city jail, not accused of anything. It later turned out we were being held as hostages for my father, in order to induce him to return.

I did my jail time in a cell with two young political prisoners, who had to look forward to long sentences. They educated me in courage and resourcefulness and when our starvation-level rations were cut in half for me, the Jew, they shared their rations equally with me. They were Socialists and lived by that ethic. I believed that I would never go free and that, if my underground work were discovered, I would end my days in a concentration camp. I learned that fear could be conquered by coming to terms with the worst possibilities and that fighting back, even in the most hopeless situations, would give rise to hope. I obsessively focused on getting out of jail in order to take my *Matura* exam — the final exam without which it was impossible ever to attend a university in Europe. The exam was scheduled for five weeks after my arrest. I wrote petitions on toilet paper, I made a pest of myself with all the guards, I asked to be taken with armed guard for my exam. No response, except the ridicule of the guards. The day after the supposed exam I was taken to a Gestapo interview and learned that all these activities about the *Matura* were in my record, yet I was returned to jail. A week later my mother and I were released and I found out that the exam had been postponed for a week in order to install a Nazi examining board. I went to the exam the next morning and passed it with honors. I also learned that my German teacher and other Nazi teachers had petitioned the Gestapo in my behalf. Since I was the only student in my school to be arrested, they were sure it was a simple mistake.

My mother and I had been released from jail only on condition that we would leave the country forthwith. Then followed three months of police harassment and threats of being jailed again, and the overcoming of systematic bureaucratic obstacles put in our way by the government. Finally, shortly before the infamous *Kristallnacht*, my mother, my younger sister, and I were able to join my father in exile in Liechtenstein.

What did I learn?

Social definitions can turn privileged citizens with rights into outcasts —in fact, by Nazi definition, into vermin that can and should be killed.

Expropriation and the taking away of citizenship accomplish the same end.

One cannot survive alone. In order to survive, one must foster courage, accept help, and help others.

In April 1939 I managed to immigrate into the United States, hoping to bring my family there later. This proved to be impossible, due to U.S. restrictions on immigration. Having experienced the force of politics and power firsthand, I early became a dedicated antifascist. My intellectual encounter with Marxism continued during the years of emigration and my years as an unskilled, underpaid immigrant. Two and a half years after my arrival in the United States I married Carl Lerner, a theater director, who wanted to work in film, and who was a Communist. We moved to Hollywood, where I became involved in radical left wing union politics and, later, in the struggle against the Hollywood blacklist. During my own years as a Communist I was involved mainly in grassroots activities for nuclear disarmament, peace, racial justice, and women's rights. For the next twenty years of my life I would live at the societal bottom level, where sheer survival comes first, action and efforts at organizing come next, and abstract thought is a luxury, a leisure-time indulgence. Still, I continued my uphill struggle as a writer, publishing short stories, a novel, and translations, and working on a musical, and film scripts.

IN THE FALL OF '63 I entered Columbia University. I was forty-three years old; my daughter was in college and my son was in high school. My husband was busy with a successful career as a film-maker and teacher of film. I had shopped around before selecting a graduate school in order to be allowed to do a biography of the Grimké sisters, the only Southern women to become agents and lecturers of the American Anti-Slavery Society, as my dissertation. Columbia was the only place where the department chairman was willing to bend the institutional regulations so as to meet my needs. The topic, on which I had already been working for four years, was approved for my dissertation, even before I had fulfilled my orals requirements. Due to this flexibility, I was able to earn both the M.A. and Ph.D. degrees in three years from the time I entered, while also teaching part-time at the New School and for the final year at Long Island University in Brooklyn.

In a way, my three years of graduate study were the happiest years of my life. It was the first time in my adult life I had time and space for thinking and learning. Greedy for knowledge, the way only people who have long been denied an education can be, I gave up all recreation, social life, and other interests. More than anything else I was driven by an urgency to learn what I needed to know in order to carry out a passionate ambition, which by then had taken concrete shape in my mind.

During the interview at Columbia prior to my admission to the Ph.D. program, I was asked a standard question: Why did I take up the study of history? Without hesitation, I replied that I wanted to put women into history. No, I corrected myself, not put them into history, because they are already in it. I want to complete the work begun by Mary Beard. This announcement was, not surprisingly, greeted by astonishment. Just what did I have in mind? And anyway, what was Women's History? The question set me off into a lengthy explanation, on which I have played variations for the past forty years. I ended in somewhat utopian fashion: "I want Women's History to be legitimate, to be part of every curriculum on every level, and I want people to be able to take Ph.D.s in the subject and not have to say they are doing something else."

As if my age and unusual background did not sufficiently mark me as "different" from other students, I set myself further apart with this little speech, as being opinionated and having grandiose ambitions. But my real difficulty in graduate school was not so much style as substance—I could not accept the content of the curriculum, the worldview I was being taught.

In the twenty-five years since I had left school in Vienna, I had been an unskilled and later semi-skilled worker, a housewife, a mother, a community activist. In all these roles I met an active group of women, who worked quietly and without public recognition, usually without pay and frequently without an awareness of the significance of the work they were doing. Political organizations were influenced by their work, yet no one would ever know of their existence through the writings of historians or through the media.

Now, in one of the best graduate schools in the country I was presented with a history of the past in which women did not seem to exist, except for a few rulers or some who created disturbances. What I was learning in graduate school did not so much leave out continents and their people, as had my Viennese education, as it left out half the human race, women.

I found it impossible to accept such a version of the past as truth. I questioned it in seminars and in private discussions with faculty, and I was quickly made the target of ridicule by my teachers and classmates. Had I been a young woman just out of college, I probably could not have withstood this social pressure. Still, after a while, I made a place for myself and even won the respect of some of the faculty for my specialized knowledge. I learned sometimes from my professors, often against them, and much by trial and error, but always I tested what I was learning against what I already knew from living. What I brought as a person to history was inseparable from my intellectual approach to the subject; I never accepted the need for a separation of theory and practice. My passionate commitment to Women's History was grounded in my life.

Professors Robert Cross and Eric McKitrick, who jointly supervised my dissertation, gave me considerable freedom in interpretation, but insisted on professional competency in documentation, for which I will always be grateful to them. Neither they nor any of my other teachers shared my interest in Women's History. The only exception was visiting professor Carl Degler, who taught a course in U.S. Social History, in which he included a section on women. He had long considered the history of women's reform activities an essential aspect of social history. I learned much from him and greatly appreciated his openness to my interests.

Still, my Columbia teachers provided me with a solid grounding in traditional history and historical method, which sharpened my already ongoing critical discourse with Marxism. I learned by studying specific examples in depth that any explanation that offered only single causes was flawed. Historical events were always multicausal. Marxist dialectics appeared more and more as a straitjacket.

When I graduated in 1966 Professor McKitrick gave me this well-meant advice: "When you go in the job market, don't tell anyone about your exotic speciality. You're a good social historian, let it go at that." I never took that advice and it is perhaps due to that obstreperousness that I owe my career.

Having experienced the best of traditional history training, I also had learned its weak points, its unconsidered omissions, and its unacknowledged assumptions. I thought I knew what needed changing. I had also studied the tactics of African American historians, extending over more than four decades, to legitimize their field of inquiry. This helped me to develop a strategic plan.

At age forty-six, I figured I had twenty years in the profession ahead of me, with luck. I reasoned I would have to have an impact on the academic world in a number of ways in order to make Women's History accepted: by actual research and writing, by proving the existence of sources, by upgrading the status of women in the profession, and by proving that there existed student demand in this subject and moving from there to designing courses and graduate programs. I made this plan in 1966 without knowledge of the spectacular progress that would be made in a short time due to the energy, zeal, and creativity of the women's movement and of Women's Studies. Fortified with my shiny credentials, I decided once and for all to stop defending what I was doing. I would just go ahead and let my work speak for itself.

During my years of independent study of writings about women I had come across Mary Beard's *Woman as Force in History*. Despite the obvious flaws in her work I was struck by the simplicity and truth of her insight that women have always been active and at the center of history. Beard recognized the duality of women's position in society: subordinate, yet central; victimized, yet active. Her greatest contribution is the insight that focusing on the concept of women as victim obscures the true history of women. Women were, and always had been, agents in history. Beard also insisted that the history of women had to reflect the variations in the status of women at any given time according to class. She did not avoid the fact that women have been oppressors as well as oppressed and that class and sex interests have often been in conflict. Reading Mary Beard raised my feminist consciousness. I consider Mary Beard, whom I never met, my principal mentor as a historian.

Essentially, Mary Beard invented the concept of Women's Studies. Her critique of the androcentric academic establishment led her to envision new models for the education of women. I adapted her example to my uses, my own time. Unlike her, I was not willing to choose amateur and marginal status in my profession. I believed that in order to write and research the history of women, historians must have the best of traditional training and practice their craft with rigorous skill, and then they must go beyond it.

For me, working in archives led to a special kind of joy. I had the great good fortune, all during my dissertation research, to be able to work in the finest private collection of women's books then in existence in the United States, the library of Miriam Y. Holden, a member of the National

Women's Party since its inception and a close co-worker of Alice Paul. She had also worked with Mary Beard, Eugenia Leonard, and Elizabeth Schlesinger toward establishing a national Women's History archives. After all their efforts had failed, Miriam Holden responded by systematically collecting printed sources on women, which were housed in her New York East Side brownstone. She abhorred the Dewey decimal system, because it made it unnecessarily difficult to elicit the hidden history of women. In her library she ignored divisions by academic fields and made no separation between books by women and books about women. This library was a protected island in which the activities and thoughts of women were dazzlingly on display front and center. Here I learned that the search for women's history must be interdisciplinary and that nontraditional methods and new questions would be needed to document women's past.

Mary Beard and Miriam Holden represented a direct, personal link to the earlier woman's rights movement for me. They inspired me to seek an alternative to the then normative model of graduate education. In 1969 the ways for graduate students to become professionally known by participating in conference sessions, offering papers or commentary, and getting articles published were deep mysteries found accessible only through a student's male mentors. The absence of women and minority group members in the functions of the learned societies was glaringly obvious. Women were not on the boards of editors of journals; they were not on the boards of professional organizations; they did not appear on the programs of the annual meetings. These conditions began to change only after women in the professional societies started to organize themselves and demand more equal opportunities. The formation of the Coordinating Committee on Women in the Historical Profession (CCWHP), a group co-chaired by Berenice Carroll and myself, at the 1969 American Historical Association convention was soon followed by the formation of Committees on the Status of Women in the major historical societies. (See Chapter 2.) For me, the culmination of that work was my election, in 1982, as the first woman in fifty years to become President of the Organization of American Historians.

In 1972 I established the M.A. Program in Women's History at Sarah Lawrence College. As were so many other of my ventures, this one was beset with difficulties, institutional resistance, and the need to secure outside funding. Still, the twelve years I spent at Sarah Lawrence were exciting intellectually. The foundation course of this program was interdisciplinary and team-taught. We created a teaching model that combined lectures, seminars, tutorials, and presentations by students based on their individual research. (See Chapter 3.)

MY SCHOLARLY WORK and writing developed at the same time that I functioned as an organizer of women historians, an administrator of graduate programs, and a teacher. I came to the study of history through my interest in doing a biography of the Grimké sisters. This work allowed me to combine my newly acquired scholarly skills with those of the writer. The book, *The Grimké Sisters from South Carolina: Rebels Against Slavery*, has had a long life ever since 1967 and has recently been reissued in a revised edition.[1]

During my research for this book I had come across many primary sources on the activities of black women in the antislavery movement. Here was another group whose history had been forgotten, due to their double invisibility as women and as African Americans. At that time this was a subject that had not yet been recognized as a valid field of inquiry. In 1972 I published *Black Women in White America: A Documentary History* with a bibliographic essay that pointed to the vast amount of source material yet to be explored.[2] I am happy to say that the book helped in the development of a new scholarly field, African American Women's History.

My comparative study of women of different races and cultures taught me that no generalization about women as a group could be valid unless differences of class, race, ethnicity were taken into consideration. The fact that I was concerned with these questions long before African American scholars attacked the predominant focus on white women in feminist scholarship derived from my life experience, the years of my living in a racially mixed community and my organizational work with black women. I have retained my interest, both in research and teaching, in the construction of differences and the ways patriarchal power exploits such differences for dominance.

Step by step, through innovations in teaching, through exposure to hitherto hidden primary sources, through organizational experience in the profession, and above all, through close collaboration with other scholars in the field, the outlines of a framework for doing Women's History began to emerge.

In the early stages of the development of the new women's history I tried to create a conceptual framework and theoretical principles for placing women in history. These were published in two collections of articles, *The Majority Finds Its Past* and *Why History Matters*.[3] Later, as I was training Ph.D. students in Women's History at the University of Wisconsin, I became more and more concerned about setting new standards for such training. I developed a "Theories of Feminism" course—essentially a historiography of feminist thought—that became a foundation course for the graduate program. I created a practicum course that enabled students to combine outreach work with their theoretical training. Above all, students needed to learn what analytic questions to ask and how to distinguish important from unimportant questions.

To me, the question of the origin of women's subordination seemed the most important. The traditional patriarchal answer to it was either religious or biological: men and women were inherently different and therefore performed different functions in society. Such explanations supported women's inequality in society by legitimizing it as God-given or natural. Modern feminists, rejecting this view, were offering a variety of explanations, many of them based on Friedrich Engels' *Origin of the Family, Private Property and the State*. It seemed to me important to explore whether an explanation based on valid historical evidence could be found. For me, this project also meant finally coming to terms with my Marxist past.

My commitment to Marxism had held up until the Khrushchev revelations, even as I became more and more disillusioned with Old Left politics. Ever since the late 1950s I believed that Marxist thought was in error in regard to race and ethnicity in its insistence that class subsumed these categories. Marxist thought was also unable to adequately explain or improve the position of women, because it dealt solely with their economic oppression.

As a strong advocate of women's agency in history, I needed to understand why women had, over the centuries, colluded in their own oppression by passing the rules of patriarchy on to their children of both sexes. I wanted also to understand why there had never been women who built important explanatory or philosophical systems.

When I began seriously to undertake a study of the origins of patriarchy, I found myself confronting the psychological obstacles other women before me must have experienced. Who was I to try such a difficult task? How was I qualified for it? My head was full of the great men of the past I would have to argue with, and there were no female guides to help me. To give me courage, I looked at who the major theorists on the subject were — theologians, philosophers, sociologists, and journalists. I discovered that none of them, including Engels, had been academically trained for their task. This encouraged me to go ahead. Since I had a Guggenheim grant for a year, I used the time to give myself a graduate reading course in anthropology and in Ancient Near Eastern studies. Still, throughout the eight years it took me to write *The Creation of Patriarchy* I frequently felt as though I had jumped off a cliff into a raging river.[4]

Engels claimed that the development of private property led to the subordination of women, which he postulated had happened as a historic event, "the world historical defeat of the female sex." His theories were based on ethnographic studies that have since been largely disproven. In my research for my book I found that while Engels had been correct in postulating a connection between the agricultural revolution of the Bronze Age, the rise of militarism, the development of private property, and the rise of the patriarchal family, he had been wrong as to causes, sequence, and historicity. It was not private property that led to sex discrimination and the formation of classes; it was gender oppression — the enslavement of women — that preceded class oppression. Slavery, almost everywhere in the world, was first used against women and children, because men had not yet learned how to subdue captured males to permanent slave service. Captured women were raped and stayed with their children. The invention of slavery as a means of recruiting a labor force taught men how to organize difference — of tribal adherence, of race, of religion — into dominance. Enslaved women and children were the first property. When archaic states were organized, they transformed these property relations into legal structures and the foundation of the state. This development took place over a period of nearly 1,500 years and was not "an over-throw." Patriarchy was instituted with the consent and cooperation of women and was, in fact, at one time a rational institution. By the time science and philosophy were invented in the first millennium BCE, the patriarchal order had already existed for centuries and was taken for granted as being normal and God-ordained. Patriarchy seemed beyond challenge.

What I learned from writing this book shattered the last remnants of my adherence to Marxist thought. It also led me to other questions. How did women survive under patriarchy? How did they resist it? I tried to answer these questions in my book *The Creation of Feminist Consciousness*.[5] Work on this book brought me to a new understanding of the ambiguous role of religion as an institution that fortified the subordination of women by asserting that it was God-given. On the other hand, religion became the location of women's most radical emancipatory assertion, developed over 700 years, namely that God spoke to women and authorized their striving for equality.

Because women were for millennia educationally deprived, they were denied the ability to develop systems of knowledge and to define the content of higher education. The most advanced women thinkers were forced into dialogue with male thinkers, while women thinkers were denied both authority and knowledge of their own history. The implication for the present is that those wanting finally to achieve women's full participation in the intellectual work of humankind need to abolish not only discrimination, but also its long-range consequences in the thinking and socialization of women.

Even though I have spent much of my career attempting to change academic institutions, I have enjoyed the long-deferred benefits of insider status. I could not have written these two books had it not been for the generous support I received from the University of Wisconsin. They supported my founding of a Ph.D. program in Women's History and awarded me two chairs, which gave me time and research assistance for my scholarly work. I am very grateful for this support and for the many foundations that have over the years helped my various projects. I take these as a recognition that the changes for which I worked were perceived as constructive and in line with the best interest of these institutions.

After my retirement from the University of Wisconsin I wrote *Fireweed: A Political Autobiography*.[6] With this work I reclaimed my voice as a writer and attempted to explain to myself and perhaps to others how I became who I am.

Up until quite recently history as a profession has spoken in the voice of exclusion, in which a small elite of trained male intellectuals has interpreted the past in its own image and in its own voice. In the short span of forty years, women scholars have challenged the absurd assumption that one half of humankind should perpetually present its own story of the past as being a universally valid story. All kinds of groups who have been previously denied a past have reclaimed their human heritage. This development has been and is truly a landmark event in world history. We have taken many steps in the direction of democratizing and humanizing the academy. We have shown that the formerly "anonymous" have voices and can tell their stories. We have unearthed formerly ignored sources and have learned new ways of interpretation. We have created networks, organized conferences, initiated over sixty graduate programs in Women's History. It has been a rich experience of sharing knowledge, of inspiring one another, and engaging in sharp and often critical debate. Theory and practice, life and thought have fused.

It has been my great privilege to be part of the most exciting intellectual movement of the twentieth century.

Notes

1. Gerda Lerner, *The Grimké Sisters from South Carolina: Rebels Against Slavery* (Boston: Houghton Mifflin Co., 1967); Gerda Lerner, *The Grimké Sisters from South Carolina: Pioneers for Women's Rights and Abolition*, revised and expanded edition (Chapel Hill: University of North Carolina Press, 2004).

2. Gerda Lerner (ed.), *Black Women in White America: A Documentary History* (New York: Pantheon Books, 1972).

3. Gerda Lerner, *The Majority Finds Its Past: Placing Women in History* (New York: Oxford University Press, 1980; reprint, Chapel Hill: University of North Carolina Press, 2005); Gerda Lerner, *Why History Matters: Life and Thought* (New York: Oxford University Press, 1997).

4. Gerda Lerner, *The Creation of Patriarchy* (New York: Oxford University Press, 1986).

5. Gerda Lerner, *The Creation of Feminist Consciousness: From the Middle Ages to 1870* (New York: Oxford University Press, 1993).

6. Gerda Lerner, *Fireweed: A Political Autobiography* (Philadelphia: Temple University Press, 2002).

chapter two

Women among the Professors of History

THE STORY OF A PROCESS OF TRANSFORMATION

When I entered graduate studies in 1963, women represented a tiny fraction of professional historians. Women entering the profession in middle age were considered "freaks" and were viewed with suspicion. Most of us never saw a woman or a nonwhite professor during our doctoral studies. Isolation, alienation, and a sense of being there on sufferance, always offered with the expectation that we would not measure up and were likely to fail, defined our environment.

I had entered graduate study after several decades of involvement in grassroots organizing and political activism. Thus it seemed natural to me to address these problems organizationally, especially since they were also reflected in the attitudes and environment of the annual conferences of historical societies. Shortly after earning my Ph.D. in 1966 I became active in the Organization of American Historians and later took a leadership role in the formation of the caucus of women historians at the 1969 convention of the American Historical Association. The following essay describes what we did and how we managed to transform the professional societies and with them the career choices for both women and men in our profession. *

As I look back to the beginnings of feminist organization among historians in the late 1960s, I am aware of the fact that I entered the field with an unusual background. I came to academic life as a mature woman, having been a committed political activist since age fifteen. A refugee from Hitler, I had experienced fascism, racism, imprisonment, and persecution. As an immigrant in the United States I worked in typical unskilled women's jobs, from domestic work to file clerk, and it took me years to work my way up to becoming a medical technician. I had long worked with women

* Based on two previously published essays: Gerda Lerner, "Women among the Professors of History: The Story of a Process of Transformation," in Eileen Boris and Nupur Chaudhuri (eds.), *Voices of Women Historians: The Personal, the Political, the Professional*, 1–10 (Indiana University Press: Bloomington and Indianapolis, 1999; Gerda Lerner, "A View from the Women's Side," *Journal of American History* 76, no. 2 (Sept. 1989): 446–56.

in their community organizations, and I knew in my bones that women build communities. But as I entered academic life as a student, I encountered a world of "significant knowledge" in which women seemed not to exist. I never could accept that patriarchal mental construct and resisted it all through my training. My commitment to women's history came out of my life, not out of my head.

I first attended a convention of the Organization of American Historians (OAH) in 1963, the year I entered graduate school at Columbia. It was a discouraging experience: I knew no one there, and there seemed to be no way of getting to know anyone. The group was overwhelmingly male; there were so few women and so very few female graduate students that one noticed each woman in the room. Yet no one seemed to want to be the first one to speak to a stranger. The social highlights of the convention were something called "smokers," organized by various prominent schools. The Columbia smoker, true to its name, took place in a smoky room without chairs, in which men, each carrying the obligatory over-priced drink, milled around trying to connect with others they knew. The few women present usually turned out to be wives. The famous professors were surrounded by a few nervous and eager young men, whom they had chosen from among their graduate students to be introduced to other important professors who might further their careers.

At that time there were no accepted ground rules for hiring and interviews. Most jobs were never advertised, but were announced informally through the old boys' network. When a job opened, a professor from that department would call his friends and contacts in other schools and elicit the names of their favorite and preferred students. The job search then took place privately, at the convention or on campuses, as a sort of competition between the pre-screened chosen few. Less favored students or those whose professors were not well connected in the network simply lost out. Women and minorities tended to be among the losers. At the smokers one could stand in a corner and watch the ballet of eminent professors introducing their favorites to other eminent professors or one could try to stand on the outer rim of a group and catch the professor's eye in hopes of being included. It was a dismal form of social interaction.

I also remember taking a number of lonely meals at these conventions and feeling miserable, until I finally decided to make my own contacts. At first, I just walked up to one or more of the nuns present and asked if I could have lunch or dinner with them. The nuns were always friendly and cheerful, and I made some splendid contacts and lifelong friendships. From this I branched out to introducing myself to other women, but many of them were busy socializing with men they knew and hanging around the important professors. It took several years before I had built up enough contacts so that I would not pass the convention in lonely misery.

I may have been particularly inept socially or, as I then believed, I was enough of a misfit among the Columbia students (too old, a married mother of teenagers, and interested in Women's History) to account for my isolation. In the '60s very few women over forty pursued graduate training. Those who did faced discrimination not only in admission to graduate programs, but especially in access to the informal networks which sustain professional development.

The ways for graduate students to become professionally known, by participating in conference sessions, offering papers or commentary, and getting articles published, were deep mysteries that students found accessible only through their mentors. If one leafs through the programs of the conventions of the major historical professional organizations in the '50s and early '60s, if one looks through their journals, the absence of women as participants and contributors is glaringly obvious. Women were not on the boards and offices of the professional organizations. The same was true for members of minority groups, only their exclusion was closer to total.

All of this changed with the organization of the Coordinating Committee on Women in the Historical Profession (ccwhp) at the 1969 convention of the American Historical Association (aha). Although only seventeen people attended the first meeting, which Berenice Carroll had organized, a public meeting held later during the convention drew a large crowd and generated a list of over one hundred who wished to participate in the new organization. We drew up a statement of purpose, a set of immediate demands, and elected officers: Berenice Carroll and Gerda Lerner, co-chairs; Hilda Smith, treasurer; and a steering committee of five members. An indication of the politics of the group was the sharp debate over what to call the organization. The more radical members wanted it to be called Women's Caucus, while the moderates, among whom I was then counted, wanted to avoid the term because of its radical connotations. I'm afraid I have to admit that I was an advocate of the somewhat klutzy name that resulted and with which we were saddled for decades. In fact, we were a women's caucus and acted as such. In organizing our group we were influenced and encouraged by the formation of women's caucuses in other learned societies, such as the Modern Language Association, the American Sociological Association, and the American Studies Association. In the early 1970s the movements for equity for women in the professional societies and the growth of Women's Studies erupted throughout the academic world; they would lead eventually to a transformation of academic disciplines and to the curtailment of the unchecked male dominance in the structures of higher education. Our efforts in the field of history were a fairly typical case study of how this transformation was accomplished.

The program of CCWHP was threefold: 1) to encourage the recruitment of women into the profession and advance the status of women at all levels; 2) to oppose discrimination against women; and 3) to encourage and develop research and instruction in the field of Women's History. Other specific demands were quickly formulated: the formation of special "women's committees" to investigate the status of women in the profession; the provision of child care at the conventions; changes in hiring practices, and the appointment of a special assistant to oversee the transition to open hiring practices; the establishment of a roster of women historians to facilitate the hiring of women; equal access of women to all committee appointments of the professional organizations; and equal participation in the formation of convention programs. In one form or another all of these demands were implemented over the next five years.

I functioned as a liaison with the Berkshire Conference group during our 1969 meeting and the next year and tried to convince its leadership that the formation of CCWHP was in the common interest and that we should closely collaborate. The "Berks" had formed in the 1920s, largely in order to help female historians overcome the sense of marginality and isolation they experienced at professional conventions. The group met once a year in the Berkshires for a weekend retreat to discuss papers, and served as a support group for its members. As it later turned out the activities of CCWHP and the spectacular growth of the Women's History movement infused new life into the group. After the notable Berkshire Conference on Women's History held in 1974, the successive Berks conferences became major social and professional events, attracting over 2,000 participants and rivaling the AHA for attendance.

CCWHP from the beginning and throughout its existence tried to engage in serious and pragmatic organizing and to avoid factionalism. Many women in CCWHP were active members of the radical caucus, others were strongly committed to feminism, and still others were more traditionalist in their politics. We certainly had our disagreements, which have heightened as the field of Women's History has become more respectable. Whenever any disagreements among us were publicly expressed, those who all along disparaged our efforts used these to prophesy the downfall of our enterprise. But I think, seen in historical perspective and compared to other radical movements, ours has been characterized by the avoidance of factionalism and by an acceptance of differences that still allow for alliances. We have benefited from the support of male radical historians and they from ours on specific issues, in which we shared a common interest, such as the broadening of the base of our professional organizations, opposition to the Vietnam War, the advancement of the status and opportunities of minority scholars, and support for the Equal Rights Amendment (ERA).

THE APPROACH OF women historians has been to work from within and with the professional organizations and to use a broad spectrum of forces to promote change. At its October 1969 council meeting, the AHA received a petition from twenty-two historians, some of whom would subsequently be among the vanguard of CCWHP, urging that the AHA appoint a committee to undertake a formal investigation of the status of women historians. After the December membership meeting the council named Professor Willie Lee Rose of the University of Virginia as chair of an ad hoc Committee on the Status of Women in the Profession. It took another year before this committee became a standing committee of the organization. Its report, issued in December 1970, provided the factual basis for setting the agenda for a massive effort to improve the status of women historians. Soon after, the OAH established its first Committee on the Status of Women in the Historical Profession. The two committees were unusual in that they had a lively constituency that prodded them along and supported their recommendations. Each of the women's committees' future demands—such as the appointment of a paid executive secretary to deal with women's problems in the profession and the publication of a roster of women historians—was at first resisted by the administration and the council, and it took repeated efforts and membership pressure to get them passed. Still, persistence paid off, and women historians, introducing innumerable resolutions at AHA and OAH conventions, returning after they were beaten and presenting them again, succeeded in initiating a series of dramatic institutional changes within the professional organizations.

In these early years Committees on the Status of Women were organized also in the regional and affiliated branches of the historical societies. They added initiative and pressure for change to the efforts started by CCWHP and helped focus attention on the need to democratize the structure of the historical societies.

Some of the most important changes were initiated quite informally by women historians and their allies and were later formally introduced as resolutions at the OAH and AHA conferences. They concerned the conditions under which historians obtained their jobs. We supported all efforts to make the hiring process open, equitable and accessible to all, and with some support from government affirmative action rules, we succeeded. We also lobbied for the appointment of women to the advisory boards of the AHA and OAH journals and as members of program committees.

We set out also to systematically demystify the process of becoming a professional historian. A few of us found out how the professional organizations worked, how program committees formed their programs, how one got to suggest a panel proposal, how one got appointed to a committee. Whatever we found out, we immediately shared with everyone. We organized graduate student workshops, issued survival manuals, organized and proposed our own panels and fought to get them accepted by program committees. The AHA Committee on Women Historians issued a "Survival Manual" that included chapters such as "Survival at Interviews," "How to Apply to Graduate School," "How to Get on a Program at a Meeting of Professional Associations," and "How to Apply for Grants and Fellowships." The manual quickly became popular with male and female historians. Panels and workshops on these subjects, sponsored by the women's committees or CCWHP, began to be featured at succeeding conventions. They provided contacts for networking and forums for airing grievances and planning future actions, and they became models for open democratic process. The CCWHP cocktail hour, which we started in 1973, quickly became an institution and soon it was *the* social event of the conventions, a good antidote to the old boys' smokers. For women, for graduate students, and for many men, we transformed the social climate during conventions, simply by modeling other possibilities. For me, from 1970 on, the two professional conventions and, of course, the revitalized Berks, have become warm social occasions, not only for learning what's new and current in scholarship, but also for meeting an ever-widening circle of close friends and co-workers.

At the time, changing the social climate of the conventions was not high on our priority list, but it proved to be an important side effect of the work of CCWHP and the women's committees. Creating an alternative to the hierarchical model of the old boys' network not only made the conventions more pleasant and more inclusive, but it helped to involve a broader group of people in the work of the organizations.

The two women's committees quantified the glaringly unequal representation of women in articles published in journals and in reviewing assignments. We monitored the articles submitted and the rejection letters; we set up meetings with editors of the journals to discuss these issues. I remember participating in several very unpleasant meetings of this kind with editors and various gatekeepers in which our efforts to gain access for women scholars and Women's History scholarship were rebuffed. The usual first response was denial; nobody ever had rejected articles by women or treated them in any way differently than articles written by men. The second response was more maddening: it was a sad "fact" that no good articles by women were being submitted to journals. If such quality articles were to be submitted, they would undoubtedly be accepted. CCWHP proposed that the OAH and AHA might try publishing separate journal issues focusing on scholarship by women. Such proposals were rejected with disdain by editors of historical journals. Were we afraid of fair and open competition? Did we wish to lower standards?

It may be difficult for younger historians to imagine the extent to which male historians' resistance to our efforts took the form of disparagement. It is, of course, an ancient tactic by those resisting change to accuse those advocating change of lowering standards. The same response greeted educational reformers in the 1840s and again at the turn of the century, who wished to include the study of American history and literature in college curricula. They, too, were accused of wanting to lower standards and dilute the value of higher education. The same accusations are, of course, made today against those advocating affirmative action and multicultural curricula. The assumption of the gatekeepers was and is that education is a zero-sum game. If new groups were to be included, it must mean that old groups would be slighted. The other, and more galling assumption, was that by definition scholarship by women was and would be inferior to scholarship by men. These objections vanished in the face of the solid scholarly work of the women and minority scholars who finally succeeded in gaining representation on the advisory boards of the journals and as members of program and executive committees.

Petitions, lobbying, and the introduction of resolutions by and about women at each of the conventions became staples of our organizing work. It was a slogging, slow, and often utterly frustrating process. We met resistance each step of the way, but in the end we prevailed. For example, the practice of CCWHP interviewing candidates for election to OAH and AHA offices regarding their views on a number of organization issues was considered divisive, unprofessional, and terribly threatening when we first started it. By now, it has become an accepted feature of OAH and AHA elections and has certainly contributed to making candidates for office more accountable to the voters. I think that our shattering of the old boys' network and transforming the hierarchical, mystified way of running the professional organizations was one of the best and most useful things CCWHP did for everyone in the profession, not just for women and minorities.

In 1969 the status of women in the profession was marginal and hedged about by discriminatory practices and an androcentric tradition. The employment situation of women historians over a twenty-two-year span was surveyed in 1986 by Patricia Albjerg Graham, then the chair of the Committee on Women Historians (CWH), in a report to the AHA. In 1950–59 women had represented 10.4 percent of the Ph.D.s in history, while in 1980–84 they represented 32.6 percent.[1]

The situation is somewhat improved. In 1998 women faculty were 29.9 percent of those employed, while in 2003 they were 30.4 percent. This must be measured against the fact that women earned 40 percent of all Ph.D.s in history in 2003. Thus, considering the available cohort of qualified faculty, women were still discriminated against in access to employment.[2]

The greatest and most positive changes have occurred in the two major professional organizations. In 1969 there were no women officers in either organization. The presidency of both the OAH and AHA had been filled by males throughout the entire period of their existence, with the exception in each case of one woman president in the 1930s. By 1982 women constituted 34 percent of the elected officers of the AHA and 36 percent of the members of standing committees. My election to the presidency of the OAH in 1982 was followed by that of Anne Firor Scott in 1984 and that of Natalie Zemon Davis to the presidency of the AHA in 1987. Since then, women have been fairly represented in the elections of both organizations. Whereas women at the 1969 AHA convention had represented 4 percent of all program participants, they numbered 25 percent in 1982 and 46 percent in 1998. In both organizations the participation of women in the annual conferences has vastly increased and with it their access to professional exposure and scholarly exchange.

In 1970 the status of Women's History was nonexistent. At a time when political and institutional history was the measure of significance and social history had only recently been elevated to legitimacy, the subject "women" was defined as doubly marginal. Women's History was not recognized as a legitimate field and to admit that one worked in it was considered the kiss of death professionally. In 1970, there were only five scholars in U.S. History who defined themselves primarily as historians of Women's History: Janet James, Anne Firor Scott, Elizabeth Taylor, Eleanor Flexner (a nonacademic historian), and myself. Carl Degler, Clarke Chambers, and Christopher Lasch had done significant work in Women's History, and Degler and Chambers were instrumental in furthering the establishment of the field. Christopher Lasch told me, probably in 1971, when I asked him what his next project in Women's History would be, that he had "taken the field about as far as it would go" and was now working on other subjects. A younger generation of graduate students was, of course, already working on Women's History topics and would shortly emerge as a self-conscious force, but there was a vast gap between them and the generation of Mary Beard, Elizabeth Schlesinger, Eugenia Leonard, and Elizabeth Massey who had, mostly outside the academy, worked to establish Women's History in the 1920s and '30s.

I was very much aware of the lack of support for Women's History during the founding period of CCWHP. A questionnaire answered by seventy-two CCWHP members in 1970 regarding what should be the focus of the organization's work revealed that 45 percent wanted it to focus primarily on the professional status of women and only 25 percent wanted to focus on Women's History.[3] My commitment was then already clear: for me the promotion of Women's History as a field had primary importance. Accordingly, I concentrated in 1970 on getting several panels sponsored by CCWHP into the programs of both the AHA and OAH. After lengthy negotiations I succeeded in organizing a panel, "Feminism—Past, Present, and Future" for the 1970 AHA convention (Chair, Anne Firor Scott; papers by Alice Rossi, Jo Freeman, and myself, with William O'Neill as commentator). During the same convention the innovative chairman of the Program Committee, Professor Raymond Grew, accepted a panel discussion, "Women's Experience in History: A Teaching Problem," organized by the AHA Committee on the Status of Women. What a triumph—out of a hundred sessions, two concerned women. These path-breaking sessions were lively and well attended. As a mark of progress, the 1971 AHA convention featured five Women's History panels. The 1971 OAH convention featured a panel on Mary Beard and two panels on professional concerns of women historians. I served as the single woman member of the 1972 OAH program committee and wrote more than fifty letters trying to get several panels on women organized, but succeeded only in getting two on the program (or perhaps three, if one wants to consider a paper on the "marriage market" as representing Women's History). One of these sessions, "The Case of the Missing Ladies," which dealt with a study of the leading college textbooks and the near-total absence of references to women in them, proved to be quite sensational, with an overflow audience and reporters present. It was written up in the *New York Times* the next day. So it went, step by step, six steps backward for every two steps gained. Yet, since 1972, at each convention, there have been panels and workshops pertaining to the professional interests of women and to Women's History.

In the summer of 1970 CCWHP reported that, nationwide, twenty-two members were offering at least one course on Women's History and that four Women's Studies programs were then being developed. That was only thirty-eight years ago. In 1972, when, with the help of a Rockefeller Foundation grant, I launched the M.A. program in Women's History at Sarah Lawrence College, ours was the first graduate program of its kind in the United States and, to my knowledge, in the world (see Chapter 3). Today students can earn an M.A. or Ph.D. with a Women's History specialization at over seventy colleges and universities.[4]

The process of gaining acceptance for this new field of scholarship was slower and even more labor-intensive than that of promoting the status of women historians. We had to advance on four fronts all at once: we had to show that there were adequate and interesting sources available in Women's History; we had to produce first-rate work based on these sources; we had to train teachers and develop bibliographies and syllabi; and we had to convince administrators and our colleagues that there was student demand for these courses.

Just as we had often been told by traditional historians that women's history was insignificant, so we were constantly met with the unproven but widespread belief that there was a lack of sources for this field. This was disproved once and for all in a project I helped to conceive, organize, and finance. In April 1971, a small group of scholars got together at the OAH convention to discuss what might be done to make sources on women more readily accessible to scholars. All of us who participated in this meeting—Anne Firor Scott, Carl Degler, Janet James, Clarke Chambers, and myself—had done primary source research on women in the archives. Janet James, with her husband Ed James and Paul Boyer, was then still editing the three-volume *Notable American Women*, the first modern reference work on the subject. We all knew that one of the difficulties for researchers on women was the fact that archives and libraries did not catalogue their material on women in a coherent way. Women's diaries, letters, and writings were lost in family correspondences catalogued under male family members' names. The records of women's organizations were not systematically collected or identified. The work and activities of women were often hidden in organizational records, government files, and church records. As long as there were no finders' guides or indices indicating that these records pertained to women, researchers could only find them by serendipity. It was a common experience to go into an archive, ask the archivist what they had on women, and be handed one or two items, when in fact the archive contained hundreds of items by or about women. The five of us decided that we needed to do a survey of archives and of their holdings about women. What was needed was a reference work, a sort of union catalogue. Clarke Chambers offered his state, Minnesota, as a testing ground and recommended that we bring in Andrea Hinding, curator of the Social Welfare History Archives, to take on the project. With the help of Dorothy Ross, who at that time chaired the AHA women's committee, we secured the cooperation of both the AHA and OAH in drafting a grant proposal for such a project. We also organized a workshop for historians and archivists at the 1972 OAH meeting, which enthusiastically supported the project.

Meanwhile, in the fall of 1971 I had been invited by historian Peter Wood, then an officer of the Rockefeller Foundation, to consult with him about how to advance work in Women's History and Women's Studies. I recommended the convening of a small planning conference to designate priorities in the development of Women's History. As a direct result of this conference at the Rockefeller Foundation, held April 8, 1972, we were able to secure grant support for the test run of the Women's History Sources Survey, which afterward was funded by the National Endowment for the Humanities and the University of Minnesota. The final project, which took four years to complete and surveyed all the states, resulted in a work of two volumes: Andrea Hinding (ed.), *Women's History Sources: A Guide to Archives and Manuscript Collections in the United States* (New York: R. R. Bowker, 1979).

Of all the projects I have ever been involved in, this, I think, was the most effective and important. Not only did we show that there were vast, and mostly unused, primary sources available virtually in every major community in the United States, but we made these sources easily accessible. The informal networks of Women's History scholars, which were then being established, helped greatly to spread the effect of this work to the broader community. Further, in the process of conducting the survey, most archives and libraries decided to reclassify their items on women in such a way that they could be easily identified. The National Archives led the way by creating a finders' guide to its Women's History materials, and other major collections soon followed. Thus, the Women's History Sources Survey project transformed the way archives were cataloguing their holdings on women and greatly aided scholarship on this subject.

The production of monographs, essays, collections, documents, and books in women's history was greatly aided by this archival project. In 1960, one could find thirteen books in print in Women's History. In 1978 I published a *Bibliography in the History of American Women*, which listed 291 titles.[5] There were then hundreds of dissertations in the field still in progress. By the year 2000 scholarship in Women's History had grown large enough to be listed separately in the annual bibliographical survey of the *Journal of American History*. In the three years 1998–2000 the survey listed 720 items of scholarship on the subject. These consisted of 150 books, 280 dissertations, and 290 articles.[6] The growth trend has continued since. Its quality is attested by the ever-increasing numbers of books on women winning top literary and historical awards.

The professional organizations of women historians contributed to this development from 1970 on. We began by publishing lists of "Research in Progress in Women's History," and we systematically distributed course syllabi and bibliographies in Women's History to all interested. Beginning in 1972 the women's committees and CCWHP agitated for the commissioning of a pamphlet on Women's History, to be sponsored by the AHA in its series of teaching pamphlets. Typically, the editor of the series refused us, with the information that such a pamphlet was not high on the AHA's priority list. When we persisted, he changed his mind. I was asked to write this pamphlet, which, when it was finally printed, turned out to be the best-selling pamphlet in the series for many years. The fact that women's history questions now appear on SAT tests in many states is the result of organizational effort by women and pressure by educators. Textbooks at all levels have begun to reflect the growth and impact of this intellectual transformation, which is at last bringing the history of the majority into the mainstream.

Networking and the sharing of work in progress was another way in which we helped to build the field. In the fall of 1969, Patricia Graham (Columbia University,) Annette Baxter (Barnard College), and I organized New York Metropolitan Area Women Historians, which soon affiliated with the national CCWHP. By December 1970 the national organization had three affiliates: the New York City group, the West Coast Association of Women Historians, and the Committee on the Status of Women of the Southern Historical Association. Today, with seventeen CCWHP affiliates, it is probably hard to realize how triumphant we felt then at our swift growth. The New York City group quickly organized a campaign, securing 600 signatures on a petition in support of the demands made by CCWHP on the professional organizations: 1) support for the office of a special assistant on the rights of women in the AHA; 2) urging history departments to increase the number of women graduate students; and 3) affirmative action in the hiring of women faculty and the setting up of timetables to effect equal ratios of men and women in departments.

It took several years longer before we could persuade Columbia University to make room among its 232 faculty seminars, which were organized by fields of historical scholarship, for *one* seminar dealing with women. Pat Graham, Marcia Wright, Annette Baxter, and I cooperated on this project. When, at last, the seminar "Women and Society" was established, it quickly became one of the most popular and best-attended seminars of all. Similar work was, of course, being done all over the country by women historians trying to promote the new field.

When I graduated from Columbia in 1966 my specialty, Women's History, did not really exist. I was advised to hide my interest in this "exotic subject" and to market myself as a good social historian. I did not take that well-meant advice, but I was aware of the fact that my special interest was a professional liability. We have come a long way since then. We have disproven the skeptics, persisting in the face of disparagement, ridicule, and tenacious resistance to change. CCWHP and the women's committees staffed in succeeding years by new and enthusiastic advocates of women and Women's History deserve a large part of the credit for the advances the field has made.

As for myself, looking back on sixty years of organizational work, mostly for lost causes, the past thirty years tell a story of spectacular, and often unexpected, success. The quest for restoring the interpreted past of half of the world's population has been richly rewarding, exhilarating, and energizing. We have proven, over and over again, that women make history and have always made history. In so doing, we have had to challenge the exclusionary and outdated patriarchal structures of academic institutions. Life and thought have merged; transforming knowledge has led us to transform institutions.

Notes

1. Patricia Albjerg Graham, "Revisiting the Rose Report," presented at the Women's Committee Breakfast Meeting, December 29, 1986, reprinted in *CCWHP Newsletter* 18, no. 1 (February 1987): 7–10.

2. Robert B. Townsend, "Federal Faculty Survey Shows Gains of History Employment but Lagging Salaries," in *Perspectives, News Magazine of the American Historical Association* 44, no. 3 (March 2006): 8.

3. *CCWHP Newsletter* 1 (Summer 1970): 6.

4. Accurate accounts of graduate training in Women's History are elusive. The figure mentioned was derived from a hand count of programs listed in Karen Kidd and Ande Spencer (eds.), *Guide to Graduate Work in Women's Studies*, 2nd ed. (College Park, Md.: National Women's Studies Association, 1994). It is likely the figure somewhat understates the number of such institutions.

5. Gerda Lerner, *Bibliography in the History of American Women* (A Sarah Lawrence College Women's Studies Publication, 3rd revised printing, 1978). In a fourth revised printing, there were 1,358 items listed. Gerda Lerner, with the assistance of Marie Laberge, *Woman Are History: A Bibliography in the History of American Women* (A Publication of the Graduate Program in Women's History, Department of History, University of Wisconsin–Madison, 1986).

6. Gerda Lerner, "U.S. Women's History: Past, Present, and Future," *Journal of Women's History* 16, no. 4 (2004): 10–27.

chapter three

The M.A. Program in Women's History at Sarah Lawrence College

The twelve years I spent at Sarah Lawrence College in Bronxville, New York, north of New York City, allowed me to translate my theoretical insights about Women's History into practice. Because I was able, in 1973, to secure a grant from the Rockefeller Foundation, supporting the start-up Graduate Program in Women's History for three years, I was able to launch the program without at the time having an overwhelming mandate from either faculty or students at the college.

As the program grew, our model not only encompassed a new structure and approach to teaching, but also institutionalized outreach to the community through innovative conferences and summer workshops. We were fortunate in attracting outstanding faculty for these ventures and in getting excellent national and local publicity. This, in turn, impressed the college administration sufficiently to overcome their initial objections to the program and led to a commitment on their part to continue the program after the grant ran out.

As we were developing our team-taught course we made progress toward creating a Women's Studies Program and won so much faculty and student support for it that it was clear that the undergraduate and the graduate programs would develop jointly and with each other's help.

I believed then and I do now that Sarah Lawrence College was unusually well suited for developing a model Women's Studies Program. Its outstanding faculty, its educational model of combining intense seminars with individual faculty-supervised tutorials, and the existence of its pioneering Continuing Education program—all these factors made it an ideal institution for a program that would be innovative in content and structure. Those of us who started planning the first course were conscious also of some of the problems of the Sarah Lawrence system: students' isolation from one another and competitiveness, the focus on learning only by close association with faculty, and the often narrow focus on small areas of concentration. We were conscious also of a need to foster a close and egalitarian community of faculty and students and to replace student competitiveness with group work.

Our goals were ambitious, both visionary and somewhat utopian. We were not merely adding some novel courses; we were offering a new way of seeing the world and the past.

We defined our goal as follows: To develop a mode of learning in which women were at the center of the inquiry; to reclaim our history and with it our true perspective on ourselves, our present, and our future; to fuse thought and action; to heal the rift between abstract knowledge and practice; to create community.

I probably learned more during those initial years than did my students. Working with a superb team of women faculty, who brought their best talents and experience to the project, made me improve as an intellectual and as a teacher. I learned how to create a non-hierarchical classroom; I learned how to involve students both as learners and as teachers; I learned how to deal with conflict and difficulties through democratic dialogue. From Amy Swerdlow and several of the superb organizers among the students I learned how to be effective within the institution, while working to change it. We all were very conscious of the fact that what we were doing ought to be excellent enough to serve as a model. And so it did.

The program got off the ground in 1972–73, coinciding with the eighteen months during which I nursed my husband through his terminal illness. While this put an enormous amount of stress on me, it also helped me to survive and to carry on after his death. I had something bigger than myself to challenge me and to force me to function in the world even during my grief and mourning. As I look back on it, I wonder how I could do that. But vision and social purpose can help to give us strength and to make us stretch beyond our reach. Whatever it cost, I was amply rewarded in spirit.

I came to Sarah Lawrence College in the fall of 1968 as a one-year replacement. In January of 1969, President Esther Raushenbush encouraged me to apply for a permanent position. I hesitated, because I had tenure at Long Island University–Brooklyn, and Sarah Lawrence would not offer me tenure, but Mrs. Raushenbush assured me that I would get consideration for early tenure after two years, and so I accepted. I did not then know that she was retiring and that a new President would be taking over.

1968–69 was the time of two student strikes at Sarah Lawrence College—a rather tumultuous time, and my support of the striking students quickly marked me as being "controversial." The fact that, in 1969, I proposed that the college start a "Coordinated Program in Interdisciplinary Feminist Studies" did not help. My proposal was ignored. Still, on April 29, 1971, I again offered a detailed report on "Restructuring the College," arguing that Sarah Lawrence was uniquely situated to pioneer in Women's Studies. I suggested that the college accept graduate students for an M.A. in those disciplines with faculty interested in participating. I offered to initiate such a course in history. I also suggested that we create a course for our students, for Center of Continuing Education (CCE) students, and for community women that would combine theory and practice.[1] I sent this proposal to the Committee on Restructuring the College with a note, "The attached report went down like a pebble in a deep well sinking rapidly and leaving no trace. I am revising it now because I think at least some of the points I made deserve fuller discussion."

I had been getting encouragement and support from Melissa Richter, then Dean of Graduate Studies, and Elizabeth Minnich, the Director of CCE, who helped me to find a format under which an M.A. in Women's History could be given. It was the same format Melissa had used for starting her pioneering program in training women in genetic studies.

Meanwhile, in December 1968, I was invited by historian Peter Wood, then an officer at the Rockefeller Foundation, to consult with the foundation about the Women's Liberation Movement. I had at that time already connected with Sheila Tobias and Florence Howe in promoting the formation of Women's Studies programs across the nation. Florence Howe had been meeting with the Ford Foundation and had won their support for some of her projects, and I thought I might possibly have a similar impact in working with the Rockefeller Foundation. I had several conversations with Peter Wood in which we discussed the differences between the Women's Rights Feminist Movement and the new Women's Liberation Movement. I explained that the new movement was multifaceted and embraced a range of positions: from women's rights advocates to Marxists, advocates of radical sexual reform, lesbians, and religious feminists. In my explanation I talked about "them"; I did not yet consider myself a part of them. I told Peter Wood that I was mostly interested in promoting Women's History. He was very sympathetic to the idea and accepted my proposal for a two-day planning meeting of about fifteen people.

On June 8, 1972, that planning conference met at the Rockefeller Foundation. It was a very productive meeting that resulted in a priority list of projects we wanted funded. The first one was a survey of archival sources on Women's History. The second was the establishment of a Women's History Program at Sarah Lawrence College. The third was Summer Institutes in Women's History.

Back to Sarah Lawrence College. Esther Raushenbush retired as President in 1969 and was replaced by Charles de Carlo. He came to us from IBM and was hailed in the *New York Times* as a "Renaissance man." Among his stated aims for the college was to increase the number of male students, toward which end he proposed to build a pool and a sports facility, which he never did. It is no exaggeration to say that from the start President De Carlo and I were on a collision course. Building Women's Studies and a feminist campus community was not part of his interest or vision. My support of striking students during the two sit-ins had made me quite unpopular with the more conservative members of the faculty. All of which resulted in my being denied early tenure when my contract was up for renewal, which according to President Raushenbush should have happened without any problems. At that time I had left a tenured position; I had published two books and several articles and had another book under contract. It was only as a result of increasing student and faculty support for my work that I finally did get tenure in April 1972.

But in September 1971 I was quite discouraged; still I did not give up on the idea of building an M.A. program. In an effort to get faculty support I posted a notice on the college bulletin board:

To All Women Faculty Members
If you are interested in developing feminist courses in your
own field and in exploring the possibility of an interdisciplinary
Feminist Studies Program, please join me for lunch in the North
Dining Room Tuesday, October 12th, 1971 at noon.

I had reserved a table for eight at the faculty lunchroom, and was delighted to find fourteen women taking part in this discussion. However, it did not go the way I wanted it to go. With the exception of Eva Kollisch, Sherry Ortner, and Elfie Stock, each of the other women applauded the idea of having Women's Studies, but explained why she could not take part in it. This included Joan Kelly, a distinguished Renaissance scholar who had just joined the faculty. She stated that, unfortunately, there was no material available on women in the Renaissance. The meeting ended with only a small committee of people willing to discuss the matter further. I invited Joan Kelly to take a walk with me. On that walk I told her that I had found enough sources on women in the Renaissance to write a small article on it during my graduate training, Renaissance Studies being a minor field for me. After some discussion, she agreed to look over the sources I mentioned. In a manner typical of her intellectual curiosity, she came back a week later with an impressive reading list and the determination to learn all she could about women in the Renaissance. She soon developed a pioneering course on the subject and wrote several path-breaking articles that defined the new field.

JOAN KELLY HAD been hired as a Renaissance historian in 1971, and her leaving CUNY to come to Sarah Lawrence was considered quite a coup by the faculty elders. While we were still awaiting a response to the Rockefeller grant proposal Joan told me of a strange conversation she had had with President De Carlo. He had offered her the position of Director of Women's Studies, in case the grant was approved. He justified this on the ground that she was a full professor and outranked me. Joan knew that I had been working for this program for more than three years and that I had written the Rockefeller grant application. She felt his offer was inappropriate and designed to publicly humiliate me. She refused it; she wanted no part of such intrigues.

We talked for quite a while about the way feminist faculty were set up to compete and fight with each other for limited resources, as had frequently been done with minority faculty, when Afro-American Studies units were being organized. We decided to strengthen our position by assuming co-directorship of the program and working closely together. We would help each other and trust each other and we would stick to a principle Joan defined: "When there is a disturbance of any kind between us, resolving it takes precedence." We stuck to this principle and dealt with any potential conflict between us before it could become public and hurt the program. We shared the directorship of the program for less than two years; then Joan returned to CUNY for reasons of her own and I continued, with the exception of two years when I went on leave, to direct the program until I left Sarah Lawrence. Joan continued to support our program through her position as chair of the Committee on the Status of Women of the American Historical Association (AHA). Our personal relationship soon became a close friendship based not only on organizational ties, but on shared research interests. It lasted until her untimely death in 1982.

The committee to design and teach the new course "Women: Myth and Reality" consisted of Joan Kelly (Renaissance Studies), Eva Kollisch (literature), Sherry Ortner (anthropology), and myself. We were given a small summer stipend to allow us to meet regularly. Gradually, other faculty got interested and helped us get off the ground.[2]

"Women: Myth and Reality" was my first experience with team-

teaching. My initial apprehension about it soon dissolved, as I participated in the rigorous and stimulating discussions in the preparation of our
course. The four of us were at different levels of commitment to feminist
thought and practice, and we found that by respectfully acknowledging
these differences and making them visible to our students we strengthened their educational experience. Joan Kelly was far ahead of any of us in
practicing what later we would call "feminist pedagogy." She had for years
developed democratic classroom practices that involved students not only
as learners, but also as teachers in course participation. The anthropologist
Sherry Ortner, the youngest among the four of us, was most outspokenly
feminist in her approach to her material. I admired the fact that she called
her seminar "Nuns and Prostitutes" and that what she was teaching was the
effect on women of gender role indoctrination. This was at a time when
the concept of gender was new and still quite controversial.

The course offered in the fall of 1972 consisted of a weekly two-hour
lecture and discussion attended by all students and faculty. In addition,
four seminars given by the four participating teachers met once a week
for two hours. The teachers also held private and group conferences with
the students in their seminar. Some of the students, who could not be
accommodated in the seminars, did independent conference work with
other faculty in a variety of fields. The four participating faculty members
also held a weekly two-hour meeting to plan and coordinate the work.
The course enrolled eighty-two students, but the lectures attracted many
more, including six or more faculty members from other colleges. Several
of them were inspired to develop new, women-focused courses in their
own disciplines and home institutions.

We planned the lectures so as to deal with a number of major themes
from different viewpoints and disciplines and encouraged student projects
to be developed around similar themes. Students then reported to the entire group on their seminar projects during the last third of the course, a
feature that greatly enhanced student leadership and commitment to the
course. Participating faculty were inspired to some of their best production: Sherry Ortner's "Is Female to Male as Nature Is to Culture?," Joan
Kelly's "Did Women Have a Renaissance?," and my "The Majority Finds Its
Past" were lectures developed and first given in this course. Students and
faculty felt tremendously inspired and energized.

This enthusiasm showed up in student activities engendered by the
course that included a month-long arts festival focusing on women, a stu-

dent film on "Images of Women," a lecture series by prominent women authors, and creation of a student committee to improve health services at Sarah Lawrence College (so as to include contraceptive information, counseling, and abortion referral).

Publicity and word-of-mouth resulted in notice of the course in the *New York Times*. In the fall of 1973 we received fifty-six applications for admission, from which we selected eight entering students. Throughout the existence of the program we yearly had hundreds of inquiries and a large number of applicants, but we were restrained in our ability to accept them due to lack of resources and scholarship aid.

One of the most interesting aspects of our early activity was the course "Women Organizing Women," which I had designed and which was written into and financed by the Rockefeller grant. That grant was the reason we succeeded in giving it at all, since the college was less than enthusiastic about it. "We don't teach organizing here. We're an educational institution," was one of the objections raised. To overcome these I was forced to change the course name to "Women in Community Activities." Nobody ever called it that, though. We offered a ten-credit seminar for equal numbers of undergraduates, CCE women, and community activists. We had over one hundred applicants for twelve openings. Fellowship holders were selected for age and race diversity and for their practical experience. We had among them a trade union activist, a day care organizer, and an officer of the first organization of women alcoholics. The learning experience for all of us who took part in this course was exhilarating. But at the end of the three-year period the course was not continued.

For me personally, the course design was and continued to be an important aspect of feminist pedagogy. Whenever I could, I made sure to have classes that included students of different ages and at different stages of learning. I built exposure to activism into my class plans and encouraged my students to participate in or initiate outreach activities. Every course I taught would have some relationship to what people had experienced, the work they had done, the application of their knowledge to wider community service. My students developed slide lectures on Women's History for elementary schools; they raised money and organized public forums and discussions. Our outreach work included a course on the history of working women, taught on company premises to AT&T employees, and a course at Bronxville High School, "Perspectives on Women." Developing outreach activities for the community also became part of my later work in Madison, Wisconsin, where my students put a lot of volunteer labor into organizing Women's History Week celebrations at the university and in the community. I convinced my department to give credit to a graduate practicum course, so that students' volunteer work was rewarded. It turned out to be a very helpful item on their vitas, as they went out seeking jobs.

The academic system, built as it was on patriarchal principles, promoted the separation of theory and practice to the detriment of its students and of the community as a whole. I firmly believed that bringing theory and practice together was one of the biggest contributions feminists could make in the academy.

Women's Studies and the graduate program at Sarah Lawrence continued to grow in popularity and range. We added a number of conferences to our offerings, which were financed by outside grants and reached out to the larger community of feminist scholars. In March 1975 we ran a conference, "Conceptual Frameworks for Studying Women's History," attended by 280 participants. The subject matter reflected a general concern among Women's History scholars, which I shared, that the conceptual framework under which we were working *was still a patriarchal framework*, that put men and their activities in the center of inquiry and made the activities of women appear to be subsidiary and marginal. It did not answer our needs. Many scholars in the field were searching for other frameworks, but there was as yet no consensus. There was a Marxist framework that did not fit Women's History well; there were many efforts at creating a Marxist-feminist framework. Some women were trying to create a framework that focused on women's sexual repression; others put unpaid reproductive work in the center of their concerns. With this conference we connected with all the major groups of scholars then working on this challenging question. The conference created a venue for discussing the various perspectives. It led to a lively exchange, but to no conclusions.

In 1976 we organized a Summer Institute for High School Teachers. This was co-sponsored by the Committee on the Status of Women of the AHA, then chaired by Joan Kelly, and received grant support from the National Endowment for the Humanities (NEH). Amy Swerdlow served as Project Director, and I was Educational Director; teachers were Carole Groneman, Sara Evans, and myself.

Amy Swerdlow was one of my M.A. students at Sarah Lawrence, who came to us with an M.A. in Art History and with impressive credentials as a leader of women. She was one of the founders and leaders of Women Strike for Peace and a leader in the women's peace movement. She was also a close co-worker of Congresswoman Bella Abzug. She became known—and notorious—for leading a women's peace delegation to Vietnam during the war. It was a pleasure and a challenge to have such an accomplished student, who soon became my colleague. She puts it differently. She always says, "I was fifty-three years old, and then I met Gerda Lerner, and I sold all my worldly goods and followed her."

In fact, I certainly learned as much from her as she did from me. Her enormous organizational ability was put to good use when she became the Co-Director of Women's Studies at Sarah Lawrence after her graduation. She succeeded me as Director of the Program, when I left, and stayed in that position until she retired. The success of the program is largely due to her ability to relate Women's Studies scholarship to social action in the women's movement.

The 1976 Summer Institute for High School Teachers of which Swerdlow was Project Director was attended by forty-three teachers from sixteen states. We utilized the educational model we developed, combining lectures, seminars, workshops, and group projects. As their class project, the participants produced nine curriculum outlines with bibliographies for the high school level. Five of the participants became motivated to continue their education by studying for a Ph.D. in Women's History.

The AHA's Committee on the Status of Women used this institute as a model for a series of similar Summer Institutes held at Stanford, the University of North Carolina, the University of Minnesota, and Rutgers, funded by the NEH. As a result, hundreds of high school teachers were trained in integrating Women's History into their curricula. The AHA also published and distributed a teaching guide on the subject (see Chapter 6).

Faculty in the Women's Studies Program published and distributed two major bibliographies in Women's History and several pamphlets based on our conferences, with all proceeds going to the college.

In 1977 we organized the conference "The Future of Housework, the Role of the Housewife, and Sharing Arrangements for Child Care." This event was jointly sponsored by Sarah Lawrence College, the Congress of Neighborhood Women, and the Union of Household Technicians, representing a constituency of academics, ethnic working-class women, and black domestic workers. I can take credit for the concept and the topics for the conference. My interest in the subject goes back to decades of organizational work in communities, when I was myself a housewife and young mother. I organized for improvements in the neighborhood schools, for peace, for support of the United Nations, and for child care centers and after-school day care centers.

When the modern women's movement began to organize, influenced by Betty Friedan's book, *The Feminine Mystique*, and by an activist contingent of young women emerging from the civil rights movement, I was appalled by the prevailing attitude toward housewives, who were treated as backward and unimportant. The young women in the movement had no knowledge of the long and radical history of housewives and mothers in community organizing; they were preoccupied with their conflicts with their own mothers.

In my book, *The Female Experience*, which I worked on in the early '70s, I had a theoretical chapter on housework.[3] To my knowledge that was the first time the subject was taken seriously by anybody in the women's movement. The Sarah Lawrence conference was an outgrowth of my practical experience and my theoretical concerns with the occupation of the vast majority of women all over the world.

The conference was an innovative attempt to cross racial, ethnic, and class barriers and to bring theory and practice to bear on a major societal problem. Amy Swerdlow and I had learned enough from our previous work to know that you could not hope to bring these disparate groups of people—white ethnic housewives, academic theorists, and African American domestic workers—together for a conference unless you first engaged them in a joint process. To this end, we wrote a pre-convention planning conference into our grant proposal. We knew also that we could not bring these groups together at Sarah Lawrence, with its aura of wealth and privilege, without inviting conflict.

The Congress of Neighborhood Women, who came from Brooklyn, pointed out that for a long time they had been coming to distant Sarah Lawrence College for meetings and it was time all of us came to Brooklyn. "We'll show you how neighborhood women organize." When we met in Brooklyn in May our friends overwhelmed us with wonderful food and great hospitality. As they did for church suppers and PTA meetings, the neighborhood women brought their favorite dishes for potluck and offered their best home-baked pies, cakes, and cookies. The academic women, appreciating their hosts' culinary skills, had a sudden insight into how their own idea of entertainment—red wine and cheese and crackers—must seem ungracious and inhospitable to the neighborhood women. The African American women had never met with white housewives on common ground, but they shared their culinary expertise and soon found they had other common interests.

At this meeting the site for the final conference was selected. Everyone agreed that it should not be at Sarah Lawrence College. Someone suggested we hold it in Harlem. Dead silence. "Where could we hold it there?" Someone suggested the federal building. Some of the Brooklyn women were obviously worried, but did not quite know how to express their concern. Would it be safe in Harlem? The black women assured us they'd protect us and show us the same kind of hospitality the Brooklyn women had shown us. And so the decision was made. Probably that was the most important thing we did at the conference—after that decision a new level of dialogue could and did take place. We moved on to a one-day Planning Conference, held May 7, 1977, at the New School for Social Research, where the agenda for the main conference was planned by the fifty-nine participants.

That conference was held on October 22, 1977, at the Harlem State Office Building. It garnered support beyond the three sponsoring organizations, being endorsed by Lieutenant Governor Mary Ann Krupsak, Representative Bella Abzug, and State Senators Carol Bellamy and Karen Burstein. It was funded by the New York Council for the Humanities. Of the 215 registered participants, 41 were academics, 4 were public officials, 22 were neighborhood women, 53 were activists in the women's movement, 27 were students, and at least 10 were domestic workers. A well-rounded action agenda, which included calls for shared housework with men and children, appeals for child care legislation, a resource manual and bibliography, and a pamphlet summarizing the work of the conference were the lasting results. The conference proceedings were broadcast live over WBAI. CBS did a program on it, and we had PR stories in the *New York Times*, *MS Magazine*, and *Vogue*.

While the conferences and Summer Institutes were highlights of our work, our program was sustained and grew because of our daily work with students. By the time I left Sarah Lawrence, eight years after starting the M.A. program, we had graduated over 120 students. Of these, 13 went on to earn Ph.D.s in Women's History at various universities. With a very few exceptions, they found employment—in archives, libraries, colleges and universities, high schools, the business world, and various political and private organizations. The outcome was great, but we faced many obstacles and difficulties in our work.

From its inception the idea of Women's Studies at Sarah Lawrence College was met with resistance by many faculty members. Why would a woman's college need a special Women's Studies Program? In responding to this objection we were forced to formulate an analysis of the difference between educating women and offering them a woman-focused curriculum. This understanding helped us to lay the groundwork for our educational goals.

Another objection was: we've been educating women all along, why introduce a political agenda? Is this just a contemporary passing fad? We were told that Women's Studies would not be financially sound. When, after the Rockefeller grant ended in 1976, we proved that it was financially sound, we were questioned as to whether it was educationally sound. From its inception the program was underfunded and understaffed. Although after 1974 the co-directors got a one-quarter teaching load reduction, this in no way compensated us for the endless hours spent in answering hundreds of inquiries, acting as an admissions committee, developing extracurricular activities, such as Summer Institutes and conferences, and endlessly writing grants to secure funding. Administrative support for the program was never adequate. The hidden cost in harassment, disapproval, lost merit increases, and constant overwork was always with us. While we managed to create a model program, we also seemed to model the formula by which such programs were administered: minimal administrative support, occasional public statements of support, and trust that the women running the program would work hard and under bad conditions because they were passionate about what they were doing. That is how Women's Studies has been built nationally: on the wisdom, enthusiasm, overwork, and underpayment of dedicated pioneers.

Over the years, an undercurrent of anxiety was always present among those opposing us: was this program promoting lesbianism? This reached its ugliest moment in 1977. Sarah Lawrence College alumna Anne Roiphe approached the college with the news that she had been assigned by the *New York Times* to do an in-depth article on the college. She was warmly welcomed by the administration in the expectation that such an article would help the college. During her time at the college she visited most programs and many classes, but never came to Women's Studies or our graduate program. I called this to her attention and invited her to see what we were doing, but she declined, saying she already knew all about us.

Her article, which appeared in the Sunday *New York Times Magazine*, featured as her main theme the proposition that Sarah Lawrence had serious problems because of a "cohesive, open, homosexual group and its vocal, political philosophy."[4] She considered the "root problem" to be a "collision between the women's movement on campus (in which lesbians form a small minority) and the administration's efforts to proceed from token to full coeducation."

The Roiphe article precipitated a political crisis on campus. At first it looked as though the President, struggling to salvage the college's reputation, wanted to respond by attacking Women's Studies and the "excesses" of campus lesbians. Many members of the faculty wanted a public statement to be sent to the *New York Times* and the errors, inaccuracies, and outright distortions of the article to be revealed. The more conservative elements wanted at all cost to avoid any conflict with the *New York Times*. The atmosphere on campus was one of confusion, homophobia, anger, and a search for scapegoats. Meanwhile, feminists on campus wanted our position to be clearly stated and debated. Women's Studies faculty and other sympathetic faculty members prepared a statement, based on my draft, that discussed the feminist position on homosexuality and focused on the problems faced by gay/lesbian students. We stressed that, as caring teachers, we had a responsibility to support our lesbian students and help them have a good college experience. We also strongly rejected lesbian-baiting and affirmed the right to free expression and the right to privacy of all students. In an open all-campus forum our position was debated and generally accepted. The President changed his tone and thereafter in his public statements defended Women's Studies. In the aftermath of these events, lesbian faculty and students felt oppressed, devalued, and forced into silence. It took years for the college to overcome the economic and psychological damage done by the Roiphe article.

Still, I believe our struggle on behalf of lesbian rights was a defining moment for Women's Studies at Sarah Lawrence College. From then on, our existence and our right to exist were never again openly questioned. It was through the growing support of male colleagues that I was later elected to the Advisory Committee, a committee that works closely with the President on college governance. When the college was evaluated by the Middle States Association, Women's Studies was singled out and praised for excellence.

It was against this background that on July 15–29, 1979, the Summer Institute in Women's History for Leaders of Women's Organizations took place. It was co-sponsored by Sarah Lawrence College, by the Women's Action Alliance, an umbrella organization of one hundred women's organizations, and by the Smithsonian Institution. The impetus for it came from Ruth Abram, who was the Executive Director of the Women's Action Alliance, which had been founded to prepare for the 1977 Houston National Women's Conference and carry forward its program. Ruth Abram was a great organizer and an inspiring leader. Her concept, which became the goal of the Institute, was to take adult women of high achievement and varying educational levels, heterogeneous as to race, ethnicity, class, and culture, and to offer them an educational experience that would lead to changes in perceptions, attitudes, and values. For the length of the Institute we created a feminist community free of competition, status-consciousness, private ambition, and prejudice. The Institute encouraged the sharing of experiences, group process, and an atmosphere in which disagreement could be taken for granted, worked through, and resolved.

Forty-three women, each an elected official of her organization, represented a full spectrum of women's organizations, among them the National Council of Jewish Women, B'nai B'rith, the YMCA, the Girl Scouts, the American Association of University Women, Women Religious (nuns), the Allianza Feminile Mexicana, the Rosebud Dakota Sioux Reservation, and many other groups. Faculty and students lived together on campus, with only one Sunday off during the fifteen days of the Institute.

The classes were team-taught by Alice Kessler-Harris, Amy Swerdlow, and myself, with six graduate students, among them three African Americans, as our team leaders. During the day, participants received the equivalent of a full semester seminar. They could chose among three topics, all within the field of American Women's History. In the afternoons the students worked in small groups, did their assigned readings, and wrote short papers. Each seminar also prepared a one-hour presentation based on research, which was then shared with the entire class.

Each evening the participants planned some cultural events. The dynamic interaction of these outstanding leaders living and working together in a "free space" — free from interruptions, free from the demands of daily

life, free to think creatively—was astounding. The evening sessions lasted
into the morning hours; the availability of living rooms and outdoor
spaces allowed for every variety of program to be arranged by the participants. The various musical groupings that evolved managed to transcend
all the usual divisions in society—the Gospel singers, black and white; the
folk singers; the aficionados of musicals and popular show tunes. Whatever
divisions might have appeared in the daytime activities were rearranged
and disappeared during the cultural events of the evenings. Difficulties
that might ordinarily have led to disputes and resentments were ironed
out during these evening happenings. People lived together and found
common ground in areas they had never expected. It carried over into the
daytime activities.

We knew that we could not expect only harmony and cooperation in
such a diverse group and that there must be space in which people could
express their dissatisfaction. If there is no space for people to express their
grievances, these will escalate and lead to explosions. We built space for
grievance sessions into our program and, since most of these were grievances against the organizers, we tried to listen respectfully and tried to
change what we could.

We encouraged the group to focus on one large group project that
would be carried out after the end of the Institute and were surprised
when the group chose as their project "making the celebration of Women's
History Week a national event." They were inspired in this by one of the
students, Molly McGregor from Sonoma County, California, who had
for years organized local community-sponsored women's history celebrations. The group understood that this was a vast undertaking that would
require them annually to secure a joint resolution of Congress and then
the President's signature. I personally thought it too grandiose an undertaking and tried to argue them out of it. After listening to me politely, one
of them said: "Gerda, you turned us on to Women's History. Why don't
you leave the organizing to us." I did, and they went ahead, undaunted and
aware of the strength of the organizations they represented. They took
on this enormous organizing job and fulfilled it. The 1980 proclamation
by President Jimmy Carter of Women's History Week was the first of its
kind—and it has been repeated every year since 1980 by different Presidents and different Congresses. Exposure to Women's History had inspired
these leaders; from 1980 on, the celebration of Women's History Week,

and later, Women's History Month, spread to every state, every county, and most communities in the United States, one of the biggest grassroots history movements in the country.

We celebrated the end of the Summer Institute with a moving ceremony at the Smithsonian Institution in Washington, D.C., at which Representative Patricia Schroeder gave the main address. The presence of a number of women politicians and activists helped to signify that Women's History now had national and public recognition. My conviction that good history must move out of the academy and become part of public culture was amply justified by our experiment in public outreach.

I LEFT SARAH LAWRENCE in 1980 in order to start a graduate program in Women's History at the University of Wisconsin–Madison, in which we could offer both the M.A. and Ph.D. Carole Artigiani, one of the graduates of our program and then its director, and faculty members Amy Swerdlow, Judith Papachristou, Eva Kollisch, Persis Hunt, Phyllis Vine, and Patricia Morola carried the Sarah Lawrence program forward.

In 2004 the graduates of the 1979 Summer Institute in Women's History for Leaders of Women's Organizations organized a reunion at the college. Twenty-seven women came at their own expense to celebrate the Summer Institute and to testify to its lasting influence on their lives. The State of New York, on this occasion, declared the Women's Studies building, where our program had started in 1972, a state landmark, and in a moving ceremony an official landmark sign was erected in front of what still is one of the shabbiest and most modest buildings on campus.

Speaking for the first, the pioneering generation, I can say that we passionately believed in what we were building, and we feel amply rewarded by the recognition and achievement of generations of our students. We believed in the strength of Sarah Lawrence's educational system and added to it some basic concepts that enriched that system:

- The concept that woman-focused inquiry is an essential aspect of education.
- The concept that Woman's History is woman's right.
- The concept that academically trained women can learn from and interact with community women — that women organizing women is a proper subject for inquiry and a good mode of giving young women a reality-based education.

Now, thirty-six years after the founding of the M.A. Program in Women's History, the college is continuing what was then started. Hundreds of graduates of the program have carried the message of women's centrality to historical events into every level of the educational system. Others have brought it to ever-widening circles in business, labor unions, and community organizations. Today, Women's History is accepted and legitimized as part of the historical narrative. The story I have here told records only a small part of the effort it took—the inspired belief in the rightness of our research; the dogged persistence in the face of obstacles, resistance, and harassment; the inspiration and strength we gathered from working together with other women—to get to this outcome.

Shortly before her death Joan Kelly dictated the text for the preface to a collection of her essays that would appear posthumously. In it she described her reaction to her discovery that there were vast and challenging sources available about women in the Renaissance:

> That turned out to be the most exciting intellectual adventure I can recall. . . . Suddenly the entire world of learning was open to me. . . . It had a new and compelling attraction and was utterly questionable at the same time. . . . Most questionable was everything I thought I had known about the Renaissance.
>
> The change I went through was kaleidoscopic. I had not read a new book. I did not stumble upon a new archive. No fresh piece of information was added to anything I knew. But I knew now that the entire picture I had held of the Renaissance was partial, distorted, limited, and deeply flawed by those limitations. . . . All I had done was to say . . . suppose we look again at this age, the Renaissance . . . from the vantage point of women?[5]

Joan Kelly, describing her own experience, gave an accurate description of the excitement and challenges women experienced when first confronted with Women's History. Quite apart from the intellectual challenge, they experienced a personal force, an energy, that engaged them in new ways and that often led to dramatic changes in career goals and life decisions. The Graduate Program in Women's History at Sarah Lawrence College managed to give form and shape to this energy and to find ways to connect its insights with the larger community. That was its strength, and that is what gives its pioneering role historical significance.

Notes

1. The Center of Continuing Education served as a transition back to college for women who had interrupted their education due to marriage and motherhood. After one year in the program, the women were able to enroll in any M.A. program the college offered. This was an educational innovation that was widely copied by other institutions and proved highly successful.

2. The other faculty members who offered courses and took part in the creation of Women's Studies were Elfie Stock, Charlotte Doyle, Gertrude Baltimore, Joyce Riegelhaupt, Katherine Rowe, Karen Romer, Charlotte Price, and Lydia Kesich.

3. Gerda Lerner, *The Female Experience: An American Documentary* (Indianapolis: Bobbs-Merrill, 1977).

4. Anne Roiphe, "The Trouble at Sarah Lawrence," *New York Times Magazine*, March 20, 1977, 21–22, 30–39.

5. Joan Kelly, *Women, History and Theory: The Essays of Joan Kelly* (Chicago: University of Chicago Press, 1984), xiii.

PART II

Doing History

chapter four

The Meaning of Seneca Falls

This chapter and the next deal with the Seneca Falls convention of 1848 and the political and social movement it engendered as an event of major significance, both in the past and in the present. In this chapter I try to place the event in its proper historical setting.* In Chapter 5 I deal more closely with the practical lessons applicable to today's struggles that can be drawn from it.

The French Revolution, with its proclamation of the "rights of man," has been deservedly treated by historians as a major event in world history. Not so for the Seneca Falls convention, which, in fact, was the first public gathering of women to proclaim the "rights of women." In either case, we are dealing with half of humankind; yet the Seneca Falls convention has been treated as a side issue, a footnote to history, generally mentioned only in connection with the fight for suffrage in the United States. It occurred to me while writing the essay that a comparison with another historical event that happened the same year, the publication of the Communist Manifesto, *might move readers to consider the Seneca Falls convention in its proper significance.*

Both events offered utopian and practical propositions in order to remedy societal evils. Both led to the creation of vast, long-lasting mass movements. Marxism foresaw revolution as the inevitable means for changing society; feminism demanded societal, institutional, and intensely personal changes to be won through persuasion—a vast cultural transformation. Comparing the worldwide results more than 150 years later might lead us to new insights into the strategy and tactics of making social change.

In 1848, according to Karl Marx and Friedrich Engels, "a specter [was] haunting Europe—the specter of communism." In that same year, the upstate New York village of Seneca Falls hosted a gathering of fewer than 300 people, earnestly debating a Declaration of Sentiments to be spread by newsprint and oratory. The Seneca Falls Woman's Rights Convention marked the beginning of the woman's rights movement.

The specter that haunted Europe developed into a mighty movement, embracing the globe, causing revolutions, wars, tyrannies, and counter-

*This article originally appeared in *Dissent* (Fall 1998): 35–41.

revolutions. Having gained state power in Russia, China, and Eastern Europe, twentieth-century Communism, in 1948, seemed more threatening a specter than ever before. Yet, after a bitter period of "cold war," which pitted nuclear nations against one another in a futile stalemate, it fell of its own weight in almost all its major centers.

The small spark figuratively ignited at Seneca Falls never produced revolutions, usurpation of power, or wars. Yet it led to a transformation of consciousness and a movement of empowerment on behalf of half the human race, which hardly has its equal in human history.

Until very recently, the Seneca Falls convention of 1848 was not recognized as significant by historians, not included in history textbooks, not celebrated as an important event in public schools, never mentioned in the media or the press. In the 1950s, the building where it was held, formerly the Wesleyan chapel, was used as a filling station. In the 1960s, it housed a laundromat. It was only due to the resurgence of modern feminism and the advances of the field of Women's History that the convention has entered the nation's consciousness. The establishment of Women's History Month as a national event during the Carter administration and its continuance through every administration since then has helped to educate the nation to the significance of women's role in history. Still, it took decades of struggle by women's organizations, feminist historians, and preservationists to rescue the building at Seneca Falls and finally to persuade the National Park Service to turn it into a historic site. Today it is a major tourist attraction and has been enhanced by the establishment of a National Women's Hall of Fame on the site. This history of "long forgetting and short remembering" has been an important aspect of women's historic past, the significance of which we only understood as we began to study women's history in depth.

Elizabeth Cady Stanton, the great communicator and propagandist of nineteenth-century feminism, has left a detailed account of the origins of the Seneca Falls convention both in her autobiography and in the monumental *History of Woman Suffrage*.[1] The idea for such a meeting originated with her and with Lucretia Mott, when they both attended the 1840 World Antislavery Convention in London, at which representatives of female antislavery societies were denied seating and voting rights. Outraged by this humiliating experience, Stanton and Mott decided in London that, as soon as possible, they would convene a meeting of women in the United

States to discuss their grievances. But her responsibilities as mother of a growing family intervened, and Stanton could not implement her plan until 1848, when Lucretia Mott visited her sister Martha Wright in Waterloo, a town near Seneca Falls. There, Stanton met with her, her hostess Jane Hunt, and their friend Mary Ann McClintock. Stanton wrote: "I poured out that day the torrent of my long accumulating discontent with such vehemence and indignation that I stirred myself, as well as the rest of the party, to do or dare anything."[2] The five drafted an announcement for a "Woman's Rights Convention" to be held at Seneca Falls on July 19 and 20, and placed the notice in the local paper and the abolitionist press.

The five women who issued the call to the Seneca Falls convention were hardly as naive and inexperienced as later, somewhat mythical versions of the events would lead one to believe. Lucretia Mott was an experienced and highly acclaimed public speaker, a Quaker minister and longtime abolitionist. She had attended the founding meeting of the American Anti-Slavery Society in 1833, which admitted women only as observers. She was a founder of the Philadelphia Female Anti-Slavery Society and its long-term President. The fact that she was announced as the principal speaker at the Seneca Falls convention was a distinct drawing card.

Elizabeth Cady Stanton's "long accumulating discontent" had to do with her struggle to raise her three children (she would later have four more) and run a large household in the frequent absences of her husband Henry, a budding lawyer and Free Soil politician. Still, she found time to be involved in the campaign for reform of women's property rights in New York State, where a reform bill was passed just prior to the convention, and she had spoken before the state legislature.

Martha Wright, Jane Hunt, and Mary Ann McClintock were all separatist Quakers, long active in working to improve the position of women within their church. All of them were veterans of reform and women's organizations and had worked in antislavery fairs.

The place where they held their convention was particularly suited for attracting an audience of radical thinkers. The region had for more than two decades been the center of reform and utopian movements, largely due to the economic upheavals brought by the opening of the Erie Canal in 1825 and the ensuing competition with western agriculture, which brought many farmers to bankruptcy. Economic uncertainty led many to embrace utopian schemes for salvation. The region was known as the "burned-over district," because so many schemes for reforms had swept over it in rapid succession, from the evangelical revivalism of Charles Grandison Finney, to temperance, abolition, church reform, Mormonism, and the chiliastic movement of William Miller, who predicted the second coming of Christ with precision for October 12, 1843, at 3:00 A.M. The nearly one million followers of Miller survived the uneventful passing of that night and the similarly uneventful revised dates of March or October 1844, but their zeal for reform did not diminish.

The men and women who gathered in the Seneca Falls Wesleyan chapel were not a national audience; they all came from upstate New York and represented a relatively narrow spectrum of reform activists. Their local background predisposed them to accept radical pronouncements and challenging proposals. Most of them were abolitionists, the women having been active for nearly ten years in charitable, reform, and antislavery societies. They were experienced in running petition campaigns, and many had organized antislavery fund-raising fairs. Historians Judith Wellman and Nancy Isenberg, who have analyzed the origins and affiliations of those attending the convention, showed that many were religious dissidents, Quakers, who just two months prior had separated from their more traditional church and would shortly form their own group, New York Congregationalist Friends.[3] Another dissident group was Wesleyan Methodists who had been involved in a struggle within their church about the role of women and the laity in church governance. Yet another group came from the ranks of the temperance movement. Among the men in attendance several were local lawyers with Liberty Party or Free Soil affiliations. Also present and taking a prominent part in the deliberations was Frederick Douglass, the former slave and celebrated abolitionist speaker, now editor of the *North Star*.

Far from representing a group of inexperienced housewives running their first public meeting, the majority of the convention participants were reformers with considerable organizational experience. For example, Amy Post and six other women from Rochester who came to Seneca Falls were able to organize a similar woman's rights convention in Rochester just two weeks later. One of the significant aspects of the Seneca Falls convention is that it was grounded in several organizational networks that had already existed for some time and could mobilize the energies of seasoned reform activists.

Most of the reformers attending had family, church, and political affiliations in other areas of the North and Midwest. It was through them that the message of Seneca Falls spread quickly and led to the formation of a national movement. The first truly national convention on woman's rights was held in Worcester, Massachusetts in 1850. By 1860 ten national and many local woman's rights conventions had been organized.

The first day of the Seneca Falls meeting was reserved to women, who occupied themselves with debating, paragraph by paragraph, the Declaration of Sentiments prepared by Elizabeth Cady Stanton. Resolutions were offered, debated, and adopted. At the end of the second day, sixty-eight women and thirty-two men signed their names to a Declaration of Sentiments, which embodied the program of the nascent movement and provided a model for future woman's rights conventions. The number of signers represented only one-third of those present, which probably was due to the radical nature of the statement.

The inequities cited and the demands raised in this Declaration were not entirely novel. Like all major social and intellectual movements, feminism has many and diverse antecedents.

By selecting the Declaration of Independence for their formal model and following its preamble almost verbatim, except for the insertion of gender-neutral language, the organizers of the convention sought to base their main appeal on the democratic rights embodied in the nation's founding document. They also put the weight and symbolism of this revered text behind what was in their time a radical assertion: "We hold these truths to be self-evident: that all men and women are created equal."

The feminist appeal to natural rights and the social contract had long antecedents on the European continent, the most important advocate of it being Mary Wollstonecraft. Her work was well known in the United States, where the same argument had already been well made by Judith Sargent Murray, Frances Wright, Emma Willard, Sarah Grimké, and Margaret Fuller.

The second fundamental argument for the equality of woman was religious. As stated in the Declaration:

Resolved, that woman is man's equal — was intended to be so by the Creator, and the highest good of the race demands that she should be recognized as such.

And one of the "grievances" is:

> *He [man] has usurped the prerogative of Jehovah himself, claiming it as his*
> *right to assign to her a sphere of action, when that belongs to her conscience*
> *and her God.*

The feminist argument based on biblical grounds can be traced back for 700 years prior to 1848, but the women assembled at Seneca Falls were unaware of that fact, because of the nonexistence of anything like Women's History. They did know the Quaker argument, especially as made in her public lectures by Lucretia Mott. They had read Sarah Grimké's *Letters on the Equality of the Sexes*, and several of the resolutions in fact followed her text.[4] They knew the biblical argument by Ann Lee of the Shakers, and they echoed the antislavery biblical argument, applying it to women.

The Declaration departed from precedent in its most radical statement:

> *The history of mankind is a history of repeated injuries and usurpations on*
> *the part of man toward woman, having in direct object the establishment of*
> *an absolute tyranny over her.*

The naming of "man" as the culprit, thereby identifying patriarchy as a system of "tyranny," was highly original, but it may have been dictated more by the rhetorical flourishes of the Declaration of Independence than by an actual analysis of woman's situation. When it came to the list of grievances, the authors departed from the text and became quite specific.

Woman had been denied "her inalienable right to the elective franchise"; she had no voice in the making of laws; she was deprived of other rights of citizenship; she was declared civilly dead upon marriage; she was deprived of her property and wages; she was discriminated against in case of divorce, and in payment for work. Women were denied equal access to education and were kept out of the professions, held in a subordinate position in Church and State, and assigned by man to the domestic sphere. Man has endeavored to destroy woman's self-respect and keep her dependent.

They concluded that in view of the disfranchisement of one-half the people of this country,

> *. . . we insist that [women] have immediate admission to all the rights*
> *and privileges which belong to them as citizens of these United States.*

It has been claimed by historians, and by herself, that Stanton's controversial resolution advocating voting rights for women—the only resolution not approved unanimously at the convention—was her most important original contribution. In fact, Sarah and Angelina Grimké had advocated woman's right to vote and hold office in 1838, and Frances Wright had already done so in the 1830s. It was not so much the originality as the inclusiveness of the listed grievances that was important.

The Declaration claimed universality, even though it never mentioned differences among women. Future woman's rights conferences before the Civil War would rectify this omission and pay particular attention to the needs of lower-class and slave women.

While grievances pertaining to woman's sexual oppression were not explicitly included in the Declaration of Sentiments, they were very much alive in the consciousness of the leading participants. Elizabeth Cady Stanton had already in 1848 begun to include allusions to what we now call "marital rape" in her letters and soon after the Seneca Falls convention made such references explicit, calling on legislatures to forbid marriage to "drunkards." She soon became an open advocate of divorce and of the right of women to leave abusive marriages. Later woman's rights conventions would include some of these issues among their demands, although they used carefully guarded language and focused on abuses by "drunkards." This was a hidden feminist theme of the mainstream woman's temperance movement in the 1880s and caused many temperance women to embrace woman suffrage. What we now call "a woman's right to her body" was already on the agenda of the nineteenth-century woman's rights movement.

It was the confluence of a broad-ranging programmatic declaration with a format familiar and accessible to reformers that gave the event its historical significance. The Seneca Falls convention was the first forum in which women gathered together to publicly air their own grievances, not those of the needy, the enslaved, orphans, or widows. The achievement of a public voice for women and the recognition that women could not win their rights unless they organized made Seneca Falls a major event in history.

WHAT PROGRESS HAS been made in the status of women since 1848?

It is useful to think of women's demands as encompassing two sets of needs: women's rights and women's emancipation.

Women's rights essentially are civil rights—to vote, to hold office, to have access to education and to economic and political power at every level of society on an equal basis with men. They include property rights, the right to one's earnings, the right to sue and be sued, and the right to dispose of property. These rights are demanded on the basis of a claim to equality: as citizens, as members of society, women are by rights equal and must therefore be treated equally. All of the rights here listed are based on the acceptance of the status quo—all women ask is to be admitted to it on a basis of equality. These are essentially reformist demands.

Women's emancipation is freedom from oppressive restrictions imposed by reason of sex: self-determination and autonomy. Oppressive restrictions are biological restrictions due to sex, as well as socially imposed ones. Thus, women's bearing and nursing children is a biological given, but the assignment to women of the major responsibility for the rearing of children and for housework is socially imposed.

Self-determination means being free to decide one's own destiny, to define one's own social role. Autonomy means earning one's status, not being born into it or marrying it. It means financial and cultural independence, freedom to choose one's own lifestyle, regardless of sex. It means freedom to define issues, roles, laws, and cultural norms on equality with men. The demands for emancipation are based on stressing women's difference from men, but also on stressing women's difference from other women. They are radical demands, which can only be achieved by transforming society for men and women, equalizing gender definitions for both sexes, assigning the reproductive work of raising the next generation to both men and women, and reorganizing social institutions so as to make such arrangements possible.

Women, just like men, are placed in society as individuals and as citizens. They are both equal and different. The demand for women's emancipation always includes the demand for women's rights, but the reverse is not true. Generally speaking, women's rights have been won or improved upon in many parts of the world in the past 150 years. Women's emancipation has not yet been won anywhere.

The movement started at Seneca Falls called itself the *woman's rights movement*—embracing the concept of the individual woman as both a person and a citizen demanding rights. As we have seen, its program, from the start, embraced both—by demanding legal, property, civil rights, and by demanding changes in gender role definition and in woman's rights to her own body. As the nineteenth-century movement matured, there developed some tension between advocates of these two different sets of demands, with the mainstream focusing more and more on legal and property rights, while radicals and outsiders, like sex reformers, birth control advocates, and socialist feminists, demanded more profound social changes.

The twentieth-century *women's movement* adopted the plural "women" to show inclusiveness and to reflect the fact that it was a broadly based, coalition-building movement. But the same distinctions and tensions as in the first wave of feminism have appeared in the "new feminism" that started in the 1960s. One wing focused mainly on women's rights—adoption of the ERA, legal/political rights, and representation and civil rights for women of different classes, races, and sexual orientations. The other wing began as "radical women's liberation" and later branched off into many more specialized groups working on abortion rights, the protection of women from violence and sexual harassment, the opening up to women of nontraditional occupations, self-empowerment, and the creation of women's cultural institutions, ranging from lesbian groupings to women's music festivals and pop culture. The two informally defined wings of the movement often overlapped, sometimes collaborated on specific narrow issues, and recently have worked more and more on bridge-building. The Women's Studies movement has struggled long and hard to bridge the two wings and encompass them educationally. Further, new forms of feminism by women of color or women who define themselves as "different" from the majority in various ways have sprung up and served their own constituencies. Their existence has not weakened the movement, as its critics like to claim, but has strengthened it immensely by grounding it more firmly in different constituencies.

Let us not forget, ever, that when we talk about women's rights we talk about the rights of half the human race. No one expects all men to have the same interests, issues, or demands. We should therefore never expect women to have one agenda, one set of issues or demands.

The women's rights demands first raised at Seneca Falls have in the United States been generally achieved for middle-class white women. They have been partially achieved for working-class women and women of color, but progress has been very uneven. The continuing horrendous gaps in life expectancy and in infant mortality and survival rates between white and African American women is but one illustration of this unevenness. The progress on economic issues, such as equal wages, equal access to credit, and equal treatment in home-ownership and insurance availability, has also varied by class and race, with much remaining to be done.

The feminization of poverty and the increasing income gap between the rich and the poor have turned many legal gains won by women into empty shells. An example is the way in which legal restrictions on women's right to choose abortion have fallen more heavily on poor women than on the well-to-do. The uneven availability of child care for working mothers is another example.

The cultural transformation on which demands for woman's emancipation build has been enormous. Many demands that seemed outrageous 150 years ago are now commonly accepted, such as a woman's right to equal guardianship of her children, to divorce, to jury duty, to acceptance in non-traditional occupations. Female police and fire officers and female military personnel are accepted without question in the United States. Women's participation in competitive sports is another area in which progress has been great, though it is far from complete. Many other feminist demands that seemed outrageously radical thirty years ago have become common-place today—the acceptance of lesbians as "normal" members of the community, single motherhood, the criminal character of sexual harassment and marital rape. The acceptance of such ideas is still uneven and different in different places, but generally, the feminist program has been accepted by millions of people who refuse to identify themselves as "feminists." What critics decry as the splintering and diffusion of the movement is actually its greatest strength today.

It should also be recognized that the aims of feminism are transformative, but its methods have been peaceful reform, persuasion, and education. For 150 years feminists have organized, lobbied, marched, petitioned, put their bodies on the line in demonstrations, and have overcome ancient prejudices by heroic acts of self-help. Whatever gains were won had to be won step by step, over and over again. Nothing was "given" to women; whatever gains we have made we have had to earn. And perhaps the most precious "right" we have won in these two centuries is the right to know our own history, to draw on the knowledge and experience of the women before us, to celebrate and emulate our heroines, and finally to know that "greatness" is not a sexual attribute.

WHAT MEANING DOES Seneca Falls hold today?

It shows that a small group of people, armed with a persuasive analysis of grievances and an argument based on generally held moral and religious beliefs, can, if they are willing and able to work hard at organizing, create a transformative mass movement.

The fact that it took seventy-two years of organized effort for American women to win the vote shows that social transformation and legal change is a slow process. The women who launched a small movement in 1848 had to learn to stay with it over nearly four generations. They had to build, county by county, state by state, the largest grassroots movement of the nineteenth century and then build it again in the twentieth century to transform the right to vote into the right to equal representation.

Revolutionaries splutter and flare up like rockets in the night. Those who transform nonviolently sign up for the long duration, through good times and bad—sustaining the warmth necessary for growth like a banked fire.

Seneca Falls and the movement it spawned show that legal changes, hard won though they are, remain useless, and can be reversed, unless social and cultural transformations sustain them.

The feminist program proclaimed at Seneca Falls spoke to vast constituencies of women. The worldwide movement of women for their rights and for emancipation has steadily progressed and is irreversible, although of necessity it has progressed at an uneven pace, due to different historical and cultural conditions in different countries.

Over the past 150 years all of the grievances listed at Seneca Falls have been resolved or at least dealt with, though new inequities and grievances arise in each generation. The "specter that haunted Europe" left some gains, but mostly bloodshed, terror, and devastation in its wake, and most of the inequities it sought to adjust are still with us. Feminism has behind it a record of solid gains without the costs of bloody war and revolution.

Although the media and many politicians with monotonous frequency declare feminism to be dead, many of its goals have been accomplished and its momentum, worldwide, is steadily rising. It will continue to live and grow as long as women anywhere have grievances they can proclaim and as long as they are willing and able to organize to rectify them.

Notes

1. Elizabeth Cady Stanton, *Eighty Years and More: Reminiscences 1815–1897* (T. Fisher Unwin, 1898; reprinted, New York: Schocken Books, 1971); Elizabeth Cady Stanton,

Susan B. Anthony, and Matilda J. Gage, *History of Woman Suffrage*, 6 vols. (New York: Fowler and Wells, 1881–1922).

2. Stanton, *Eighty Years and More*, 148.

3. Judith Wellman, *The Road to Seneca Falls: Elizabeth Cady Stanton and the First Woman's Rights Convention* (Urbana: University of Illinois Press, 2004); Nancy Isenberg, *Sex and Citizenship in Antebellum America* (Chapel Hill: University of North Carolina Press, 1998).

4. Sarah Grimké, *Letters on the Equality of the Sexes and the Condition of Women; Addressed to Mary Parker, President of the Boston Female Anti-Slavery Society* (Boston: Isaac Knapp, 1838).

chapter five

Midwestern Leaders of the
Modern Women's Movement

*It all began with a feeling of personal discontent in 1967, a year after the founding of the
National Organization for Women. I was one of the founders, but as the media began to
transmit information about the new movement, the stereotypes of its members began to
emerge, and people like me—a mother of two in her late forties, community activist for
decades working on women's issues—disappeared, as though we did not exist. Years later,
when the first accounts of the movement were written, the error was perpetuated. Since
I am a nineteenth-century historian, I was not going to do any research on this myself.
Only, in my teaching, I always felt uneasy about the story of the discontinuity of women's
activism in the 1920s and its spontaneous re-emergence in 1966.*

*Shortly after I came to the University of Wisconsin–Madison in 1980 in order to estab-
lish a graduate program in Women's History I met Kathryn (Kay) Clarenbach, a political
scientist and member of the Outreach and Political Science Departments. I soon realized
she was a national treasure and an enormously important figure in the history of the modern women's movement. With the aid of a modest grant, I was able to record her oral history, which revealed a to me an entirely unknown aspect of women's history, namely the
role played by the members of various State Commissions on Women in disseminating and
promoting the modern feminist movement. Further research convinced me that this and
the story of the Midwestern leadership of this movement needed to be recorded and become
part of the historical record.*

*After identifying, with Kay Clarenbach's help, twenty-four subjects for interviews and
gaining their assent as well as pledges by some participants to donate their relevant papers
and documents to the Wisconsin State Historical Society, I secured the co-sponsorship of
the State Archivist and the Director of the University Library for the project. Hoping to
win at least three assistantship positions for graduate students in my program, I drew up
a grant proposal in 1989 to be submitted to the National Endowment for the Humanities
(NEH) for a three-year oral history project. Planning and actual work on the proposal took
over a year. The NEH rejected the proposal, but invited us to make some changes and resub-
mit. We did so, even though it meant losing another year.[1] Meanwhile, I proceeded with a
back-up plan. This meant writing three more grant proposals to local funding agencies and*

wheedling a money commitment out of the Graduate School for a project reduced to two rather than three years. When the NEH again and finally rejected the proposal, the back-up plan allowed us to proceed. Thus, in the fall of 1991, we finally launched our oral history project, "Midwestern Leaders of the Modern Women's Movement."

After all the interviews were finished, we concluded the project with a conference titled "Bridges That Carry Us Over: Midwestern Leaders of the Modern Women's Movement," held at the University of Wisconsin–Madison on November 20–21, 1992, at which we honored the participants. For some of them, this represented the first recognition ever given to them for their work for women. This chapter is partially based on an article derived from my lecture at that conference.* The tapes and documents supporting this project, as well as a separately recorded tape of Kathryn Clarenbach, are available to researchers at the Archives Division of the Wisconsin State Historical Society in Madison.

Those writing history depend on records and sources as interpreted by succeeding generations of historians. For nearly four millennia the sources most likely to be preserved concerned the activities of men in public life, warfare, conquest, and political and economic power. For nearly all of the centuries in which trained historians practiced their craft of interpretation, the historians were male, and what they described were the activities of men. Thus it came to pass that most of the historical record omits or marginalizes the activities of women. To put it another way, for most of recorded historical time, women have been deprived of their history.

Yet women have always struggled for some kind of knowledge of women's activities and work. This is shown in the centuries of women's making and passing on to others the lists of famous or worthy women—a rudimentary form of history-making.

Late in the nineteenth century, the leaders of the woman suffrage movement began to be concerned with collecting the raw materials for women's history and with preserving, state by state, the record of their own achievements in educational and reform institutions, churches, women's clubs, and communities. What they were then documenting was the record of daily activities, the immense community-building work of ordinary women. Whether they knew it or not, this effort links them with the long line of list-makers, who tried to tease the existence of a history

---

*The article was published as Gerda Lerner, "Midwestern Leaders of the Modern Women's Movement," *Wisconsin Academy Review* 41, no. 1 (Winter 1994–95): 11–15. The present chapter is a revision and expansion of this earlier article.

of women out of the scraps available to them from the history of educated men.

The most self-consciously feminist effort of this kind was represented in the six-volume *History of Woman Suffrage*, compiled by Elizabeth Cady Stanton, Susan B. Anthony, and Matilda Joslyn Gage, with contributions from women in every state.[2] The feminists engaged in this effort realized that the first need for those creating history is the existence of sources. They were aware of the danger that their movement—which, combined with the women's club movement, was the largest mass organization and the largest coalition built in the nineteenth century—might fall into oblivion if its records were lost. To preserve the record was uppermost in the minds of the editors. Their somewhat haphazard assemblage of the documents they could find was an immense contribution, despite its shortcomings.

History of Woman Suffrage is an incomplete and heavily biased assemblage of sources. The strongly secular bias of its editors and their disenchantment with the organized churches in regard to the struggle of women for their emancipation is reflected in the way they defined the movement as mostly political and constitutional, disregarding the important feminist struggles in the various churches during the nineteenth century. It is also factionally biased in its downplaying of the role of women who in 1869 split with Stanton and Anthony, a distortion that is particularly striking in regard to the virtual suppression of the contributions to the movement of Lucy Stone.

Yet these volumes have provided the basis for over one hundred years of history-writing on this subject. It is to this source we owe the story of the origin of the nineteenth-century woman's rights movement, which has been faithfully and uncritically repeated ever since: the crucial meeting of Elizabeth Cady Stanton and Lucretia Mott at the 1840 antislavery convention in London, at which the idea of a movement for woman's rights first took shape; Stanton and Mott meeting socially with three other women over tea in 1848 and deciding to hold a convention at Seneca Falls; their inexperience, which caused them to ask a man to preside over their meeting; their reliance on political documents—the Declaration of Independence and the Constitution—to direct their movement into secular, political channels; the origin of their ideas in the antislavery movement; the crucial importance for the future of the movement of Stanton's daring resolution asking for woman suffrage; and above all, the leading role of Elizabeth Cady Stanton in holding what her version of the story stressed was the first

national woman's rights meeting. The story is true and, through omissions
and shifts of emphasis, it is also false.

What the story omits is the decisive role of women other than Stanton
and Mott in initiating the movement; the long years of organizational
experience many of these women had in reform, especially in religious reform movements; and the continuity of this reform effort and its breadth.
Historians Judith Wellman and Nancy Isenberg have shown that the idea
of a woman's rights movement was talked about in a number of reform
groups before 1848; that the Seneca Falls meeting was a local meeting; and
that the first truly national woman's rights convention was held in 1850
at Worcester, Massachusetts. Studying the activists in the pre–Civil War
conventions, they show that most of them came from dissident religious
groups and from reform movements of various kinds and that the woman's
rights movement from its inception depended on the existence of a radical
reform network, based largely in several dissident churches.[3] Thus they
give us a much broader and richer interpretation of both the origins and
the early decades of the movement than does the traditional version. Isenberg also uncovers and highlights the role of several other great leaders and
theoreticians besides Stanton.

There is an interesting parallel here to the history of the origin of the
twentieth-century women's rights movement. In historical and in media
accounts we have been told that once women got the vote in 1920 they
ceased to struggle for their own rights. The decades from the 1920s to the
1960s, and especially the 1950s, have been generally viewed as a period
devoid of feminist activities. Then, almost as if by magic, the movement
started suddenly as the result of Betty Friedan's book, *The Feminine Mystique.*[4] In a somewhat deeper analysis, historians have identified several
"roots" of the twentieth-century women's movement: women's organizations among some of the churches, such as the Methodists; the small band
of former suffragists who rallied around the National Women's Party; the
civil rights movement of the 1960s; and the student movement of the same
period.[5] The media version of the origins of the modern women's movement has perpetuated certain commonly held misconceptions: that it was
a movement that arose largely in several East and West Coast centers and
in Chicago; that it was led and organized by young, radical women, most
of them college students; and that, from its inception, the movement's
membership was white and middle-class.

Without in any way wanting to diminish the importance of Betty

Friedan's book and her organizing energy, or discounting the burst of initiative and the creative energy of young women out of the civil rights movement (disenchanted with that movement's sexism) and the breakthrough of theoretical insights and organizing genius of lesbians and others involved in the sexual revolutions, I would argue that up to now we have insufficiently recognized the contributions to the movement made by other groups of women.

AS IT HAPPENED, many of the founders of the major modern women's organizations, such as the National Organization for Women (NOW) and the National Women's Political Caucus, came from the Midwest and particularly from Wisconsin—so much so that in the 1970s they were jocularly known among movement leaders as the "Wisconsin Mafia." In 1966, of the 196 founding members of NOW, 134 came from the Midwest, among them 8 nuns. It is these Midwestern activists who were the focus of our oral history project. Their stories, as personally told by them, document their leadership roles in national and local movements and their important organizational work in launching the modern feminist movement.

In order to appreciate the full importance of the contribution of Midwestern women to the creation of the modern women's movement attention has to be given to the crucial role of the Commissions on the Status of Women (CSW). When, in 1961, President John F. Kennedy, at the urging of his Secretary of Labor, Esther Peterson, created the first national commission, the mainstream women's rights movement gained national legitimacy and an institutional base. By 1967 Governors' commissions had been set up in all states. Their membership included government officials, leaders of women's organizations, and representatives from labor, business, and reform organizations. The charge of the commissions was to monitor legislation on women, to fight sex discrimination, and to promote opportunities for women in public employment. In 1970 this network of women leaders was united in the National Association of Commissions for Women, an umbrella organization of the state CSWs, chaired from 1970 to 1972 by Kay Clarenbach. This appointment put her at the center of a national network of women activists and grassroots leaders.

Kathryn (Kay) Clarenbach (1920–94), the mother of three children, was Director of University Education of Women, 1962–67 and Specialist in Continuing Education for Women, 1967–72, at the University of Wisconsin–Madison (see Appendix A for a fuller biography). As Professor of

Political Science she continued her work in Outreach until her retirement in 1988.

Due to her years of activism among faculty women and on behalf of women students, Clarenbach was at the center of a strong network of activists when she became Chair of the Wisconsin Governor's CSW in 1964. All the women we interviewed named her as the key person and organizer of their group, when they participated in the founding of NOW in 1966. She was elected as Chair of the first Board of NOW (1966–70), member of the NOW Advisory Council, and President of NOW Legal Defense and Education Fund (1982–83). She was, in fact, the chief organizer of NOW in its early years and, as such, she was able to bring the concerns of a small movement promoting radical ideas for cultural and economic reform into a long-established national movement represented by women in the various state CSWs. Through her and through the women she mobilized, radical feminist ideas began to become part of mainstream women's organizations, while in turn these groups influenced the feminist movement to support a legislative agenda and work for equity for women in government appointments.

Clarenbach continued her central organizing role as Executive Director of the U.S. Commission for Observance of International Women's Year (1975–76) and deputy Coordinator of the Houston National Women's Conference (1977). Again, she acted as organizer, networker, and coalition-builder. She continued her leadership in national women's organizations and in women's education until her retirement.

The twenty-two women we interviewed were identified by Kay Clarenbach as being representative of the Midwestern leadership of the modern women's movement—and included Clarenbach herself. Their demographic profile differed sharply from that commonly ascribed to modern feminists. As a group, these were not young women, but rather women well into middle age. In 1966, just prior to the formation of NOW, the two youngest women in the group were thirty-seven and thirty-eight years old; the three oldest were fifty-four, fifty-five, and sixty-three years old; and the others were in their forties.

Two of the women were nuns: Sisters Joel Read and Austin Doherty of the School Sisters of Saint Francis. Of the remaining twenty women, fifteen were married and thirteen had children. Here again, their demographics vary greatly from the standard of their contemporaries: six women had one or two children each; two had three; one each had four, five, or six children. Political activist and State Representative Midge Miller had four children of her own and, after her husband's death, married a widower with five children. Addie Wyatt had two children and, after her divorce, raised them and five of her own siblings.

Again contrary to stereotype, there were three African American women among the group: Addie Wyatt, Nellie Wilson, and Clara Day. It is also striking that seven women out of twenty-two, not counting the two nuns, had strong religious backgrounds and were activists in their churches before they became interested in women's issues. Several of them continued their church activities down to the present and one, Addie Wyatt, became the minister of her Church of God after retiring from her union work.

As we look at brief biographies of their lives and see them functioning in several circles of activism, we can get a deeper understanding of the way grassroots activism is initiated and sustained. (See Appendix A for more information on the women mentioned here) We can view each woman as the center of activity that radiates outward and draws in larger groups of participants to the causes to which she dedicated herself. We can notice the way their advocacy of women's rights was sustained over decades and took organizational shape and direction after 1966, when they became part of the leadership of the new women's movement. We can get glimpses of the richness and diversity of that movement, when we see how it turned these grassroots Midwestern community leaders into national figures. Their stories have not adequately been told, and their roles in the movement have been hidden from view. Let us now look at several of them in their affinity groups.

Seven of the women were trade union leaders and lifelong activists.

Mildred Jeffrey, after working for the Amalgamated Clothing Workers and the War Production Board during World War II, worked for the United Automobile Workers (UAW) in leading positions. She was the first director of the UAW Women's Department, 1945–49.

Following Jeffrey in UAW leadership was **Dorothy Haener**, who became the union's International Representative in 1952 and director of the Women's Department in 1960, working in the latter capacity until her retirement. As chair of the Women's Department, Haener worked for passage of the Equal Pay Act and for adding the category "sex" to the executive Order on Equal Employment Opportunities. She served on the President's Commission on the Status of Women. She chaired the NOW Task Force on

Poverty. As a member of the organizing committee for the 1977 International Women's Year Conference in Houston she helped develop the plank on employment adopted by the conference.

The UAW was exemplary in the labor movement for its positive attitude toward its female members, many of whom advanced to leadership positions. The union's Women's Department, founded in 1937, pioneered in negotiating equal pay and equal job training opportunities for its 200,000 women members in every contract. The maternity leave clauses in UAW contracts became models for maternity protection in other industries, businesses, and academic institutions. The union's demand for government- or business-funded child care centers was more difficult to implement and has yet to be achieved.

Another UAW activist was **Doris Thom**, who broke new ground for women when, in 1961, she became the first and only woman to serve on the union's Executive Board, a position she held for seven years. In 1965, as a result of her filing a complaint with the Equal Employment Opportunity Commission (EEOC), she became the first woman at the plant to move out of the wholly female trim line into a job category previously reserved for men only.

Helen Hensler worked in the office of the Steelworkers Union. She held various leadership functions and served as President of Local 9 of the Office and Professional Employees International Union. She served on the County Labor Council and founded the Women's Committee of the Wisconsin AFL-CIO, serving as its chair from 1970 to 1986.

The three other union women were African American. **Clara Day** helped to organize her shop for the Brotherhood of Teamsters and later worked full-time for the union, including as Executive Board member and Trustee.

Nellie Wilson was active in the Steelworkers Union, the first woman elected to office in her local and later on the union's Executive Board. She joined the staff of the AFL-CIO and worked with the Milwaukee Labor Council.

Addie Wyatt worked in a Chicago meatpacking plant; her co-workers were white men. Yet she was elected in 1952, first as Vice President, then as President of Illinois Meat Local 56, the first woman and the first black person to win a union leadership position. She continued as a staff member of the United Packinghouse Workers of America until her retirement in 1984.

On our original list of leaders to be interviewed there were two other union women: Catherine Conroy (Communications Workers of America) and Caroline Davis (UAW), who unfortunately died before the project was funded. Had they been included, nearly half of the group would have been trade union activists.

It is noteworthy that these women all had years of factory experience, even though several of them advanced to staff and organizational leadership positions. Thus they were able to bring the experiences of shop workers to the women's movement and to their middle-class allies. They lived with the daily reality of job discrimination. Addie Wyatt reported on the situation in the Chicago Armour meatpacking plant, where in the 1940s in the canning room women made 62 cents an hour and men 76 cents for the same job. As typists, a white woman could make $18.00 a week, a light-skinned black woman $12.00 a week, and a dark black woman, like herself, $8.00 a week. Such real life experiences taught women the inseparable linkage between race and sex discrimination.

The union women in our project all reported that they had had to fight sexism and racism not only in employment but within their unions. When Addie Wyatt attended a union meeting for the first time, she was deeply impressed that there was a room full of people of different ages, sexes, and colors "talking about the problems of decent wages and working conditions. But in addition to that, they were talking about the struggle of black people, Hispanic people, women. . . . I wanted to be a part of it." This experience started her on her remarkable thirty years of union leadership. Union women fought for an end to sex discrimination by businesses and within unions and gained the support of the wider women's movement for those issues. They advocated equal job rights for women, by which they meant access to job opportunities regardless of sex and equal pay for comparable work. In short, they were fighting against the gender-segregated job definitions that inevitably categorized a woman's job as lower skilled and lower paid than a man's. But they also were aware of the reality of women's dual roles as workers and family members and wanted them supported in both aspects of their lives. In this respect they differed, at times sharply, from the middle-class women who saw access to job opportunities as the main issue and who believed family obligations and equally shared household responsibilities could be gained by private negotiations and by education. Both groups agreed on working for access of women to nontraditional jobs, and their coalition helped to win startling successes in a relatively short time span. Today, women's equal job status as police, fire-fighters, construction workers, and within the military is taken so much for granted, it is easily forgotten that these were hard-won gains of a militant feminist movement.

Midwestern women played a prominent role in the formation of a special labor organization to help union women achieve leadership positions and take part in political action. The Congress of Labor Union Women was formed in 1974 by Clarenbach, Day, Wilson, Haener, Hensler, Jeffrey, and others as an advocacy and political action group for union women.

The National Women's Political Caucus (NWPC), another group formed in the 1970s, had the broader goal of advancing legislation beneficial to women on the national and state level and of acting as a training group for women in politics. Among our interviewees, seven were NWPC founders and activists: Gene Boyer, Clarenbach, Ruth Clusen, Mary Eastwood, Haener, Jeffrey, and Miller.

The trade union leaders represented in this group worked all their active lives within their unions, where they worked on economic and social women's issues. Their activity for women workers brought wider and wider circles of union women into activism on other feminist issues, such as opposition to rape and violence. The very existence of this core group of trade union activists gives the lie to the constantly repeated stereotype that the modern women's movement was middle-class.

When we now look at the women who made political careers, we see a pattern of their moving from local, grassroots work to state and national leadership. **Martha Griffiths**, a lawyer and a Democrat, was elected to the Michigan state legislature in 1949. Winning a seat in Congress in 1954, she served for twenty years and won many "firsts" as a woman. Although she did not consider herself a feminist, she made crucial contributions to winning women's rights.

Mary Eastwood, after a decade of local activism and various government jobs, became staff lawyer to the President's Commission on the Status of Women. Her research into the legal status of women led to her publication, co-authored with African American Pauli Murray, of the highly influential publication "Jane Crow and the Law: Sex Discrimination and Title VII." This work led Eastwood to become a strong supporter of the Equal Rights Amendment (ERA) and the EEOC, a founding member of NOW and of the Woman's Party. She continued her legal feminist work as an Equal Opportunity Officer in the Justice Department, in various feminist organizations she founded, and finally as President of the National Woman's Party from 1989 to 1991.

Arvonne Fraser worked for Hubert Humphrey's Senate campaign and then worked as secretary in the Democratic Farmer-Labor Party. In 1950 she married lawyer and activist Don Fraser, with whom she would have six children, and managed his election campaign for Minnesota State Senator. Still, Fraser moved into Farmer-Labor party leadership in her own right. When Don Fraser was elected to the U.S. Congress in 1962, the family moved to Washington, D.C. There, she continued work as Administrative Assistant in her husband's Congressional office. In 1981 President Carter appointed her Coordinator of the Office of Women in Development at the United States Information Agency. Since then, she has been active for women on the international scene.

Judith Goldsmith, who had been raised in Wisconsin, lived in Buffalo during a brief marriage, where she taught English on the university level. In 1977 she divorced her husband and lived with her daughter in Manitowoc, Wisconsin. There she founded the local chapter of NOW and in quick succession became State Coordinator, National Executive Board member, and Vice President. She was National President of NOW from 1982 to 1985.

After her Washington work with NOW, she served as Special Consultant to the Chancellor for Equity and Affirmative Action at the University of Wisconsin–Stevens Point.

Mary Jean Collins became involved in the women's movement at Alverno College in Milwaukee, where she earned a B.A. in history. After a marriage, and divorce in 1975, she began to identify herself as a lesbian. She became active in the Milwaukee chapter of NOW and, after her move to Chicago, became President of that chapter. She advanced from regional leadership in NOW to membership on the National Board. From 1975 to 1980, she worked as Representative for the Illinois Nurses Association and won a first statewide union contract. She became Executive Director of Chicago NOW and directed the state campaign for ratification of the ERA until 1982. She moved to Washington, D.C., and served as Action Vice President of NOW, focusing on reproductive rights, lesbian rights, and issues of economic discrimination. She later continued her organizational work with Catholics for a Free Choice.

The next group of women to consider is those whose main political career was in the state of Wisconsin. They are a highly educated group:

Virginia Hart, Sarah Harder, and Midge Miller earned M.A. degrees, and Miller added three years of graduate study in theology. Harder had a long academic career, first as a teaching professor, then as Assistant to the Chancellor for Affirmative Action. Mary Lou Munts earned a law degree. Kathryn Clarenbach, who was a professor of Political Science at the University of Wisconsin–Madison for twenty-six years, also belongs in this group.

Sarah Harder taught and held administrative positions at the University of Wisconsin–Eau Claire. Her political work centered on the American Association of University Women, whose President she became 1985–89. After attending the Houston Conference in 1977 she worked for the implementation of the women's agenda passed at that conference through coalition-building in the state, which led to the creation of the Wisconsin Women's Network in 1979.

Virginia Hart's organizational work dates back to the 1930s, mostly in the YWCA, then in unions. She fused her commitment to organizing and social action by teaching in the School for Workers in Madison and by activism in Democratic Party politics. When she was appointed Secretary of the Department of Labor and Regulations by Governor Patrick J. Lucey in 1973, she became the first woman to hold a cabinet position in Wisconsin, and she continued in state government service until 1983.

Marjorie "Midge" Miller started her organizational work in the YWCA and continued that work, together with her husband Dean Leeper, as YMCA missionaries in postwar Japan. She was pregnant with her fourth child when her husband died in a typhoon in 1954. She continued her academic studies and in 1962 married Edward Miller, a physics professor and widower with five children.

Miller focused her work on Democratic politics, beginning with Eugene McCarthy's presidential campaign. She attended all but one Democratic National Convention and served on the party's National Committee from 1975 to 1984. Between 1970 and 1984 she was a member of the Wisconsin State Assembly. She worked for sex equity in state employment and authored legislation against domestic abuse.

Mary Lou Munts was a leader in the national student movement while she was at Swarthmore College, and for ten years, while living in Washington, D.C., with her husband and four children, she was active in the civil rights movement. In 1967, when the Munts family moved to Madison, Mary Lou worked as an organizer for several Democratic Party campaigns and studied for a law degree, which she earned in 1976. She was elected to the state legislature in 1972 and over the course of six terms became known as the most productive legislator of her time. Her major accomplishments were divorce reform and marital property legislation and her leadership of the Wisconsin Women's Network. In 1982–84, when she served as Chair of the Joint Finance Committee, she was the most powerful woman in state government. She served on the Public Service Commission from 1984 to 1991.

Ruth Clusen was another Wisconsin-based leader, whose main organizational work was in the League of Women Voters (LWV). She was President of the Green Bay chapter, then of the Wisconsin LWV, and then of the national organization (1974–78). In the latter capacity she organized the presidential debates in 1976. She was also active on environmental issues, which resulted in her appointment as Secretary for the Environment in President Carter's administration. She also served on the University of Wisconsin's Board of Regents.

Although several of the women interviewed achieved distinction in the field of education, perhaps most prominent as educators were Sisters Joel Read and Austin Doherty of Alverno College.

Sister Joel Read joined the School Sisters of Saint Francis (SSSF) in 1942 following graduation from Loretto Academy. She earned her B.A. from Alverno College and her M.A. in History from Fordham University, where she also pursued doctoral studies. She joined the Alverno College History faculty in 1955 and served as department chair before becoming College President in 1968, a position from which she recently retired. Together with Sister Austin Doherty, she initiated and supervised curriculum reform that was strongly influenced by their work with secular women's organizations. Alverno replaced grades with achievement assessment, involved students in self-assessment, and created a close connection with local businesses that enabled students to go from college to jobs by a graduated combination of academic learning and internships. Alverno's educational plan has proven spectacularly successful in helping racial minorities and economically deprived students to complete higher education. It has become a nationally acclaimed model. Sister Joel Read has been highly honored by awards and appointments, among them a presidential appointment to the National Endowment for the Humanities (1978–84).

Sister Austin Doherty entered the order of the SSSF in her mid-twenties and taught at the high school and college level while earning an M.A. in

History at Marquette University and a Ph.D. in Psychology at Loyola University in 1968. Within her religious order she has been engaged in the reassessment of the role of women religious following Vatican II and in the transformation of her order. This work strengthened and inspired her educational pioneering.

She chaired the Psychology Department at Alverno College for seven years. As Assistant Dean for Curriculum Development between 1975 and 1978 she led the college's transformation from a standard liberal arts college to a model in competence-based learning. Since 1982 she has been Vice President for Academic Affairs.

The two businesswomen in our group combined their vocations with political work, as did the educators.

Gene Boyer and her husband, a baseball player in the military, settled in Beaver Dam, Wisconsin, after their daughter was born. They purchased a furniture store, which they ran jointly. Gene Boyer began her public activism when she was denied membership in the local Chamber of Commerce because she was a woman. She responded by organizing protests and finally founding a Women's Division of the Chamber. She helped to form a Mayor's Commission in Beaver Dam and was a leader in women's organizations in Wisconsin.

Nancy Wood left a job as a high school math and physics teacher to become a full-time homemaker and mother of five, while her husband held various jobs in Illinois. During World War II the family moved to Chicago and Wood worked on the Manhattan Project of the University of Chicago, making radiation detectors. Unlike her male co-workers, she was not recruited by private industry after the war, so she founded her own company producing radiation detectors.

She began working on women's issues in Zonta, an international organization for the advancement of women in business and the professions, in the 1950s. A charter member of NOW, she served on the national board from 1967 to 1975 and founded Chicago NOW, in which she continued working on sex-integrating all-male businesses and advocating social security for homemakers.

THE FACT THAT ten women among the twenty-two we interviewed were members of either the President's or a State Commission on the Status of Women speaks to the high level of leadership they represented. As a group, these Midwestern women were firmly rooted in their communities and represented years of activism at the grassroots level. When NOW was organized in 1966, it embraced a more radical agenda than had the State Commissions. Styled on the organizational model of a civil rights organization, NOW advocated cultural changes such as the taking on of child care responsibilities by fathers, women's right to safe and legal abortions, and the promotion of civil rights for lesbians. NOW chapters engaged in consciousness-raising and in direct action to secure equity for women in access to nontraditional jobs, to outlaw sex-segregated job advertisements, and to end gender-based discrimination. While NOW's program appeared radical at the time compared to the way traditional women's organizations had worked, it would soon be considered reformist and traditional compared with the truly radical demands of the women's liberation movement that emerged a few years later.

The women in our study acted as bridge-builders between NOW and the older-style reform organizations. Nine of them were founding members of NOW, with several assuming national leadership positions. The trade union members brought an awareness of working women's demands to NOW's platform, while its explicitly feminist agenda for cultural change in women's role definitions began to impact the older mainstream organizations. All of these women worked for passage of the ERA, and after it failed to receive ratification, they continued pressuring for equal rights and opportunities for women to be enforced by the EEOC and by laws targeting specific abuses. Nine of those interviewed moved into political activism on the state and local level and worked for feminist goals such as property rights reform, divorce reform, protection of women and children from rape and violence, and improvements in women's health care. An issue uniting the several women's constituencies was the struggle for equity in educational opportunities for girls.

If we now look at the organizational work of these twenty-two women over a lifetime span, we find an unexpected pattern. In our interviews we asked the women to list their organizational work up to the year 1991, the year when we took their oral histories. As we analyzed their replies, we found an astonishing record of activism. Sixteen out of twenty-two women had engaged in organizational activism for a period of 30 to 52 years (50+ years = 3 women; 49–40 years = 3; 39–30 years = 10); five had done so for 20 to 29 years, and one had been active in organizational work for 16 years. We measured their activism simply by their activity and leadership in women's organizations or in educational work for women.

What is most remarkable is that their organizational work was carried on uninterrupted, even though many of them had mothering responsibilities and full-time work. For this particular group of Midwestern feminist leaders, we can prove that the 1940s and 1950s, a supposedly dormant period of women's activism, was instead a period of intense organizational commitment.

Just as in the 1850s, the modern women's movement in the 1960s did not arise from discontinuity, but was instead built on continuity in the organizational work of women.

WHAT CAN BE LEARNED from this oral history project?

We can learn how complex and broadly based social movements are. Comparing the "official" versions of the origins of the nineteenth- and twentieth-century women's movements, we can see that the women who collect the documents and write the first historical accounts are not necessarily the decisive players. Those who command the communications networks of their time — the media players — are not necessarily the only builders of the movement, nor are they ever the most important organizers. All mass movements depend on a network of grassroots activists and on people able to build coalitions on the state and local level.

We can learn about the variety of strands that build a mass movement. The official pronouncements of the "stars" of a movement do not necessarily describe the full appeal and breadth of it. Elizabeth Cady Stanton rightly deserves praise and recognition for her advanced views on the ballot and on the right to divorce, but the women long active in their churches, fighting for an upgraded role for women before Stanton ever came on the scene, represent an equally important strand of the movement. Similarly, the impact of trade union activism on the second women's movement has long been hidden, but was nevertheless important to its success and to its future. The stereotype of the "white, middle-class movement" wipes out the memory and activism of large numbers of women of color and working-class feminists.

We can learn about the continuity of women's efforts to organize for social change in their own communities long before the modern women's movement revitalized that effort. The work of the Commissions on the Status of Women and of the women sustaining their work needs to be further studied and documented if we wish to understand the history of the modern women's movement.

We can learn about steady and continuous leadership that does not necessarily depend on recognition by the mass media.

Our knowledge of the grassroots underpinnings of powerful mass movements can provide encouragement and sound perspective to those trying to work for social change in times of repression.

Finally, we can learn about the national significance of Midwestern leaders and the strength of their grassroots activism.

The Midwestern women who played such an important part in the founding of the modern women's movement showed all the characteristics of leadership: commitment to a great ideal, the ability to inspire others and influence them through organizational work, and an understanding that social change rests upon long-range effort. They were not easily discouraged, and they transcended difficulties, hostility, and backlash. They were indeed among the movers and shakers of the twentieth-century women's movement.

Notes

1. Unfortunately, out of the twenty-four women we had planned to interview, two—Catherine Conroy and Caroline Davis—died before we could secure enough grant money to support the launch project. Thus, we actually interviewed only twenty-two women.

2. Elizabeth Cady Stanton, Susan B. Anthony, and Matilda J. Gage, *History of Woman Suffrage*, 6 vols. (New York: Fowler and Wells, 1881–1922).

3. Judith Wellman, *The Road to Seneca Falls: Elizabeth Cady Stanton and the First Woman's Rights Convention* (Urbana: University of Illinois Press, 2004). Wellman's dissertation, on which her book was based, was available to scholars years in advance of the book's publication. Nancy Isenberg, *Sex and Citizenship in Antebellum America* (Chapel Hill: University of North Carolina Press, 1998).

4. Betty Friedan, *The Feminine Mystique* (New York: W. W. Norton, 1963).

5. For a discussion of the role of the Methodist Church youth movement, see Sara Evans, *Personal Politics: The Roots of Women's Liberation in the Civil Rights Movement and the New Left* (New York: Vintage Books, 1980). For the role of the National Women's Party, see Leila J. Rupp and Verta Taylor, *Survival in the Doldrums: The American Women's Rights Movement, 1945 to the 1960s* (New York: Oxford University Press, 1987). For varying interpretations of the sources of the modern women's movement, see Maren Lockwood Carden, *The New Feminist Movement* (New York: Russell Sage Foundation, 1974); Flora Davis, *Moving the Mountain: The Women's Movement in America since 1960* (New York: Simon & Schuster, 1991); Barbara Sinclair Deckard, *The Women's*

Movement: Political, Socioeconomic, and Psychological Issues, 3rd ed. (New York: Harper and Row, 1983); Susan M. Hartmann, *From Margin to Mainstream: American Women and Politics Since 1960* (Philadelphia: Temple University Press, 1989); Judith Hole and Ellen Levine, *Rebirth of Feminism* (New York: Quadrangle Books,, 1971); Rita J. Simon and Gloria Danziger, *Women's Movements in America: Their Successes, Disappointments, and Aspirations* (New York: Praeger, 1991); and Sheila Tobias, *Faces of Feminism: An Activist's Reflection on the Women's Movement* (Boulder, Colo.: Westview Press, 1997).

chapter six

Women in World History

This chapter is based on a paper I gave at a conference on World History.* I was asked specifically to speak on how women might be included in the World History survey. It was a question I had encountered in various forms wherever I spoke on Women's History. The traditional training historians had received and their years of practice had led to the development of a canon, which seemed immutable and of eternal validity. Gradually during the development of Demographic and Social History, this canon had to be expanded to allow for the inclusion in the traditional narrative of masses of ordinary people, who had hitherto been left out of the historical account. Throughout the twentieth century, new groups of such people—African Americans, Hispanics, women, Native Americans—raised their claims for inclusion, which eventually led to the expansion and enrichment of the traditional historical narrative. In each case, traditionalists bemoaned the "splintering" of history and glumly predicted a lowering of standards. They raised the specter of having to exclude "important" people on account of these newcomers. But history is no straitjacket and no zero-sum game. Its narrative has always been altered to fit new constituencies and new concepts.

From the late 1960s on, when I had become a spokeswoman for Women's History, I had endlessly to respond to the same questions and objections. I replied as simply as I could. From its inception what we call history had been concerned only with the activities of half the human race. It should properly be called the history of men. To correct that profound error of omission, it was time to question the criteria of selection by which historians defined historical significance.

The development of Women's History and the history of oppressed minority groups began in the 1980s to call attention to the social construction of identities and with it to entirely new fields of inquiry: Gender History, Gay and Lesbian History, the history of sexualities. Challenges to the predominance of European-centered history and the realities of globalization led to a growing interest in developing World History courses. Conferences and institutes were organized to better train teachers for the demands of the new field. I was often invited to speak at such conferences on the subject of how to include women in World History courses.

*Presented on the panel "Gender in World History" at the World History Association Meeting, Boston, June 23, 2000.

In a pamphlet written for the American Historical Association series on teaching his-
*tory—*Teaching Women's History*—I outlined how to broaden our historical under-*
standing by the use of fifteen analytical questions that would bring women into view (see
the Introduction for more about my approach to writing this pamphlet). Since many teach-
ers found it very useful in developing Women's History courses, I decided to use twelve of
these analytical questions, applying them to World History.

The problem of how to integrate women into courses in World History
is similar to that faced in all other fields, such as U.S. History, Medieval
History, Social History. The fields have already been defined in such a way
that they exclude and marginalize women; the courses have a finite number of weeks assigned to them, and there already exists a body of material
to be learned. Material on women is available in abundance—the prospec-
tive teacher shudders at the thought of somehow having to make room
for it. And the first question that arises is "What do I have to leave out in
order to put women in?"

We have all been through that stage, which leads to token representation, frustration, and a general sense of unease, both in teachers and students.

A favorite strategy is to identify one or two topics in which women
have been recognized as historical actors, such as "woman's suffrage" or
"women and the family" and to spend one or two class hours on these
special topics, and be done with it. One certainly can usefully discuss the
struggle for woman's suffrage or the impact of demographic changes in
the family upon women and their lives, but these topics encompass only a
small part of women's role in societies. To make such units stand alone or to
combine them with the inclusion of a few famous women, usually queens
or women noted for scandalous or deviant behavior, only reinforces the
marginalization of women in the totality of the history course.

Another favorite teaching strategy is to treat women as we often treat
"minorities" and include in the course only stories of their victimization
and oppression, with here and there an example of heroic resistance to
such oppression—Joan of Arc, Anne Hutchinson, Rosa Luxemburg. While
inferior status and oppressive restraints have been aspects of women's historical experience and should be taught, the limitation of this approach
is that it casts women into passive roles or deals with them merely as victims. It fails to elicit the positive and essential ways in which women have
functioned in history. Women have *always* been agents in history. The true

history of women is the history of their ongoing functioning in a male-defined world, *in their own terms.*

Let me suggest that the first precondition for successfully teaching about women is that the teacher must believe that what women did, experienced, and thought in the past actually matters. The teacher must go beyond the patriarchal conceptual framework in which he or she was trained and fully accept what it means that women are half of humankind. Women are in fact, in many places, including the United States, the majority, and they are distributed through all classes and categories of society. Their history inevitably reflects variations as to class, race, religion, ethnicity, and any number of other categories, as does the history of men. But the overriding fact is that women's history is the history of half of humankind.

It follows logically that it is inconceivable that there should have been any events in history in which women were not actively participating in one form or another. But historians have defined and categorized the activities pursued by men as being by definition significant, while the activities pursued by women have been deemed insignificant. Thus, for example, the acquisition and distribution of real estate and property have been considered significant and form the bulk of Diplomatic and Military History, while the building of communities and the rearing and educating of children have been deemed insignificant and somehow trivial. Women's History challenges the assumption, which underlies all traditional scholarship, that man is the measure of all things. It demands that women and men be made the measure of significance.

Once we have made that shift from patriarchal assumptions to gender-neutral assumptions, a series of simple analytic questions can help us to bring women into view. These questions help to turn any history topic into Women's History.

Question 1. Who are the missing women and where are they?

Question 2. What did women contribute to this or that movement?

The first two questions replicate the historiography of Women's History. Wherever the field is first developed, the early stage is the history of "illustrious women"—usually women who have done what men have done. The next stage is "contribution history"—a study of traditional movements, organizations, stages of development. We add women by asking what women "contributed" to these movements or events.

This strategy can be quite useful. In World History, studying the varying ways women were affected by and contributed to modernization can be very illuminating. Or, for earlier periods, what did women contribute to the development or spread of Christianity? What was women's contribution to various wars or revolutions? What was women's contribution to various trade union movements and struggles? The applications of these questions are endless. Picking one or another of these themes for illustration of the role of women is a useful way to introduce students to women as agents in history. It also helps to balance the male dominance in the historical narrative. But note that this approach leaves the categories by which the material is organized untouched.

Question 3. What did women do while the men were doing what the textbook tells us was important?

The discussion of major historical periods and of major movements all lend themselves well to this approach. Answers to the question illuminate the fact that men and women did different things or that they did whatever they did in different ways. This can lead to a discussion of *gender*—the different roles assigned to men and women in a given society. Comparisons of gender role assignments in different societies can further students' comprehension of the force of gender in history. It can lead to a discussion of how criteria of selection are defined in the writing of history and how such criteria take on a coercive force. The value judgment made over thousands of years that women's brains were less developed than those of men and that their intellect was inferior did, in fact, serve to justify the vast and persistent educational deprivation of women, which is worldwide. How did such educational deprivation of half the population affect women? How did it affect men? What was its impact on the development of a given society?

Question 4. How was it different for women?

This question opens up almost any topic to a woman-focused analysis. How was immigration different for men and women? How about marriage? Private property? Modernization? The possibilities are infinite. It needs to be stressed that in answering this question a woman should always be compared only to her brother. Very often the question is posed by comparing a woman to her grandmother, which always results in a rosy story of progress. But if one compares a woman to her brother, one holds all other factors, such as modernization, urbanization, and better health care, steady, so that one focuses solely on gender differences.

Question 5. What was the female experience at a particular time and place? What were the hopes, aspirations, frustrations, and actual lives of women of the past?

This question leads to the use of primary sources: autobiographies, letters, and diaries of women. It allows the teacher to introduce female voices of the past into a narrative usually confined to the male voice.

Demographic data—life expectancy, age at marriage, birth rates, death or survival rates of children—are frequently used to answer these questions and to draw cross-national comparisons. This is useful, but insufficient. Figures and graphs can make students forget that what they are describing are the life experiences of actual human beings who suffered pain, joy, hope, and despair. Students should learn how to translate such abstractions into the life cycles of women of the past. If a woman in premodern society bears a child every two years, what does this actually mean in the life of women? Birth statistics do not record miscarriages or aborted pregnancies, but one may assume they occurred at an even higher rate than do such events in contemporary society. It means that a woman of child-bearing age in premodern society was either pregnant or nursing or recovering from a miscarriage or birth most of her life, since women's life expectancy did not exceed the child-bearing years. What does this mean in terms of the choices for self-development open to women?

Demographic data concerning maternity should also always be taught together with demographic data about single women. Historians have estimated that throughout history on average 35 percent of all women were single (never married, divorced, widowed). For women's history the study of single women is highly significant. As long as single women are considered deviant and their economic needs are not met by employment or work opportunities, marriage becomes the chief economic role for *all* women. When, for women, being single becomes an acceptable alternative to marriage, the status of all women, single or married, is raised.

Question 6. Who defined women's sexual lives? Who controlled them and how? How were marriages contracted? Who controlled information pertaining to reproduction?

These questions open up vast areas for consideration. Marriage, family practices, and laws—such as bride price, dowry, and gender-determined inheritance—are the building blocks for social institutions. They determine class and racial relations and the distribution of resources in any given society. Sexual regulation under patriarchy is always different for men and women, and the difference has been used consistently in the service of power. For example, the fact that in all the major political revolutions in Europe since 1792 the victorious revolutionists began their rule by restricting the sexual and reproductive freedom of women is something worth considering in its political implications.

The provision for widows and their treatment in various societies is another illuminating topic. Single women have historically been particularly vulnerable to the threat of being defined as deviant, whether as witches, spinsters, loose women, strong-minded women, or lesbians. A study of these stereotypes and control mechanisms, especially when combined with similar mechanisms used to control racial, ethnic, religious, or colonial groups has a great deal of meaning for students.

Prostitution, rape, and violence against women are other themes that can be dealt with under this heading. In any course on World History the international sex trade and traffic, which overwhelmingly victimizes young women of impoverished population groups, needs to be considered as a topic. Prostitution has, for centuries, remained the second-largest employment category for women, next to domestic service. In the post–World War II period, with the spread of electronic media and the growth of a mass market for pornography, the international sex industry is a growing and highly profitable commercial enterprise. Do women truly make an individual choice in entering that industry and in staying with it? Do they profit by their sex work? What are their working conditions? Their health risks? Does legalization of prostitution and sex work benefit the women involved?

Definitions of sexuality have often been used by societies to target certain groups as deviants and outcasts. This has been the case for homosexuals, whose status and history can also be considered under the heading "the construction of deviants and outcasts." The struggles of organized groups of gays and lesbians for their rights can be told as part of the emancipation struggles of other minority groups. But it has a special significance in regard to the emancipation struggle of women, since the accusation of sexual deviance against feminists has for centuries been a potent weapon discouraging women from working for their own emancipation.

Question 7. What are the economic and social consequences of women's unpaid household work?

If there is one valid generalization to be made about all women, it is that the overwhelming majority of them—regardless of whether they hold a paid job or not—are engaged in the unpaid labor of food preparation, maintenance of the home and clothing and, if they are mothers, child rearing. The unpaid housework women do demands considerable expenditure of time and energy and hourly availability, but it is not counted as part of the nation's GNP. The work confers neither pay nor rights nor benefits on the woman. Regardless of the woman's class, "occupation housewife" fixes the woman into dependence on a male breadwinner.

Class and race divisions are shown in different functions of the housewife's role. The middle- and upper-class housewife can replace her daily services by paying another woman to perform them or by substituting consumer services for them—commercial laundries, take-out food and restaurants, babysitters. Working-class and rural housewives, who frequently do double duty as part-time paid workers, actually help sustain the family or keep it from sinking into poverty by bargain shopping, home-cooking and baking, making and repairing clothes. The unpaid services of the homemaker enable the family to weather substandard wages and periods of unemployment. For many working-class women or women of minority groups, doing someone else's housework is the single occupation for which they are always in demand.

Woman's place as homemaker is firmly embedded in the economic and familial relations of society as a whole. The modern sexual division of labor masks woman's actual economic role by making the housewife invisible in the economy, as women have been invisible in history. The historian must address the position of the housewife as an essential aspect of social and economic organization.

Question 8. What kind of paid work do women do and what are their working conditions?

This question is well suited to making women visible as workers within the structure of traditional history. The question should be enlarged, as follows:

Question 9. What were the contributions of working women to family income and home maintenance? What determined their decision to enter the paid labor force and/or to leave it? How did women's workforce participation vary by class, race, and ethnicity?

Women have always worked and contributed to the family economy; their decisions about work participation are based on a complex interplay of ethnic/racial traditions, economic opportunities in particular localities, and family strategies. Whether unmarried daughters take factory or domestic work, whether mothers take in boarders or do home sewing, whether young daughters are taken out of school to mind babies or grandmothers take over that work—these are all decisions that affect the economic survival of rural and working-class families. Worldwide patterns show that women are structured into low-paying, low-status service jobs and face structural obstacles to upward mobility. Industrialization, although emancipating some working women through unionization, has reinforced their overall subordination and powerlessness, while maintaining their double burden of work for pay and as unpaid homemakers.

A sexually segmented labor market also discriminates against women in skilled and professional jobs. "Women's occupations" take on the characteristics of low pay and low status. This happened in the United States in such diverse fields as domestic service, nursing, librarianship, and social work. In the former Soviet Union medicine became defined as a female occupation, with the same bad consequences for women.

Question 10. How did women see their world? How did they relate to other women?

With these questions we move into the realm of "woman-defined history." By using diaries, autobiographies, and oral history sources for class assignments, research topics, and lecture material, the teacher can bring a long-needed corrective to androcentric history into the World History course. One way of doing this is to add women's personal narratives as additional readings in the traditionally structured World History survey. Another successful strategy is to give one written assignment based on women's autobiographies in such a course. The teacher also needs to make sure that examples cited in lectures do not always focus only on men.

To add women's voices to the overwhelmingly male discourse of traditional history is all to the good, but it is not sufficient. In order to elicit the important role of women's networks and women's organizations in the struggle for women's emancipation, it is essential to ask how women related to other women. We need to counteract a tradition that has for millennia seen women mainly through male eyes. When it has focused on women at all, it has considered their relationship to men as primary in importance. Women's relationship to other women has been entirely neglected or has been deemed to be trivial and insignificant. Recent Women's History and Gay History scholarship has offered an important corrective to this distortion and has thereby uncovered hitherto unknown aspects of women's agency in home and society.

Question 11. How did women respond to their subordinate status and what were the consequences of these responses? How did individual consciousness develop into collective consciousness?

These questions lead to the theme of women's long struggle for their own emancipation. This subject can be treated as a separate unit, which would include various women's movements, the struggle for suffrage, campaigns for equal pay for equal work, for maternal and child protective legislation, and for civil rights. For the past hundred years it would include the struggle against rape and violence against women, against sexual exploitation, and for lesbian rights. Teachers may want to explore some of these subjects one by one, or they may use a comparative, cross-cultural, cross-national approach.

A cross-national approach to the struggle for women's suffrage reveals important similarities in very different national settings: Women won suffrage frequently after wars or revolutions in which they performed roles unusual for their sex; they won suffrage because men in power tried to enhance their political power by doubling it; they won the vote as a result of massive and long-range coalition-building and organizing.

Question 12. What would a World History course be like if women were fully integrated in it and if it were seen equally through the eyes of women and men?

This question will be essential for those wishing to design an entirely new course. It will address the initial question: What do I leave out in order to bring women in? For such a course one would have to abandon the traditional patriarchal value distinctions by which historians decide what is important and what is not. One would have to assume that the activities of men and women are equally important and one would have to allot time and space accordingly. If the biographies of "significant men" are included, one would include also the biographies of significant women. If illustrations or examples of events are given, one would make sure that not all the examples are males. Since the historian never can tell everything that happened in the past in its entirety, one would probably omit some events concerning politics and diplomacy in favor of events that help students conceptualize the functioning of societies of the past in a holistic way.

If one is teaching history in a way that includes women, the story of the existence of slavery in the world and of the struggles for its abolition would never be told without noting the crucial historical fact that everywhere in the world the first enslaved persons were women and their offspring and that the means of keeping women enslaved was to rape them. Pregnant women could not escape, and enslaved mothers usually stayed in captivity in order to protect their children as best they could. The close and persistent interconnection between physical enslavement and sexual exploitation is a universal, cross-cultural feature of the history of slavery.

For another example, the story of the Reformation is usually told in terms of a contest between Luther and the Pope or states against other states. The diplomatic and military battles certainly need to be explained, but the story might also focus on the outburst of religious enthusiasm among peasants and artisans; on the itinerant preachers in the marketplace, male and female; on the explosion of education among sectarian groups; and on the theological emancipation of Protestant women who took it upon themselves to interpret the biblical text without benefit of clergy. The story would include the persecution of heretics and witches and the rise of organized misogyny as an instrument of state power.

The struggle of women for access to education, for the right to learn, to teach, and finally to define the content of knowledge is another major story for cross-national overview. The systematic educational deprivation of women compared to their brothers is a universal societal phenomenon. It occurs with persistent regularity across time and place, but its abolition varies with cultural and political circumstances. Why is this universal? Who benefits by it? How does it affect the general status of women in given societies?

Each of these themes and subjects could be the topic for a separate course. Yet adding one or another of them as a subtheme to a more general course can also be transformative and intellectually challenging. This is especially true for female students, nowadays representing more than half of the undergraduate student body. Many girls and young women have experienced the traditional history course as vaguely oppressive. Unlike literature, sociology, and real life, all populated by female actors as well as male, traditional history has reinforced the idea that women have not had a part in the building of societies and in the shaping of historically important events. When young women encounter a gender-neutral narrative and some important female historic figures, and when they learn of women's agency in the shaping of events, their entire worldview changes. Often, they begin to engage with history seriously for the first time. They are inspired by female heroines and begin to think of themselves as potentially more capable than they have before. Many teachers, who have adopted a more holistic approach to their courses, have noticed this phenomenon.

The more inclusive, gender-neutral World History course would not only be grounded in social history, it would also incorporate more primary sources and sources from other disciplines, such as literature, art, and music. Saint Hildegard of Bingen would stand side by side with Saint Bernard of Clairvaux; Mary Wollstonecraft would stand next to Rousseau; Jane Austen and George Eliot would be discussed with Balzac and Dickens. The struggle of the Ibo market women would be cited together with other colonial liberation struggles.

Placing women into history and restoring to half the human race its legitimate past are exciting and intellectually challenging tasks, which demand the best efforts of scholars and teachers, and will bring out, in turn, the best efforts of students.

chapter seven

Taming the Monster

WORKSHOP ON THE CONSTRUCTION
OF DEVIANT OUT-GROUPS

Having tried in all my years of teaching to do justice to the problem of "differences" among women and finding various approaches inadequate, I finally, in the 1980s, struck out in a new direction.

Tired of merely describing the social construction of differences in society, I tried to find out why hierarchical governments everywhere constructed "deviant out-groups" and what ends they served. Perhaps, by understanding the system of "deviance-formation" one could learn how more effectively to interfere with its working.

These questions led me to develop a lecture course and, later, a workshop on the subject. I tested out the workshop by teaching it twice at the University of Wisconsin–Madison to different groups of administrators and the staff of the Dean of Students Office. I taught it in New Zealand, where my students were Women's Studies faculty from different universities; in Dortmund, Germany, where the participants were graduate students and faculty; in Salzburg, Austria, where the participants were graduate students and faculty in History, Sociology, German Studies, and Education; and at the University of Arizona, Tempe, where my students were Women's Studies faculty and graduate students.

The course described below has proven to be a powerful tool for understanding and learning to resist what I call "the Monster"—racism, sexism, anti-Semitism, homophobia, and all other categories of hating deviant out-groups. It is structured in ten units, following the usual three-hour seminar format. It can also be offered in a five-day format, with morning and afternoon sessions. Teachers wanting to adapt this course will have to select lecture topics and illustrative materials that fit their own specialization and knowledge.

The workshop uses a combination of intellectual work and group exercises that mobilize the participants' experiences and feelings. Changes in attitudes toward others cannot be accomplished solely by intellectual effort. The aim is to practice empathy based on one's own experiences.

The workshop is described in brief below. The detailed syllabus and exercises for the workshop can be found in Appendixes B and C respectively.

In all hierarchical societies there are groups that the dominant society considers "out-groups." The outsiders may be conquered prisoners of war; they may be ethnic, racial, or religious minorities; they may be persons with a different lifestyle or sexual orientation. They may even represent half of the population, women. They become designated as being "the Other," the group against which the society defines itself. From such a definition of "Otherness" it follows quickly that the out-group is regarded as deviant, separated from the main group and negatively defined against it. By looking at how the Other is created, why it is created, and what function this creation serves, we gain insight into the actual workings of state societies. We look at the subject of "discrimination" not from the standpoint of the victims, but from the point of view of the dominant group in society. The creation of deviant out-groups is an essential aspect of hierarchical states, which depend on it to form their identity, to cohere, and to keep their system of dominance intact.

In the earliest days of societal development, men learned that it is possible to use existing differences among people to build systems of dominance and power. When men first made this discovery, they laid the ideological foundation for all systems of hierarchy, inequality, and exploitation.

I have detailed the historic developments that led to the institutionalization of this process in the archaic states of the Ancient Near East during the Bronze Age.[1] At the time of the formation of the archaic states non-slaveholding men accepted the bargain of being dominated and exploited in regard to resources by more powerful men of their own group, because they were simultaneously offered the chance to dominate and control the resources of others, the "different" others, namely the women and children of their own class. Even to men who did not themselves hold slaves, the existence of an underclass raised their own sense of status and made them accept their own relative inequality as a fair arrangement. Once the system of dominance and hierarchy is institutionalized in custom, law, and practice it is seen by the dominant as well as by the dominated as natural and just. People no longer question it, unless historical circumstances change very dramatically. The dominated, once the system is institutionalized, learn to survive under it, even though they may regard it as exploitation based on arbitrary power.

What I have briefly outlined here is a pattern of development that takes many hundreds of years to consolidate. It shows, in its simplest and most rudimentary form, the connectedness of various forms of difference-turned-into-dominance. It shows that *sex, class, and race dominance were interrelated and inseparable from the start.* The difference between men and women was the first, most easily noticeable difference between people and therefore dominance by men could first be established over women. But class and race dominance developed almost immediately upon this first human "discovery" of how to use power so as to benefit people unequally. *The function of all designations of Otherness or deviance is to keep hierarchy in place for the benefit of the dominant.* I am not here trying to set up priorities of oppression. Which system of oppression came first and which second is insignificant, if we understand that we are dealing with one, inseparable system with different manifestations.

My bias is that I think differences among human beings are what makes life interesting and worth living. We should neither strive to wipe out differences (assimilation, the melting-pot) nor stress them in an exclusionary fashion (separatism). *What we need to abolish is the notion that the existence of difference entitles some to dominance over others who are different.*

At the University of Wisconsin–Madison, as at many universities, in recent years racial and ethnic tensions have increased, often leading to ugly confrontations. One of the institutional answers has been to sponsor "sensitivity training seminars" for various groups of faculty, administrators, and students. Some of these were given by outside groups specializing in such training. They were based on various approaches that demand consciousness-raising on the part of whites and try to induce them to become sensitive to historic discrimination and the constant negative impact of prejudice, stereotyping, and disparaging humor directed against minorities. I have seen some of the visual materials used in these workshops and have found them hard-hitting, usually quite accurate, although one-sided in their presentation, and exceedingly discomforting. I have no way of scientifically measuring the effect of these presentations, but I doubt that they are as effective as they should be. I judge from impressions of students who were taking these workshops and from my own reaction to the materials seen. They made me acutely uncomfortable, despite my having a long-range and deep commitment to working for racial justice. When I am acutely uncomfortable, I tend to be at my worst, not my best, and I think other people react the same way.

I wanted to try to develop a teaching tool that would deal with these issues without creating discomfort and guilt, but which would strongly appeal both to people's intellect and to their emotions. I wanted to induce people to make real and lasting changes in their attitudes toward people who are different from themselves and make these changes voluntarily, because they learn that the system of creating deviant out-groups hurts not only others, but could and often does hurt them as well.

I developed a workshop based on the following principles:

There would be a maximum of self-expression and class participation without anyone being made to feel uncomfortable or guilty.

We would depart from the binary conflict model—black versus white, ethnic versus black/white; female versus male. Instead, my model would show the ways in which various groups are oppressed by similar means, the similar ways they respond to this oppression, and the commonalities they share. I would stress what groups that are different have in common with each other, rather than stressing what divides them.

The emphasis would be not on placing blame and guilt, but on making people understand how the oppressive system works and how it can be resisted and reformed.

Students would be exposed to examples from different cultures and different periods of history, illustrating the creation and treatment of deviant out-groups. This would make it possible to show the long-range consequences of discriminatory policies and reveal patterns and commonalities between groups that usually seem to have little in common, for example, medieval heretics and racial minorities in modern United States.

In order to achieve a cooperative, guilt-free environment in which to discuss differences, the workshop leader must make sure that the hot-button issues of the particular time and place are *not* included in the model and class discussion. These issues are on the students' minds and the students will think about them on their own. But in order to understand the abstract model, it is best to illustrate it with materials that are emotionally neutral. When I taught this workshop in New Zealand, where there was conflict between Women's Studies and Maori Studies, I was asked by the organizers of the workshop to include these issues in the discussion. I refused, using the excuse that I had no knowledge of New Zealand politics and less of Maori issues. Instead, I urged the class to discuss race relations in the United States with me and then to see if this did not help them to deal with their issue in a better way. As it happened, the two leading

Maori faculty women were part of the workshop. Initially they sat with their arms folded and did not participate in the discussion. By the end of the workshop they were interacting fully with all the participants and honored me by inviting me to the Maori House, which was normally closed to non-Maori people.

When I taught the course in Germany and in Austria, I included anti-Semitism among the discussion topics, but it was medieval anti-Semitism I discussed, not modern. The students at first expressed some outrage at the "omission," but they quickly got the idea that they could make the connections to the modern problems themselves. By not including their hot topic, I eliminated defensiveness and the guilt feelings underlying it and freed students to think with some detachment. Nobody living today is to "blame" for medieval anti-Semitism, but everyone can recognize the similar process by which Jews were vilified and made "deviant" in the Middle Ages and in the modern world. When I taught the workshop in the United States, I made sure that all the illustrative materials were historical, from prior to the twentieth century. That had the same effect I describe above. Since the purpose of the workshop is to engage students intellectually and emotionally, it is a good teaching strategy to let them make comparisons and inferences about contemporary problems by themselves and not have the teacher lay it all out for them.

The basic model for the workshop is quite simple.

> **How do societies create deviant out-groups?**
> By turning difference into dominance.

This is done in the following way.

1. **Mark the difference.**
   Note the difference: racial, ethnic, sexual, lifestyle.
   Mark the difference where an obvious visual difference does not exist.

2. **Stigmatize the group.**
   Declare that group members have different characteristics from *us*. Assign those characteristics to *all* members of the group, whether such a designation fits or not.

3. **Institutionalize discrimination against the group.**
   Restrict the group's access to resources and privileges.

Restrict the choices and opportunities of members of the group. Observe the results of such discrimination and blame it on the group. This serves as reinforcement of previously defined differences.

4. **Allow for personal exceptions.**
   Take, for example, the phenomenon of the "Exception-Jew" in Nazi persecutions: "Every Jew has all the designated negative characteristics, except the one Jew I know, he is different." By this mechanism conflict between the irrationality of the system of discrimination and people's common-sense observation is suppressed. The exception is allowed, but the irrational system is not threatened.

5. **Scapegoat the group when society is in a period of stress.**
   They are the Other. It is all right to do things to them one would not do to members of the in-group, people like oneself. By putting the blame for the crisis in society on this out-group one can avoid dealing with the problem, while pacifying popular outrage.

Who benefits from this system of discrimination?
   The dominant elite in any given society
   Individual members of the dominant elite
   Members of otherwise disadvantaged groups who identify themselves as being "superior" to the deviant out-group

I usually present the model to the class in the first session and then spend the rest of the course illustrating each item listed with historical evidence. It is important to use at least two different examples from different periods for illustration. The lecture should discuss each case of deviance-formation in historical context and show differences among the examples, as well as likenesses. Teachers are encouraged to develop examples from their own fields of expertise. Some alternative possibilities for the lectures: the treatment of Hispanic immigrants in historical overview, changes in attitude toward Irish immigrants between 1840 and 1940, the construction of poor mothers into "welfare queens," the construction of homosexuality as a deviance.

Illustrative Material for the Model

1. Marking the Difference

Where obvious physical differences between the target group and the dominant group do not exist, mark the difference artificially, with a different haircut, an item of clothing, some sort of brand. The first slaves, in the kingdoms of the Ancient Near East, were branded on the forehead or given a distinctive haircut.

In the case of Jews, they set themselves off as being different by their religious beliefs and practices. They insisted on monotheism in a polytheistic environment. Later, they did not accept Christ as the Messiah; they refused to convert to Christianity. In the high Middle Ages, when they had already assimilated to the countries in which they lived, and could not so readily be identified, they were forced to wear hats and garments that marked them as different. The yellow star worn as a means of designating Jewishness, which the Nazis picked up for the same purpose, was first used in medieval Europe.

In the case of women, they are readily marked by biological differences. But it is noteworthy that in all patriarchal cultures women were also marked by dress and hairstyle as beings different from men. At times, such "markings" were cumbersome, painful for the wearer, and restrictive. Examples are bustles and crinoline skirts, the bound feet of Chinese women, the burkas and chadors of Muslim women, and the stiletto heels of modern women.

In the case of heretics or political dissidents, marking generally did not happen, which necessitated complex and drawn-out identification procedures, such as the Inquisition or legal hearings to identify the deviants.

2. Stigmatization

Members of the group are assigned peculiar characteristics, which must be given to all members of the group, whether the facts fit the case or not. These assigned characteristics are always defined as being inferior.

Slaves, whether of the same race as the slaveholders or of a different race, were always stigmatized as inferior. Beginning with Aristotle, such stigmatization was used as a rationale to excuse the practice of enslavement. Slaves were those people designated to serve the rulers, being themselves inferior. Therefore it was excusable to enslave them. In various cultures and at various historical periods the conditions of enslavement varied, but the principle of stigmatization did not.

Jews in Christian Europe were first characterized as being worse than heathens. They were labeled as "Christ killers," which was a patent distortion of historical fact, even when applied to the generation living in the time of Christ. But this designation was given to all Jews for nearly two millennia and each individual Jew was supposed to share in that "blood guilt." Similarly, at the time of the Crusades, when the first European holocaust was under way, the lie that Jews used the blood of Christian children to bake into *mazzot* caused the deaths of thousands. In the modern period, the persistent lie that all Jews are rich bankers and money-lenders was used together with or in substitute for the quite contradictory stigma that *all* Jews are revolutionaries and subversive of state power.

The stigmatization of women ascribed to them gender-defined qualities, both good and bad, that made them supposedly "naturally" different from men. They were nurturant, emotional, intuitive, peaceful (or timid), gentle. They were inferior in intelligence, incapable of logical thinking, noncompetitive, unsteady, unreliable, and lacking in initiative. As to their sexuality, two opposing stigmas were asserted simultaneously: on the one hand, women were seen as oversexed, insatiable seductresses, while on the other hand, they were supposed to be frigid, lacking in sexual drive and erotic capacity.

When one compares these stigmatizing characteristics across the various groups designated as deviant, it is striking how these vastly different groups are being characterized in often identical terms. So-called "female" characteristics (emotionality, intuitiveness, lack of intelligence and analytic ability, excessive sexual drive) have been ascribed to slaves of both sexes and to racial minorities. The stigma of engaging in deviant sexual behaviors has been applied to women (prostitutes and witches), to heretics, to slaves, to Jews. Various ethnic groups, when they are defined as deviant out-groups, are also charged with such stigmatizing behavior (Irish, Italians, Gypsies). When one looks at it this way, it appears obvious that these ascribed stereotypical characteristics distort the reality of the people being described in order to serve the construction of deviance.

3. Institutionalized Discrimination

The targeted group's access to resources and privileges is restricted by laws and custom. After some years the effect of such discrimination will be apparent, and it can then be blamed on the targeted group. As a result of long-term discrimination the group is now actually different, which serves as a reinforcement to the assertion of group inferiority.

Thus, Jews in medieval Europe were gradually restricted from certain occupations, barred from owning and tilling the land, from military service, and finally from attendance at universities. They were, by means of these discriminatory rules, forced to live by peddling, selling old clothes and rags, trading, and money-lending. Forced to pay higher taxes than Christians, they survived by lending money to kings and noblemen in exchange for protection. Jews were then condemned as being physically weak, cowardly for not doing military service, overrepresented in commerce and usury. The negative characteristics provable by one or two examples could then be ascribed to the entire group—they were secretive, stingy bankers and pawnshop owners, hence Shylocks.

African Americans, during slavery, were forbidden schooling, even the basics of reading and writing. They were kept from all cultural expressions and self-improvement. Rituals connected with their African heritage, such as funeral services and drumming and dances, had to be performed secretly. Poorly clothed and housed, the group showed all the characteristics of poverty and forced ignorance, which were then cited against them as "proof" of their "inferiority." A similar process of keeping African Americans in poverty and poorly educated continued even after the Civil War and, in some ways, continues to the present day. Resources are denied or restricted; the resulting low school performance, low motivation, and high crime rates are then cited against the group and reinforce racial stereotypes.

In this section it is important to make the students understand the difference between personal discrimination and prejudiced behavior (sections 1 and 2) and institutionalized discrimination (section 3). The way these two aspects of deviance-formation mutually reinforce one another should be discussed.

4. Creation of the Concept of the "Exception-Jew," the Nazis' Exzeptionsjude

Each member of the dominant group who actually knows one Jew, knows that the stereotype does not fit that particular person. The concept that the person one knows is an exception permits the whole system to function. In the case of medieval Jews, each nobleman or king had his "Exception-Jew," whom he protected in order to take advantage of his services.

In the case of racial minorities, stigmatizing generalizations were usually made while citing exceptions: the faithful house servant, the Mammy.

In the case of heretics or political outcasts, there are no exceptions granted, unless one betrays one's group. The renegade witness becomes transformed by the dominant into a person of high integrity, good motivation, and trustworthiness.

5. Scapegoating

When society is in a period of stress, members of the out-group take the blame. They are the Other, and it is acceptable to do things to them one would not do to people of one's own group. Thus, after having lived for 900 years without too many restrictions and under fairly good conditions among their European neighbors, Jews were decimated in succeeding assaults and pogroms from the eleventh to the fifteenth century. Accused as heathens during the Crusades and murdered with the sanction of the church, the surviving Jews were the scapegoats for the Black Plague, which they were accused of causing by poisoning wells. Within 200 years entire Jewish communities in England, France, the Netherlands, Switzerland, Germany, and northern Italy were wiped out. A century later, in 1492, Spain and Portugal expelled all Jews. The surviving remnants fled to what are now Poland and Russia, as well as to Turkey.

I am stressing these examples from medieval history, because most of us are familiar with the European pogroms of the late nineteenth and early twentieth centuries and, of course, with the modern holocaust. But the history of the Jews is a history of one holocaust after the other, with short intervals of peaceful assimilation or acculturation.

I have illustrated the way the system of hierarchy and dominance works in the case of Jews. The same step-by-step process of marking, stigmatization, and scapegoating makes deviant out-groups of African Americans, various ethnic Americans, and Native Americans. It works as well for lower-class people, homosexuals, people with AIDS, and welfare mothers. The group cohesion of privileged elites is strengthened by the designation and scapegoating of deviants. The victim is not only shamed, pilloried, and psychologically programmed for failure, but he or she is also blamed for the consequences of discrimination.

The system works by giving each group of the dominated enough benefits over other groups of "deviants" so that they will cooperate with the system.

In the American setting the primary scapegoated groups are defined by race. The relative freedom of the American Jewish community compared to those in other countries, and its long existence under conditions of tolerance and open access to the resources of the society, is no doubt due to the American Constitution and its protection, but it is also due to the existence of racial minorities that have been the primary target for discrimination, hatred, and scapegoating. This is not to minimize the existence of a history of anti-Semitic discrimination, nor is it to suggest that Jews are to blame for these patterns of selection. But we must recognize that Jews, as whites, have had privileges and benefits from the racially segmented labor market and from housing and job discrimination against people of color, just as have non-Jewish whites. Moreover, the way the system of competing out-groups works, there is an incentive for members of one minority group to display their assimilation, their Americanism as it were, by participating in institutionalized racism. Thus some European Jewish immigrants and other ethnics, who in all their lives had never seen a person of color, learned racism in short order, once they assimilated to American society. Conversely, some Blacks, to prove their commitment to their own people and in response to the seriousness of their own condition, found Jews an easier target in their attack on discrimination than other Americans. Black anti-Semitism and Jewish racism are deplorable outgrowths of one and the same system of creating deviant out-groups and pitting them one against the other in the struggle for resources. The same system of discrimination attempts to turn women against men, Blacks against Jews, Jews against other ethnic groups, the straight against the homosexual, and on and on.

In the workshop I assigned students various target groups—ethnic minorities, gays and lesbians, welfare mothers etc.—and asked them to test out how the basic outline for creating deviance would work for each of those groups. These homework assignments were then read and discussed with the whole group. This gave us a broader base of reference for making comparisons and observing patterns.

6. How to Stop the Vicious Cycle of Hatred and Discrimination

There is a way out of the vicious circle; *the way is refusal to cooperate*. This can be expressed in various ways:

A. ACCEPT DIFFERENCE

Once we understand that it is not "difference" that is the evil, but the stigmatization of difference, we can accept difference without dominance. We need to fight the difference-dominance connection and to expose it wherever we can, whether it applies to us or to another group.

We need to accept difference, celebrate difference — and then forget all about it.

Acceptance of difference means developing trust in oneself and in others. If we happen to be members of the dominant group, we will not be diminished by accepting that we are not the model, the norm, the universal standard. If we are members of one of the target groups, we can take pride in the accomplishments and distinctiveness of our group without feeling the need to diminish persons in other groups.

Celebrating difference means allowing those who are different from us to have their own voice, their own expression, their own identity. It means giving respect to those who are different from us. Respect, not just tolerance. It means making space for those who are different from us in the center of power and decision-making and recognizing that their way of doing things, though possibly different from our own, may be as good or better than our way.

B. FORGET ABOUT DIFFERENCE

We meet a new person and note that her hair is black and her eyes are green. These external differences may make her unusually beautiful in our eyes, or they may not. But once noted, these "different" characteristics do not form the basis on which we evaluate the person. We note them and then forget about it, paying attention to other qualities. This approach can only be used together with or after the "accept and celebrate difference" approach. The two approaches toward difference are personal practices that address individual prejudices. But we must always keep the distinction between individual prejudices and institutionalized prejudices clearly in mind. The abolition of individual prejudices can help improve personal relationships, but only the abolition of institutionalized prejudices can make a basic change in the situation of members of target groups.

In the United States we are today often urged to give up and forget "race-specific" laws and practices, such as affirmative action or racially balanced representation. In the absence of prior reform—without abolition of *all* discrimination and the equalization of opportunities—such "forgetting" merely reinforces racist maldistribution of resources. Forgetting difference is a personal practice that can come only after acceptance and recognition of difference. Forgetting difference in the public realm can work only after institutional barriers have been removed.

C. REFUSE TO STIGMATIZE PEOPLE

We can refuse to stigmatize people; we must insist that no person represents the group. Any group. No person should be held accountable for anyone but him- or herself. If we encounter unpleasant incidents or individuals from designated groups, we must resist the temptation to generalize from them to the entire group. No person is responsible for anyone's action beyond his or her own.

D. BE SENSITIVE TO THE PAIN OF PEOPLE WHO HAVE BEEN DESIGNATED AS "DEVIANT"

In order to stop the vicious cycle, we must be sensitive to the long history of pain each dominated group has suffered. There is no point in ranking or comparing victimizations. There is a lot of point in accepting with sensitivity that the pain of others has not been our pain and ours not theirs, yet the same system has hurt us both.

The coalitions we can form with others who have been or are designated as deviant out-groups will be difficult and frail, but they are inevitable and essential. We cannot free ourselves without freeing others. The coalitions must be based on allowing for disagreement on a broad range of issues, while forming alliances over the issues on which we agree. We must and can stand under different banners as long as we agree that difference is no excuse for dominance.

E. FIGHT INSTITUTIONALIZED RACISM,
SEXISM, HOMOPHOBIA

These are the unseen dimensions of the system of discrimination that constantly reinforce it. Discriminatory laws, practices, and customs legitimize the system and lend it force. Break the chain of primary discrimination and its reinforcement.

F. SEEK CONNECTIONS AND TRANSCEND DIFFERENCES

Each of us is potentially a member of a target group—we might become handicapped, aged, outsiders, the dissenting minority among a conforming majority. Finding connections enables us to move from altruism to true empathy. Self-interest dictates that we oppose the *system* of discrimination, since we, too, are not secure in our unchallenged position, as long as others can be victimized by it.

Group Exercises

The workshop structure and content lends itself to adaptation by the teacher, depending on his or her interests and teaching strength. But under any circumstances, the group exercises, which are described briefly below and fully in Appendix C, are an essential aspect of this workshop. They have proven highly effective and are powerful teaching tools.

Exercise I. What's Your Name?

This exercise sharply raises the question of identity. Who makes the naming decisions? What are the consequences of having been assigned a particular name? In the workshops people named Mary or Christina expressed lifelong unease with having been saddled with a name so heavily fraught with religious meaning. Others reported their efforts to change this effect by choosing a nickname, such as Marie or Chris. People reported either loving or hating their names, accepting or refusing to accept the burden of being named for a dead relative, and trying to fit into the predetermined characteristics of a name they were given. Very few people were neutral or indifferent on the subject of their names. Why is naming so powerful? A discussion of that question based on the group's personal evidence led us to a new understanding of the negative power of name-calling. It also opened the question of the social construction of identity to further consideration.

Exercise II. How Have I Experienced Being "Different" in a Way That Implies Inferiority?

This exercise builds trust among the group, as they share difficult or traumatic experiences with each other. It builds empathy, as they perceive others having had painful experiences similar to their own. The teacher needs to encourage a positive and supportive atmosphere by ruling out hurtful or critical comments or any attempt at competition in victimization. Students are often surprised at the ubiquity of these negative experiences.

During this exercise, which takes place quite early in the workshop, some people use self-censorship by reporting only a very minor incident of discrimination. As the workshop progresses and they develop more trust in the group, they report deeper and more painful experiences. This exercise allows the teacher to gauge the level of emotional involvement of the students.

Exercise III A and B. Re-Definition, and Chairs and the Structure of Power

In A the students are asked to rearrange the seating order so as to maximize their power position; in B they arrange the seating order so as to minimize power differences. This two-part exercise engages the students' playfulness and creativity. It demonstrates the power of re-definition. The powerless do not necessarily have to continue in that position; they can redefine the situation. One can break through the unseen barriers; one can rewrite the script. We discussed the consequences of such acts of resistance. What happens when the traditional classroom structure is replaced by sitting around in a circle, with no one designated as "the boss"? Are such re-definitions merely symbolic gestures or do they carry larger political meaning? This discussion prepares students for the topics discussed in Class VI.

Exercise IV. Target Groups: Where Do I Fit In?

This exercise should be tailored to the needs of the group. Students are encouraged to add categories. Each participant is asked to write down which target group he or she now belongs to or conceivably might belong to in the future. It is possible to define oneself as belonging to several groups, that is, to have several identities. This discovery should be noted and can lead to a stimulating discussion on the subject of identity politics.

In my experience this exercise is the only one that may encounter considerable resistance. Some people say they cannot understand it; others think it does not apply to them. If they are gently encouraged to persist with it, it has a powerful effect. Students gain the shocking insight that they might become victims of the system of creating deviance. Students come to understand how arbitrary the divisive categories are and how strongly everyone living in society is enmeshed in the systems of discrimination that work to turn difference into dominance.

When I gave the workshop to the staff of the Dean of Students at the University of Wisconsin–Madison, the participants included five or six men. Several of them were quite resistant to the exercises and the discussion and indicated in various ways that, while we were discussing real problems, they happened not to apply to them. They participated, but only at a remote and fairly superficial level. This changed with this exercise, when someone added "alcoholic" to the target list. One of the men added "political radical," another "disabled." It seemed we had struck a chord: these were target groups with which they could identify. All of a sudden they were no longer neutral outsiders to the discussion, but they owned a part of it.

THIS WORKSHOP IS NOT only intellectually challenging; it is also innovative in structure and teaching techniques. I assume that prejudices people have held all their lives, sometimes unconsciously, are well defended psychologically and can be unlearned only with difficulty and great resistance. Always having had extraordinarily positive responses to the workshop, I am convinced that it is a helpful and effective way of combating the monster of socially constructed deviance and of engaging students emotionally with the subject matter. I hope to interest teachers in using the concepts, framework, and exercises described here to construct their own courses or workshops to that effect.

Note

1. Gerda Lerner, *The Creation of Patriarchy* (New York: Oxford University Press, 1986).

chapter eight

Autobiography, Biography, Memory, and the Truth

I have worked as a writer for most of my life. Like most writers, I have used my own life as a source for the imagination, writing autobiographical novels and short stories, as well as poetry, inspired by lived events and remembered feelings. I have also, late in life, written an autobiography. Having been interviewed frequently, concerning both my life and my written work, I have experienced how easy it is to slip over the boundaries of memory and written work. Did the event happen the way I remember it or the way I wrote it? Can I remember only what I wrote?

I have worked and written for forty-three years as a historian. My published work includes a historical biography and a biographical essay on my mother. I have also collected, used, and published many oral histories. The problems connected with using autobiographical sources as a historian have been perplexing. Can diaries and memoirs be trusted as coming closer to the truth than accounts by less self-interested authors? How can they be used without unwittingly reproducing the authors' biases? How can these accounts be verified or evaluated?

A special problem concerned biographies of nineteenth-century women reformers who have experienced special friendships with other women as the main emotional support of their lives. The term "lesbian" and the concept of lesbianism did not then exist, yet such special friendships existed and were recognized by contemporaries as important and positive. In my research and reading notes I began to refer to such women as "woman-oriented women." Yet biographers of women were strangely silent on the subject. Obviously, there were taboos still operating in the present that needed to be broken. I also feel strongly that it is important for heterosexual feminists to deal with lesbian history and treat it as a normal and legitimate part of the history of women. That is why I have included a discussion of several of these women in this chapter.

Biographies and autobiographies tell life stories; they focus on the individual life in history and strive to give that life special meaning. The writing of biographies antedates the writing of autobiographies; the former were generally commissioned by powerful individuals to celebrate and give form to their heroic exploits. They were instruments for enhancing the power of the powerful, usually kings, rulers, and the heads of religious orders.

Autobiographers tell the story of their own life; the subject of the story being also its object. The genre lies across the boundaries of literature and history, and part of its fascination for the reader consists in the challenge to sort out the literary, the fictional, from the historic and verifiable. Autobiographers act on the daring assumption that their stories deserve telling, that they carry special meaning, even though the subject is not necessarily an important and recognized public figure. This lends the autobiographer greater credibility with the reader than has the biographer, who has to rely on external evidence only. Presumably the autobiographer knows his story intimately and will share his private insights with the reader. Who is likely to tell a more truthful story? Considering how closely autobiographers rely on memory, can autobiographies be considered a reliable source for the historian, the teacher, the general reader? I will explore these questions, using representative and well-known examples spanning several centuries.

THE EARLIEST AUTOBIOGRAPHIES, written in the Middle Ages, all dealt with religious experiences. The autobiography as the record of the quest of the self-defined individual finds its earliest expression in Saint Augustine's *Confessions.*[1] Born in North Africa in 354, Augustine was baptized at the age of thirty-three and became a priest four years later. In 396 he became Bishop of Hippo, and he wrote his autobiography as the Vandals invaded the coast of North Africa on their way to attacking Rome.

The book is one long dialogue with God. The narrator looks back on his own life and development from the point of view of a devout Christian. More than half of the work is taken up with an extraordinarily detailed and unsparing description of his earlier sinful life and his intellectual struggle to become a Christian. He details his adherence to various doctrines and belief systems he now considers false and describes his inability, even after having become convinced of the rightness of Christian doctrine, to give up his enjoyment of material and sexual pleasures. Most of all, he is unable to give up his enjoyment of inquiry and rational thinking. Throughout his struggle he is strongly guided by his mother's prayers and tears and by her simple devotion to the Christian way of life. The last third of the book continues in the form of prayer, but the focus is less on his personal quest than on the development of a philosophical and theological Christian doctrine.

Bishop Augustine set an example that enormously influenced later autobiographers, both religious and secular. The *Confessions* became the prototype for the quest story—the hero's search for self-development and fulfillment through a cause greater than himself. The work is unique for its author's introspection and psychological insight. The fact that he was unsparing of his ego and pride and described his sins in great detail gives his account an air of truth. His was the first prototype of the story of the redeemed sinner, a *persona* who would serve as a model for others.

Saint Augustine's major work was the development of Catholic theology, which profoundly influenced religious thought in the Middle Ages and into the present and which earned him designation as one of the four Fathers of the Church. One aspect of this theology was its strong misogynist bias that influenced church doctrine for millennia. Woman, declared Saint Augustine, was not created in God's image, but in his "likeness," and she showed a greater propensity for sin than did man. After the Fall, hers was "a condition similar to slavery." Nearly a thousand years later, the Dominican Thomas Aquinas reinforced this doctrine by arguing that the male was created with greater capacity for knowledge and rationality, whereas the woman was created chiefly as an aid in reproduction. Since rationality was a natural ability reserved to men, presumably by divine design, women, lacking this capacity, were preordained to ignorance and intellectual and social dependency. As a result of such thought, taught to children of both sexes by their parents and their priests, women were also, quite incidentally, excluded from the ranks of autobiographers.

There was, however an ancient tradition preceding Christianity and continuing in it, which allowed for another mode of enlightenment. Mysticism asserted that spiritual knowledge comes not through rational thought or through doctrine, but through a way of life, through inspiration and sudden revelatory insight. Mystics saw God as immanent in all of creation, accessible through love and concentrated devotion, ascetic practice and prayer. This form of knowledge was open to women as well as men. Among the earliest religious autobiographers, women mystics predominate. Male mystics in the Middle Ages all were clerics, who needed no other authorization than that of their religious training to assume a public role. Mysticism provided a way for some women to authorize themselves to speak of their own experiences, because they were empowered to speak by God. Women mystics testified in public to their revelations, their visions, their dialogue with God. They believed in the truth of their visions and made their contemporaries believe in them. Some told complete life stories; others only highlighted their ecstatic experiences. Most mystics recounted that they at first resisted their visions and that they struggled long and hard before they finally submitted to God's will to publicly attest to them.

Female mystics appear in clusters. The great twelfth-century mystics, Hildegard of Bingen and Elizabeth of Schoenau, both of whom died before 1180, were followed by the Beguine mystics Hadewijch of Brabant and Mechthild of Magdeburg and the remarkable nuns of Helfta, whose teachings flourished in the thirteenth century. The fourteenth century brought female mysticism to Holland, Germany, England, France, and Italy. Female preachers making prophetic claims appeared among Catholic and Protestant sectarians in the sixteenth and seventeenth centuries. The mystic mode of expression continued in Protestant sectarian movements, such as the Shakers, the Spiritualists, and many smaller evangelical movements in the nineteenth century.

Mystics told their stories not to celebrate or display their individuality; they saw themselves merely as instruments of divine revelation, often considering their gifts true burdens, which they reluctantly assumed. Hildegard of Bingen, one of the most accomplished women of her day, an adviser to kings, bishops, and popes, called herself "God's little trumpet." The thirteenth-century mystic Mechthild of Magdeburg described how she perceived "the great tongue of the godhead. . . . with the pitiful ears of my nothingness."

Mystics told of the reaction of their contemporaries to their unusual experiences: first doubt, then disbelief, finally acceptance of the special gifts the mystics had received. Many mystics won the approval and support of those closely in contact with them, but met censure and disbelief from strangers and church authorities that did not know them well. Those who were accepted as truthful witnesses by their contemporaries often wielded considerable public influence and acquired historical fame, such as Saint Hildegard of Bingen, and later Saint Catherine of Siena and Saint Teresa of Avila. Obviously, mystics whose accounts were disbelieved by their contemporaries did not get a chance to record their lives, and their stories were lost to history. Some of them were tried as heretics and died for their vision. An example of the latter is Joan of Arc, whose trial record gives an account of her life, mission, and divine revelations.

ANOTHER GENRE OF autobiographical writing developed in the form of witness stories. Witnesses tell of their experiences of terrifying events or of the evils of certain political systems in order to heal themselves and to influence others to empathize with the victims and to take action against the oppressive system.

Slave narratives form an important subcategory of witness stories. Since slaves were forced into illiteracy, most of these narratives were dictated by slaves to some white amanuensis, most likely an abolitionist. Inevitably, the white writer cast the story into a popular narrative form and not infrequently edited out certain passages he or she deemed redundant or unsuitable. Sometimes, as in the case of Harriet Jacobs' autobiography, the editor, Lydia Maria Child, specified that she edited only for grammatical correctness and helped with the structure of the story, but did not otherwise alter the manuscript. There are a few other authentic slave narratives written by the slaves themselves: Frederick Douglass, Moses Grandy, William Wells Brown, Solomon Northup.[2] These ex-slave narrators all had acquired literacy, and several had edited newspapers. Their style showed the influence of the Bible, *Pilgrim's Progress*, and the oratory they had heard from the pulpit and at political rallies. They favored an educated, elevated style, since their act of writing was to serve as testimony to the intellectual ability of their race, defying the racist slanders of their oppressors.

All slave narratives offered dramatic accounts of the evils of slavery, of the hardships and abuses suffered by slaves, and of the various ways slaves resisted their treatment. They provide a counterweight to the slaveholders' version of the past, which dominated historical writing in the United States for decades after the end of the Civil War. It is worth noting that they were the first form in which African American literature found expression.

Slave narratives also told stories of individual heroism and of the specific struggles by which slaves made themselves into free men and women. In this regard they resemble quest narratives. But unlike in typical quest stories, the emphasis is on the hero or heroine as a representative of the race, not as an individual. Ex-slaves saw themselves as models to be emulated; their stories were inextricably linked with that of their race.

Present-day historians and literary critics have pointed out that there are obligatory scenes in most of these narratives: the abuse of an innocent slave; the whipping; the runaway slave; the market scene, where slaves are separated from their families; the sexual abuse of slave women; and the neglect and abuse of old slaves. Such scenes have been deemed to represent antislavery clichés and stereotypes that have crept into these narratives, either put into them by white abolitionists or included in order to please white audiences. This order of causality is difficult to prove. It is just as likely that the reverse happened: antislavery writers took some of these main themes from slave narratives and used them in their own writing and rhetoric. Harriet Beecher Stowe drew most of the information for *Uncle Tom's Cabin* from slave narratives and the oral testimony of fugitive slaves. Lydia Maria Child, Theodore Weld, Henry Stanton, and Abby Kelly all drew on such sources for their writings and antislavery oratory.

Some narratives of elderly survivors of slavery were preserved as oral histories in the New Deal period. These were collected by white and some African American interviewers. There are differences in the tone and in the content of the narratives, depending on the race of the interviewer. When one wishes to use these narratives as sources, it is therefore particularly important to read widely in them and to use a comparative analysis. These oral histories were made when their subjects were quite elderly. Many of them recall some almost idyllic aspects of their childhood, which run counter to the slave narratives written earlier. One may wonder if, in recalling childhood events seventy and eighty years later, the narrators unconsciously exercised selective memory. On the other hand, since the oral histories do not have the literary quality and style of the earlier slave narratives, they have an immediacy and simplicity that makes them compelling and believable. They are full of homely details. One woman described that her mistress would give the black children white bread and milk for supper. "When she [mistress] died it liked to kill me. I just cried and cried. . . . I thought when she died she carried all the white bread with her. Folks was saying, 'Look at that po little nigger crying 'bout her Mistress,' but I wasn't crying 'bout mistress, I was crying 'cause the white bread was gone."[3] This kind of description has the ring of truth.

As a genre, slave narratives avoid certain themes, such as any indication of conflict between ex-slaves and white abolitionists. While almost all of them deal with the abuse of slave women by white men, none of them deals with women's sexuality from the point of view of the slave women.

The sole exception is the remarkable narrative of Harriet Jacobs. The historian Jean Yellin has verified all the extraordinary events described by Jacobs and has been able to find historical evidence for all of the figures that appear in this narrative under pseudonyms. She has climaxed this accomplishment by writing a biography of Harriet Jacobs that covers not only the events narrated by Jacobs, but decades of her life after her writing of the narrative.[4]

Harriet Jacobs' *Incidents in the Life of A Slave Girl* (1861), written under the pseudonym Linda Brent, tells the story of a slave woman's struggle against the repeated attempts of her master to make her his concubine.[5] Linda Brent was literate and had done considerable reading. Her story follows the traditional romantic plot of innocence and seduction, victim and victimizer, and virtue triumphant. But it tells it with a cruel twist: because Linda Brent is a black woman and a slave, she can have no hope of retaining her virtue. Instead, she chooses to become an agent of her own destiny by selecting a white man she considers friendly to her to be her lover. When she has two children by him, she reveals that fact to her master, thinking he would sell the children to their father and stop pursuing her. Her white lover betrays her by planning to sell off her children, and her white master continues to pursue her. Linda Brent disappears, actually hiding for seven years within proximity of her master in the attic of her grandmother's house. There she catches glimpses of her children, as they grow up over the years, cared for by her grandmother, who is a free woman. She finally succeeds in fleeing slavery with her children, but the traditional happy ending eludes her. She is able to support herself and her children, but as a woman who has sinned against society she can find neither husband nor home. Only by fictionalizing "Linda Brent" can Harriet Jacobs survive her daring act of going public with her tainted sexual life. Her insistence on exposing the racist double standard, whereby no black woman can keep herself "respectable" as long as she is in bondage and no white men are held accountable for their assaults on black women, was an act of political rebellion unique in her time.

Another significant slave narrative was written as a novel. Harriet E. Wilson's *Our Nig; or Sketches from the Life of a Free Black* (1859) is a powerful indictment of the cruelty of white women toward their black household servants.[6] Its fictional heroine, "Frado," lives in the North prior to the Civil War, working as a domestic servant. She suffers a great deal under her mistress's tyranny and details her resistance to it. Frado tells her story of an unrelenting struggle against poverty and prejudice, a sort of quest auto-biography, but she refuses to construct a happy ending. At the end of the book, Frado is homeless, abandoned by a shiftless husband, sick, and the sole support of her child. But she has raised herself from virtual slavery to the autonomy of a writer, a creative artist, who has found her authorial voice. The only way she could tell this story, with its harsh indictment of Northern racism, was to turn it into fiction.

In the twentieth century, witness stories have proliferated as victims of oppressive regimes, of wars and civil wars, and of religious persecution record their struggle for survival. Holocaust literature has become a sepa-rate academic field of study, as aging survivors have testified to their lived experience for the historical record. As with all witness accounts, the his-torian has to read widely in the literature to verify and compare events and practices that appear in many accounts. This genre, too, has its conventions and obligatory scenes, but just because they have been told so often that they appear as clichés is no reason to question their veracity.

IN THE QUEST stories genre the typically male author describes his edu-cation or his process of becoming who he is. They are stories of self-made men who regard themselves as exemplary and who see their lives as worthy of emulation by others. They chronicle their humble beginnings, their constant search for education and self-improvement, the men who helped them advance, and the obstacles they overcame.

Quest autobiographies are expressive of the culture of developing capitalism, in which the role of the individual is celebrated above that of family, clan, and class. Medieval knights could not develop such a literary genre. Quest autobiographies coincide with the growth of biography as a literary form and reinforce the concept that outstanding individuals shape historical events.

In the United States Benjamin Franklin's autobiography is the outstand-ing example of this genre.[7] His rise from being a poor printer's apprentice to become a framer of the Constitution and founder of the new nation, Postmaster-General, diplomat and negotiator of the peace treaty ending the Revolutionary War, then Ambassador to Great Britain and France would alone entitle him to serve as an example of civic leadership. But Franklin had an equally illustrious career as a scientist and inventor. His discovery that electricity is a basic force in nature was recognized with the awarding of honorary degrees from Harvard, William and Mary, and the

University of St. Andrews in Scotland, and by his election to the Royal Society in England. His many practical inventions, such as the Franklin stove, the lightning rod, and bifocal lenses, were widely acclaimed and distributed.

Franklin, the autobiographer, does not stress these most significant and celebrated accomplishments of his life. He wrote the autobiography in three sections over a period of nineteen years, finishing the work in the last years of his life. The first part, published during his lifetime, is the longest of the three and covers his youth and his rise to prominence in Philadelphia. Part Three was written in the last years of his life, when he was ill and taking morphine daily to ease the pain of his gout. With all his accomplishments behind him Franklin ended his autobiography in 1758, and thus his major role in the American Revolution and his significant work as a peacemaker and diplomat at the end of the war are not included in it.

Franklin mentions those who obstructed his rise with unforgiving venom. He gives credit to those who helped his rise, but always stresses the self-discipline, cunning, and planning that made his success possible. According to Franklin, what counts in life is not substance, but appearance. As a young businessman in Philadelphia he kept a diary listing his virtues and vices and planned every day carefully both for self-improvement and for promoting his image as an exemplary good citizen. He boasts that his method toward success can be repeated by anyone willing to discipline himself.

Franklin admits to some failings, which he playfully calls his "errata": trivial errors he committed and which he treats quite lightly. He admits to some youthful indiscretions with "low women." He does not mention his womanizing as a married man during his various stays in London and Paris. Yet he is forthright and quite unself-conscious in relating the calculated negotiations about dowry he carried on with the father of a woman he considered marrying. He tells us frankly:

> Ms. Godfrey projected a match for me with a relation's Daughter, took opportunities of bringing us often together, till a serious Courtship on my part ensu'd, the Girl being in herself very deserving. The old Folks encourag'd me by continual invitations to Supper, and by leaving us together, till at length it was time to explain. Mrs. Godfrey managed our little Treaty. I let her know that

I expected as much Money with their daughter as would pay off my remaining Debt for the Printinghouse, which I believe was not then above a Hundred Pounds. She brought me the word they had no such Sum to spare. I said they might mortgage their House in the Loan Office. The Answer to this after some Days was, that they did not approve the Match. . . . and therefore I was forbidden the House, and the Daughter shut up. . . . Mrs. Godfrey brought me afterwards some more favorable Accounts of their Disposition, and would have drawn me on again: but I declared absolutely my Resolution to have nothing more to do with the family.[8]

This is followed by his equally hard-nosed bargaining in negotiating terms for his marriage to Deborah Reed, a woman to whom he had earlier been engaged. He had broken off that engagement, but resumed his courtship after his other prospect failed. He described his conduct in this affair as an "erratum" he was able to correct.

Negotiated marriages of the kind Franklin described were quite common during the eighteenth century, and many of them led to relations of friendship and even love. Franklin never advanced to that stage, nor did he seem to strive for it. He praised Deborah as "a good and helpful helpmate, [who] assisted me much by tending the shop." He brought a son, William, into the marriage, but never revealed who the boy's mother was. He described the death of his infant son with cool indifference. The fact that Deborah feared the ocean and did not want to undertake a sea voyage did not discourage Franklin from repeatedly undertaking overseas assignments. When Deborah was quite ill and pleaded with him to come home to see her once more, he found it impossible to do so.

Franklin gave no hint of the lighter side of his character. The witty, humorous Benjamin Franklin, the flirtatious ladies man who charmed French society, stayed in the background of the autobiography. Its *persona* is the disciplined self-made man, the prototype of the New American. Whether due to his age and infirmities at the time of the completion of the autobiography or due to a deliberate choice, Franklin did not give us a rounded picture of his life. He seems to have been more interested in his creation of the *persona* of the American entrepreneur, risen from poverty to wealth, than in leaving a balanced story of his life and accomplishments. As such, his book has served generations as inspirational moral uplift and celebration of American uniqueness.

Quite beyond that he wrote a powerful quest story, crafted like a work of fiction, in which the omissions are as important as are the told facts. Unlike the biographer, the autobiographer is under no obligation to tell the whole story, nor does he have to give a balanced and reasoned interpretation of the meaning of the entire life. He can tell us what he considers important at the time of the telling. The reader is left with the task of rounding out the life.

Many quest autobiographies by statesmen, generals, presidents, and politicians follow a formulaic outline, tracing their hero's struggle from humble beginnings, over many obstacles, to the triumphant achievement of high office, power, and fame. Their straightforward narrative sounds simple and believable, even if insight, contemplation, and authenticity are missing.

Quite unlike these autobiographies in tone, *The Education of Henry Adams* turns the quest story on its head.[9] The author describes his highly successful life as a series of failures and turns his autobiography into a metaphor for the decay of American society. He moves from the assumption of political power as a family prerogative to the stance of the minor political bureaucrat unable to influence events positively. His "failed" education becomes a symbol for the decline of democratic ideals and practices. The *persona* of his autobiography is used as a tool for ironic commentary and for detached, pessimistic observation. In order to carry forward this literary device, in which "success" stands for failure, he omits major events in his personal life, such as his marriage and his wife's illness and her death by suicide. Despite these tragedies Adams succeeded in becoming one of the great historians of his time, celebrated and respected for his work and achievement in his profession, an aspect of his life barely mentioned in the autobiography.

The Franklin and Adams autobiographies illustrate that autobiographers are not necessarily reliable sources on their own life histories. Franklin turned the *persona* of his story into the new American hero, the urban entrepreneur, a forerunner of the fictional heroes of Horatio Alger. Adams, by his ironic conceit, used his story to offer a scathing critique of American progress. Still, the quest autobiography continued to flourish and enjoy a wide readership.

Leaders of social, religious, or political movements wrote autobiographies for self-justification and self-celebration, as did other outstanding figures, but also in order to promote and advance the movement they led. Their *persona* becomes that movement, becomes its symbol. The hero's quest is fulfilled only through the movement. Examples are the autobiographies of W. E. B. Du Bois, Booker T. Washington, Walter White, Malcolm X, and Mohandas K. Gandhi.[10]

FOR CENTURIES THE WRITING of autobiographies was entirely a male preserve. The creation of an authentic self that defines its own creativity was possible for women only much later in history than it was for men. The authority of male thinkers was unquestioned; a man's right to use his own experience as an exemplar was undisputed, and he could develop his thought in discourse with the great male thinkers before him. For millennia women were so constrained in their social role and so convinced of their mental inferiority that they could write about themselves only with great difficulty. They were denied all preconditions for being able to write autobiographies.

Women's lack of self-confidence and their fear of offending their contemporaries simply by their act of writing led them to use devious strategies for their self-expression. They apologized for their daring undertaking; they wrote biographies of their husbands or fathers and embedded their autobiographies in them; they asked male family members to certify to their domestic skills and accomplishments in order to justify their writing as a sort of hobby. Above all, they wrote thinly disguised autobiographical fiction. To write about one's own life implied that one thought one's life was significant, an assumption that ran counter to women's gender indoctrination. By fictionalizing, women could avoid the distress and embarrassment they might cause to friends, acquaintances, and neighbors by making their lives the subject of books. The novels of Jane Austen and the Brontës are of this type, as are those of Louisa May Alcott and Mary Wollstonecraft's *Mary*.

Virtually the single exception to this self-silencing of women's authorial voices is Christine de Pizan's *The Book of the City of Ladies* (published in 1405), a remarkable secular text that aimed to create a history of women by listing women of achievement.[11] She gave her treatise an autobiographical framework by telling of her disappointment and pain upon finding that most of the works she read denigrated and attacked women. She wished to defend women against the slanders of men, and with the aid of three allegorical female spirits, Reason, Rectitude, and Justice, she built a city in which all women might find refuge and peace. Her allegorical city, filled with heroines of worth and valor, is the first attempt by a woman to construct women's history as a means of raising women's self-esteem.

In the sixteenth and seventeenth centuries many writers, both male and female, constructed lists of "women worthies." Two centuries later biographical compilations of women's lives were used to argue for women's claim to education and equality. Biographies of eminent women became a popular genre in England, Europe, and the United States in the nineteenth century. Yet women's autobiographies were still rare exceptions, although many women kept diaries.

It was not until the Progressive period and the beginning of the twentieth century that U.S. women began to match men by celebrating women reformers and social movement leaders. These biographies represent a search for heroines, a desire to legitimate women as agents in history. They are often poorly written, haphazardly documented, and inevitably hagiographic. They tend to suppress women's private lives and to avoid any hint of ambition in their heroines. The same tendency is shown by autobiographers. Women of great independence and fierce ambition, such as Jane Addams, Frances Willard, and Margaret Sanger wrote about their search for meaningful work and for a mission, their rebellion against traditional gender restraints, their struggles for education and for financial independence. Yet they described their awakening as somehow thrust upon them, almost accidentally; they pictured themselves as motivated only by the desire to do good. They denied their agency, even though their actual lives speak clearly for their strong ambition, their careful planning, and their incredible perseverance. Anything hinting at lack of respectability was omitted. Elizabeth Cady Stanton in her autobiographical writing never mentioned the difficulties in her marriage. Jane Addams' autobiography is the memoir of Hull House more than that of its founder. Hull House, a cooperative settlement house, was highly unconventional in Addams' day and offered a home to highly unconventional women. But Addams does not mention this aspect of her work, nor does she mention that all her life she lived and partnered with a woman.

Jane Addams was not alone in hiding this important aspect of her life from her public. Biographers, using autobiographies as their source, compounded this silencing. The early biographers of great women leaders of the nineteenth and twentieth centuries tended to be their collaborators and admirers. They shared their subjects' conviction that the public and private lives of these women were separate entities, that the public life predominated and the private life had to conform as much as possible to Victorian respectability. What strikes the reader most in reading the autobiographies and biographies of Susan B. Anthony, Elizabeth Cady Stanton, Frances Willard, Jane Addams, and others of their stature is their single-minded, almost fanatical dedication to organizational life.[12] These biographies have tacitly reinforced the notion that a woman who plays a decisive role in public life is really not quite human; she is a superwoman and a deviant.

The autobiographies of African American women leaders, such as those of Ida B. Wells and Mary Church Terrell, follow the same pattern.[13] They are essentially histories of organizations and social movements and offer the reader just brief glimpses of the private person at the center of the story.

TOWARD THE END of the nineteenth century there appear a number of prominent women reformers who center their private lives on women and live a lifestyle we would today characterize as lesbian. In their autobiographies and in the biographies by contemporaries this aspect of their lives is simply ignored in favor of discussing their public lives. Similarly, their twentieth-century biographers, while carefully unearthing what evidence of the private lives they could, also avoided or denied any implication of homoerotic relationships.

It became a sort of formula for historians to acknowledge the existence of intense, intimate, and long-lasting friendships among women by citing Carroll Smith-Rosenberg's pioneering essay on the subject, and then avoiding any further reference to the troubling "problem" of sex, as though the historians were modern-day Victorians.[14] Reluctance to treat these relationships as one would treat heterosexual ones often surfaces in the form of a concern with "evidence." Why do we need a smoking gun before we can describe a relationship as homoerotic? No one expects historians to have or to need such evidence of the sexual/erotic relationships between men and women. We simply use the primary evidence of letters and journals and evidence inferred from recorded behavior; most important, we examine the impact of the private relationship on the person's public life. We assume that any relationship of such intimacy and duration would have had an intellectual as well as emotional influence and would deserve more than passing mention. Precisely this is what historians seem to be hesitant to do when dealing with homosexual relationships. They seem to be wrestling with the ghosts of homophobic judgments here: if these relationships were erotic and sexual, biographers fear they might diminish the authority and seriousness of the subjects' public lives.

A case in point is Frances Willard, the founder and organizer of the Woman's Christian Temperance Union (WCTU), the largest mass organization of her time. She goes into great detail in her autobiography about various proposals of marriage she rejected. Yet she only hints discreetly at the existence of "the real romance of my life." In a 704-page book she has only this to say about her companion, Anna Gordon, with whom she shared a home for most of her life: "The rarest of my intimate friends . . . she has been a solace and support in all my undertakings."[15]

If Willard was reticent in revealing her emotional and sexual life, her biographers had ample evidence of her private life and psychological struggles. Frances was a tomboy as a child and adolescent, and in her autobiography described vividly her agony on being forced in her teens to wear skirts for the first time. Her most recent biographer, Ruth Bordin, omits this incident from her biography, though she notes that Willard was known to her schoolmates at the Northwestern Female Academy as wild with the girls and not at all interested in the boys.[16]

At twenty-one, Willard accepted an engagement with Charles Fowler. Shortly thereafter her brother Oliver became engaged to Mary Bannister, Willard's intimate friend. Willard acknowledged feeling jealous, thinking that Mary would not love her as before. Soon after, she broke off her own engagement. Bordin refers to several other near-romantic relationships Willard had with men; but none of them led to permanent attachments.

Bordin describes the friendship between Kate Jackson and Frances Willard as that of "intimates." Jackson followed Willard around on her travels and lived in the same place as Willard for most of her life. She was jealous of other female attachments Willard formed; she often supported her financially. In 1877, when Willard, for once, was not accompanied by Kate Jackson, she met Anna Gordon, who became her intimate friend and later replaced Jackson as her "companion," to use Bordin's term. Gordon made her home with Willard and her mother for twenty-two years and was Willard's main emotional support.

Frances Willard represented an unusual mixture of respectability and radicalism. This evangelical Christian, defender of home and domesticity, redefined "home protection" in its most radically feminist way as women's defense of the home against the excesses of male abuse. She managed to translate the "do everything policy" of the WCTU into a wide-ranging program of community betterment, social welfare innovation, and female collective initiative for community welfare. Willard embraced Fabian socialism, was closely allied with the embattled labor movement in a period when it was losing popularity, and helped in the formation of the Populist Party. She worked for child labor legislation and for improved factory working conditions. Toward the end of her life she declared that if she had to live her life over again, she would work for socialism, by which she meant an American Christian socialism.

Bordin is obviously sensitive to the nature of Willard's long-standing female relationships and rightly points out that the language of love and passion in her correspondence with these women is different from that of her letters to other women whom she loved and respected as coworkers in the woman's rights cause. Yet she still insists that all Willard's relationships with other women were "homosocial," in the phrase coined by Carroll Smith-Rosenberg. Yet, by all indications Willard's relationships with other women were not homosocial but homoerotic.

Another case in point is that of Carrie Chapman Catt, the woman suffrage leader. Robert Booth Fowler manages in his biography to make Carrie Chapman Catt come alive as a person and to locate her solidly within the context of her time.[17] He argues that one of her main characteristics was a profound anger at female subordination, tempered by self-discipline, and that she believed strongly that the winning of the vote would destroy, in her words, the "obedience of women in the home."[18] While she realized that these radical ideas would not appeal to the mass of women, she was deeply motivated by them. At the heart of Catt's suffrage work, Fowler tells us, was a challenge to patriarchal ideas.

Catt emerges as a Progressive who saw woman's suffrage not as a panacea but as an instrument for liberating women, increasing their autonomy, advancing their education, and unleashing their energies for peace and a reconstituted democratic polity.

Catt was married twice, and in her widowhood she formed intimate and long-lasting relationships with women, including one of "unique intimacy" with Mary Peck. Their letters are explicit in expressions of love. Robert Fowler states,

The Catt-Peck friendship deserves to be described as a romantic attachment. This was most obvious in regard to Peck. Peck was in love with Catt for decades and everything one can discover about Peck's feelings and behavior suggests that she was in love with Catt in an erotic sense as well as in others.

   . . . While Catt's replies do not match this spirit, in time her love for Mary became unmistakable.[19]

Fowler takes Catt's relationships with women exceptionally seriously. Still, he feels it necessary to assure us that if Catt and Peck "were lovers, they were so only as far as Catt's traditional and unquestioned acceptance of heterosexuality permitted."

The evidence shows overwhelmingly that an important group of leading American and British women—reformers and women's rights advocates—lived their lives without emotional attachments to men or to any single man. For all or part of their lives they derived their emotional and affective sustenance from close association with networks of women and with one or more women, with whom they shared their lives, their homes, their finances, and their fate, in the manner of married couples.

Perhaps Alice Paul, Frances Willard, Carrie Chapman Catt, Susan B. Anthony, Anna Dickinson, Jane Addams—to name just a few—were simply what Victorian "lesbians" looked like. Just as it was possible for an educated middle-class white woman of great respectability to be a socialist in the 1890s and not lose standing or status, so it was possible for her to be woman-identified and homoerotic in her private life and lose neither respectability nor standing in her public life. In either case, public opinion of a later period would brand her as deviant.

As historians attempt to recreate the lives of their subjects from within the consciousness of the subject and from within the context of time, a more forthright, less self-conscious and thereby more respectful treatment of the subjects' homoerotic relationships is slowly emerging. The scholarly development of Gay and Lesbian History has already fostered biographies of twentieth-century women that deal openly with their lesbian lives. Examples of these are Blanche Wiesen Cook's *Eleanor Roosevelt* and Susan Ware's biography of Molly Dewson, *Partner and I*. New work, such as Victoria Bissel Brown's biography of Jane Addams, helps us to better understand the women concerned; it breaks our own stereotyped notions

of respectability and better enables us to comprehend the connection between public *persona* and private person.[20]

ANOTHER GENRE, that of autobiographical fiction, has become more
and more popular in contemporary literature and has tended to blur the
boundaries between the lived life and the account of it.

Anzia Yezierska's life and work illustrate the contested boundaries
between the *persona* of the writer and the actual person. Eight-year-old
Yezierska and her family came to America from Poland in 1890. They lived
in an Eastside tenement, the daughters working in sweatshops, while the
father continued to live the life of an old-world Talmudic scholar, con-
tributing nothing to the family's subsistence. Yezierska wrote several autobiographical novels, collections of short stories, and two screenplays. She
wrote in a raw, homespun style, a primitive English literally translated
from the Yiddish. She first won acclaim in 1918, when her short story
"Hungry Hearts" won the O. Henry Prize. The publication of a short story
collection in 1920 resulted in her going to Hollywood to write the screenplay for a film based on "Hungry Hearts." Disenchanted with the film industry, she returned to New York. In 1926 one of her novels, *Bread Givers*,
won wide acclaim, and she became celebrated as the very embodiment of
the American immigrant success story. Yet for the next decades her work
fell into oblivion. Then, in 1950, she published another autobiographical
novel that got rave reviews, but few sales.

Bread Givers tells the first-person story of the immigrant Jewish daughter fighting against a tyrannical father who has forced his other daughters
into unwanted, unhappy marriages.[21] The heroine leaves home, acquires
some learning, and becomes a writer. In a moving final scene she returns
home, after she is financially successful and happily married. She finds her
father destitute, homeless, and sick. The two are finally reconciled and she
provides for his care.

While some of the facts in her novel are autobiographical, many are
not. Yezierska had a stormy sexual life, with many love affairs, several marriages, and a great hidden romance with John Dewey. She wrote of parts
of this in her several autobiographical books. After her death, her daughter
published a book about her mother's life in which she tried to disentangle
the truth from the fictionalized version.[22] Yezierska described herself as
self-taught, deprived of formal education, although in fact she earned a

degree at Columbia Teachers College in 1904. Her primitive dialect style is a highly sophisticated invention, since she was well educated by the time she wrote her autobiographies. She freely invented incidents, transposed characters, omitted facts and distorted others, all of which her daughter meticulously documents. The reconciliation story she tells in *Bread Givers* was untrue; her actual attempt at reconciliation with her father was a dismal failure: the old man rejected and cursed her, and she never saw him again. She also entirely suppressed her romance with John Dewey, which she described in a successfully disguised form in another novel.

Yet Yezierska's fictionalized autobiographies give quite an accurate picture of the milieu and culture out of which she came. Better than most writers before and after, she described the young woman's "hunger . . . to become a person" in her own right, not just a daughter, wife and mother. Her autobiographical novels impact the reader more powerfully than do the "truthful" compendia of movement history written by Jane Addams, Frances Willard, and Carrie Chapman Catt.

The autobiographical works of Benjamin Franklin, Henry Adams, Anzia Yezierska, and the other figures discussed above reveal in their omissions and silences that such works have to be read critically and tested against outside evidence. For the historian it is especially important to evaluate the sources used in historical biographies and autobiographies. In both genres these are quite similar: diaries, letters, primary sources of contemporaries, oral histories, and the usual sources for background.

GENERALLY, READERS TEND to think of diaries as being truthful in offering direct access to the writer's thoughts and emotions. When we ask for whom and for what purpose a diary was written, the complexity of this kind of source becomes evident. Diaries are written for many purposes and for many audiences. In the nineteenth century parents encouraged their children to write daily diaries, recording their thoughts on moral and religious questions. Bronson Alcott, the father of Louisa May Alcott, required his daughters to do so. Each night, he and his wife read the diary entries and used them as the basis for moral instruction. In using such diaries as a source, it is difficult to distinguish whose views are being recorded, the diarist's or the parents'.

Other diarists write in order to make themselves feel better or in order to survive difficult periods of their lives. Anne Frank recorded the harsh reality of her experience in hiding in Nazi-occupied Amsterdam, but she also used her diary as a companion, a friend with whom to be in dialogue.

The diaries of Anaïs Nin, on the other hand, are much more literary and self-conscious. They are crafted with a reader in mind and make a *persona* of the diarist.

In autobiographies, the main source is the author's memory. People writing their own lives tend to trust their memories uncritically. But memory is a treacherous source. In general, we remember what was pleasant and feels healing and positive at the time we remember. We remember best what makes sense in the current interpretation we have of our own life.

Memory often suppresses painful, traumatic, or embarrassing experiences. Most autobiographers have no way of checking such suppressions and compensating for them. Citing my own experience as both a biographer and autobiographer, I can report that I was quite aware of the fallibility of memory and tried, wherever possible, to use written documentation, relying on letters and diary entries to test the accuracy of my memory. Still, I experienced quite a shocking example of the suppression of memory. In my autobiography, *Fireweed*, the crucial event of my life, the Nazi takeover of Austria and its immediate consequences, are described in Chapter 5.[23] After I had finished all but three chapters of the book, I was at an impasse and could not go on writing. To help myself over this writer's block, I decided to reread the entire manuscript, from the start, something I had not done before. I was appalled to find that I had no copy of Chapter 5 on my computer. Suspecting a computer foul-up I spent more than a week searching all my computer files, my back-ups, and my paper files to find the missing chapter. I knew exactly what was in it. I had written about this event once before, in a work of fiction, but that was fifty years ago, and this chapter, written in the first person, was considerably different from my account in the novel. To my amazement, I had to finally conclude that I had never written Chapter 5. It was clearly a case of my memory suppressing the most traumatic event of my life, while substituting a false memory of having written the chapter. I used a lot of background research and all the tricks of the historian to help me over the psychological block and write the missing chapter. It worked, and I was able to complete the book.

Memory often suppresses what is not socially acceptable to readers. In the cases of the social movement leaders of the nineteenth century discussed above, the authors internalize social taboos and suppress certain aspects of their private lives. Sometimes such omissions of evidence are made quite deliberately, as in the case discussed below. The silences and omissions of autobiographers need to be questioned, because they often reveal more biases than does the narrative.

When I wrote the biography of the Grimké sisters, two Southern women of the planter class, who left the South and became agents for the American Anti-Slavery Society, I relied on their diaries as sources for their early lives and on another valuable primary source, a memoir of Angelina Grimké Weld written by her husband after her death.[24] One of the troubling questions for the biographer was to explain why Angelina gave up her brilliant speaking career after her marriage. Contemporaries speculated that she had sold out her convictions; other biographers hinted that her husband, Theodore Weld, was to blame for it. Weld, in the memoir, mentioned two "injuries" that befell Angelina and that turned her into a virtual invalid. Since I could not find any corroborating evidence of any injuries, I doubted his version. It took much work for me to tease out of other sources what had actually happened: Weld used "injury" as a euphemism for a female condition that may have occurred between her first and second pregnancies and which was greatly aggravated by succeeding pregnancies following quickly one upon the other. In correspondence with her friend Harriot Hunt, the first female medical practitioner in the United States, Angelina's sister Sarah referred to this condition as a prolapsed uterus, which caused great pain. This condition is easily corrected with modern medical knowledge, but was incurable during Angelina's lifetime. The second injury referred to by Weld may have been a miscarriage or possibly a hernia. Again, these were incurable conditions at that time. For the biographer, it makes a great deal of difference whether Angelina Grimké's abandonment of her career as a lecturer was due to accidental injuries or due to too-frequent pregnancies and inadequate obstetrical care. Interestingly, Sarah Grimké in her later radical attack on patriarchal marriage cites women's sexual subordination as the cause of too-frequent pregnancies and birth-related ailments.

In the case of the Grimké memoir, Theodore Weld, its author, was falsifying the record in order not to violate contemporary proprieties.

ANOTHER DIFFICULTY IN trying to tease the truth out of autobiographical writing is the life told in anecdotes. Every human being tells a story—or a number of stories—about his or her life. Our life-story changes over time, as our understanding and our representation of our own life changes. Our life-story defines who we are and how we represent ourselves. With our life-story we try to make a good impression on others; we also try to give some sort of coherence, some pattern to events in our life. In the telling of our life-story we frequently make use of anecdotes; these anecdotes become part of our rhetorical repertoire and tend to improve over time, as they are repeated.

Anecdotes are shaped memories, usually shaped to make a point, to teach a lesson, to create a character or to embellish our tale with some humor. Anecdotes are crafted remembrances; they frequently reshape the truth. The tendency in anecdotes is to hide negative feelings or actions and to bring the story to a dramatic climax. Anecdotes are oft-told tales; the more frequently they are told, the more they take on the veracity of life. Autobiographers tend to lose the boundaries between anecdotes and actual memory. It is often easier to remember the anecdote than it is to remember what actually happened.

In reading contemporary autobiographies, especially those of politicians or other famous personalities, it is startling to realize how much of the story is made up of anecdotes. Consciously or unconsciously, autobiographers use anecdotes to avoid the necessity for a deeper probing into the motivation and meanings of their past actions. Many biographies follow the same pattern. The historian using both genres as a source needs to be aware of the shortcomings of both memory and anecdote.

THE HISTORIAN MUST evaluate first-person primary sources, diaries, and autobiographies critically and compensate for their inadequacies, omissions, and distortions with additional research. Autobiographical fiction must be read with the understanding that its author must serve the story first and foremost and is under no obligation to be truthful. It can also be read against the grain, by noting omissions and silences and questioning those for insight into the author's motivations.

The biographer has more tools at her disposal than has the autobiographer and the writer relying on memory. The traditional tools of the historian—verification, the consideration of various viewpoints in interpretation, a multiplicity of sources—can serve the biographer to come closer to the truth than do first-person accounts. Historical biography, disciplined by strict verification and enlivened by skillful writing, can come nearest to the truth in placing the individual life in history.

Notes

1. Saint Augustine, *The Confessions*, John E. Rotelle (ed.), *The Works of St. Augustine*, Part 1, Volume 1 (Hyde Park, N.Y.: New City Press, 1997).

2. Frederick Douglass, *Narrative of the Life of Frederick Douglass, an American Slave* (Boston: The Anti-Slavery Office, 1845); Moses Grandy, *The Life of Moses Grandy, Late a Slave in the United States of America* (Boston: Oliver Johnson, 1844), in *Five Slave Narratives: A Compendium* (New York: Arno Press and the New York Times, 1968); William Wells Brown, *Narrative of William Wells Brown, a Fugitive Slave, Written by Himself* (Boston: The Anti-Slavery Office, 1847), in *Five Slave Narratives*; Solomon Northup, *Twelve Years a Slave* (Baton Rouge: Louisiana State University Press, 1968).

3. Ophelia Settle Egypt, J. Masuoka, and Charles Johnson, "Unwritten History of Slaves: Autobiographical Accounts of Negro Ex-Slaves," Social Science Source Documents No. 1 (Nashville, Tennessee: Fisk University, Social Science Institute, 1946), bound typescript, 113–17.

4. Jean Fagan Yellin, *Harriet Jacobs: A Life* (New York: Basic Civitas Books, 2004).

5. Harriet Jacobs, *Incidents in the Life of a Slave Girl, Written by Herself* (Cambridge: Harvard University Press, 1987).

6. Harriet Wilson, *Our Nig; or Sketches from the Life of a Free Black Woman* (New York: Vintage Books, 1983).

7. Leonard W. Larabee (ed.), *The Autobiography of Benjamin Franklin* (New Haven: Yale University Press, 1964).

8. Ibid., 127–28.

9. Henry Adams, *The Education of Henry Adams* (New York: Modern Library, 1931).

10. W. E. B. Du Bois, *Dusk of Dawn: An Essay Toward an Autobiography of a Race Concept* (Millwood, N.Y.: Kraus-Thomson, 1974); Booker T. Washington, *Up From Slavery* (New York: Doubleday Company, 1965); Walter Francis White, *A Man Called White: The Autobiography of Walter White* (Bloomington: Indiana University Press, 1970); Malcom X, *The Autobiography of Malcom X* (New York: Grove Press, 1965); Mohandas K. Gandhi, *An Autobiography* (Boston: Beacon Press, 1957).

11. Christine de Pizan, *The Book of the City of Ladies*, Earl Jeffrey Richards (trans.) (New York: Persea Books, 1982).

12. Rheta Childe Dorr, *Susan B. Anthony: The Woman Who Changed the Mind of a Nation* (New York: Frederick A. Stokes Company, 1928); Elizabeth Cady Stanton, *Eighty Years and More (1815–1897): Reminiscences of Elizabeth Cady Stanton* (New York: European

Publishing Company, 1898); Frances Willard, *Glimpses of Fifty Years: The Autobiography of an American Woman* (Chicago: Published by the Woman's Temperance Publication Association: H. J. Smith & Co., 1889); Jane Addams, *Twenty Years at Hull House, With Autobiographical Notes* (New York: The Macmillan Company, 1910).

13. Ida B. Wells, *Crusade for Justice: The Autobiography of Ida B. Wells*, Alfreda M. Duster (ed.) (Chicago: University of Chicago Press, 1970); Mary Church Terrell, *A Colored Woman in a White World* (Washington, D.C.: National Association of Colored Women's Clubs, 1968).

14. Carroll Smith-Rosenberg, "The Female World of Love and Ritual: Relationships between Women in Nineteenth-Century America," *SIGNS* 1, no. 1 (Autumn 1975): 1–29.

15. Willard, *Glimpses of Fifty Years*, 641.

16. Ruth Bordin, *Frances Willard: A Biography* (Chapel Hill: University of North Carolina Press, 1986), 26.

17. Robert Booth Fowler, *Carrie Catt, Feminist Politician* (Boston: Northeastern University Press, 1986).

18. Catt, cited in ibid., 64.

19. Ibid., 53–54.

20. Blanche Wiesen Cook, *Eleanor Roosevelt*, vols. 1 and 2 (New York: Viking Press, 1992); Susan Ware, *Partner and I: Molly Dewson, Feminism, and New Deal Politics* (New Haven: Yale University Press, 1987). Victoria Bissel Brown, *The Education of Jane Addams* (Philadelphia: University of Pennsylvania Press, 2004).

21. Anzia Yezierska, *Bread Givers: A Struggle Between a Father of the Old World and a Daughter of the New*, with an introduction by Alice Kessler-Harris (New York: Persea Books, 1975).

22. Louise Levitas Henrikson, *Anna Yezierska: A Writer's Life* (New Brunswick, N.J.: Rutgers University Press, 1988).

23. Gerda Lerner, *Fireweed: A Political Autobiography* (Philadelphia: Temple University Press, 2002).

24. Gerda Lerner, *The Grimké Sisters from South Carolina: Rebels Against Slavery* (Boston: Houghton Mifflin Co., 1967); Gerda Lerner, *The Grimké Sisters from South Carolina: Pioneers for Women's Rights and Abolition*, revised and expanded edition (Chapel Hill: University of North Carolina Press, 2004).

PART III

Living in History

chapter nine

The Historian and the Writer

In 2002 I was awarded the Bruce Catton Prize for Achievement in History and Writing, given by the Society of American Historians.* The purpose of that society is "to encourage literary distinction in the writing of history and biography."

I have been a writer far longer than I have been a historian. Since I have done most of my writing in English, which for me is a second language, I have had to acquire the writer's craft by conscious effort and have never had the luxury of relying simply on intuition and a talent for languages. My good knowledge of French, six years of high school Latin, and years of studying medieval ballads and poetry in Middle High German were skills that helped me become a bilingual writer. What helped me the most was my intense interest in languages and linguistics and my wide and deep reading in German literature. When I became an American historian at the age of forty-six, I had already published a novel and several short stories and written a screenplay in English. Years of apprenticeship as a writer had also resulted in an unpublished novel and a file drawer full of unpublished short stories and articles.

I could not help but bring my writer's consciousness into my historical writing. My writer's habit of repeatedly editing, revising, and polishing every text served me well in academic writing, and my trained sense of style gave my writing a distinct voice. But what my writing background provided most meaningfully was an ability to express complex ideas and facts in a lucid, jargon-free style, something reviewers and readers frequently noted.

In this essay I touch briefly on the need to respect the form inherent in every content. This has been one of my deeply held convictions, which I have striven to put into practice whenever I could. It helped me to open my biography of the Grimké sisters with a dramatic moment that occurred decades into their career. It inspired me to open my book The Majority Finds Its Past with a long, autobiographical essay, at a time when such a practice was not only unheard of, but discouraged by respectable historians. That essay was the most popular part of the book and has been more frequently reprinted and taught than have the other essays. It has also opened the way for other historians to dare to inject

*This chapter reprints the text of my acceptance speech, given at the society's annual dinner, May 10, 2002.

themselves into a book of serious academic scholarship and to make their "standpoint" clear, thereby challenging the myth of historians' neutrality in regard to their research. My conviction that "form is the shape of content" allowed me to reorganize the manuscript of my autobiography, once I had found the metaphor "fireweed" suitable as both framework and title. My respect for form has often allowed me to banish the jewels of research findings into the endnotes and to confine my text to what is necessary to tell a coherent story. The telling of the story is the foremost obligation of the writer; it has seemed to me to be perfectly compatible with the historian's obligation to tell a thoroughly documented story.

I am deeply honored by this award and profoundly thank the Society of American Historians and the selection committee for including me among the outstanding historians and writers previously given this honor.

I would like to briefly speak about history and writing.

Carl Becker said: "Since history is . . . an imaginative reconstruction of vanished events, its form and substance are inseparable." Many historians would disagree with Becker's concept of an "imaginative reconstruction." Instead, they would point to history-making as a judicious assemblage of facts and data, put in a context of already established facts and data, which are interpreted and re-interpreted in the light of insights provided by succeeding generations. Becker would counter that, "left to themselves, the facts do not speak."[1] Until they are interpreted and made into a story, the facts are pebbles on the ground, and on the seashore. This is where history and literature intersect.

I would like to focus on that area of mutuality, overlap, and interpenetration. History-making, just like literature, means form-giving and meaning-giving. It is a creative enterprise by which we fashion out of scraps of memory and selected data from the past a coherent story that makes sense to the present. The form we give to this narrative determines its impact on the reader. In this act of form-giving, the historian and the creative writer are bound by certain strictures, if they wish to hold their audiences. The writer, seemingly free to invent as she chooses, can do so only within a framework of assumptions common to reader and writer. If she wishes to depart from that unwritten contract, as is the case for writers of utopias or science fiction, the framework and references must be made explicit, so that the reader is willing to suspend disbelief and follow the narrative.

The same constraint holds true for the historian, but she operates under the more rigorous discipline of having to construct her story out of actual events, loosely called facts of the past. Not only is she not free to invent her data, she must also document them scrupulously. And yet, her story must be coherent and must make sense, therefore it must partake of the imagination. "Making sense to the reader" means that somewhere in the process of finding the right form, a field of resonance, of interaction between writer and reader is created that makes conversation possible. Without such conversation, the writing has no impact. Of course, there are countless examples of historical writing that are shapeless, turgid, incomprehensible, and lacking in resonance. Others are written in mystifying specialized jargon comprehensible only to a small coterie of the initiated. Such works get published; we even award Ph.D.s for them; I will grant that some of them may have some merit, but they are neither great literature nor great history-writing.

Constraints are good for the imagination. Christian artists over thousands of years had to limit their subject matter to certain traditional scenes and to a conventional iconography, which forced them to give their works as much individuality and richness of texture and design as possible. So the constraints imposed on the historian can work to foster a deeper search for quality of writing and sharpness of style.

The overlapping of history-writing and literature is greatest in the field of biography. Here, too, the need to stay within the confines of given facts, the known data of an actual life, constrains both the writer and the historian. In the act of interpretation, the giving of meaning, it may appear that the writer has more freedom and a greater potential for success than the historian. He can invent dialogue without documentation, speculate as to motivation, and interpret more imaginatively. Yet I think the self-imposed discipline and constraint of the historian often force him to greater effort, more thorough research, more inventive construction of context and connections.

The greatest challenge in the writing of history is the fact that the outcome is known. There is no element of suspense and drama. The historian cannot construct alternative scenarios, even if the story cries out for it. Mozart cannot finish the Requiem; Lincoln must die from a gunshot wound; the enactment of woman suffrage does not bring equality for women. The historian must manage, within the imperfections of events and the ironies of human failings, to endow his narrative with meaning and purpose. I would suggest that freer and more skillful use of literary devices, such as analogy, metaphor, and irony might help. The historian who develops his or her distinct style and voice has a better chance of holding the reader's interest than has the author who writes in a neutral, supposedly objective style.

UNFORTUNATELY, IN OUR TRAINING of historians, we pay no more than lip service to developing distinctive writing. Most of the time we are willing to settle for merely competent writing. I have yet to see a graduate history program in which reading fiction and essays is a requirement and in which attention is given to developing style and voice. Academic historians are generally not rewarded for taking time and effort to impart literary skills. That is a pity. In the long run, it deprives us of wider audiences and diminishes the impact of history on society in general. The Society of American Historians, in its attention to writing and literary merit, serves as a remarkable exception to the general indifference to form and style.

In the pop-culture and media-driven world in which we live, attention to form and style is considered at best quaint, if not old-fashioned and elitist. I beg to differ. Form is the shape of content. I believe strongly that there is only one right form for each content and that it takes an act of creativity and imagination to discover and elicit that form. Once one has found it, there is a recognition reflex; one knows that it is right. What is formless, or wrongly formed, does not affect the reader. The right form holds the reader and directs his or her attention to the meaning of the story.

Style is the voice of the interpreter—the I and the eye that sees, the camera angle and aperture, the framer's choice of boundaries. Style is the connective tissue that assures continuity, the texture of the weave that gives strength and resilience. Far from being elitist, form and style can open history to new voices, new ranges of vision.

Up until quite recently history as a profession has spoken in the voice of exclusion. A small elite of trained male intellectuals has interpreted the past in its own image and in its own voice. More destructively, it has pretended that such narrow and selective representation is universal and inclusive. "There is something very absurd," said Tom Paine, "in supposing a continent to be perpetually governed by an island."[2] In making that rather obvious observation, he shattered centuries of established wisdom. In my lifetime, centuries of history based on exclusion have been challenged and overthrown. Women have, like Tom Paine, observed that it seems rather absurd that one half of humankind should perpetually present the past exclusively in its own image. This development has been and is a truly historical event in world history. All kinds of groups, who have been denied a usable past, have reclaimed their human heritage. Members of formerly subordinate racial or ethnic groups, former colonials, and, finally, women have asserted their right to a meaningful and interpreted past. We have opened up the profession of history and democratized it in an unprecedented way. We have shown that the formerly "anonymous" have voices and can tell their stories. We have unearthed ignored sources and documents; we have had to learn ways of listening and interpreting; we have had to question what activities we designate as historically significant.

What has happened to historical scholarship is akin to the momentous shift in viewpoint that occurred in the canvases of Pieter Bruegel the Elder: the traditional core, the main story of Christ on the road to Calvary is still in the picture, but it is no longer up front and in the center.[3] It is now part of an immense study of human life in its multilayered complexity. Christ stumbles under the weight of the cross, yet the focus is not on him, but on the boys playing around him. Greedy for sensation, indifferent to the tragedy they are witnessing, hucksters and peddlers, women, children, and peasants crowd the canvas, while behind them soldiers and guards wend their way toward the place of execution. Dogs fight in the background; thistles flourish on the roadside. The meaning of this decentered tragedy is powerfully obvious: all around Christ's route of suffering daily life goes on, ordinary, messy, and insistent.

The core of traditional history, its function as cultural tradition, unifying national memory, legitimizing ideology for those holding power—that core still holds. But it no longer provides the only story, nor is it necessarily always in the foreground. The clamoring voices of those so long denied their history insist on telling many stories of daily struggles for life and existence, of heroism without badges and honors, of defeats and disillusionment, of bitterness and injustice. As in Bruegel's paintings, the canvas has become crowded, perhaps more confusing, but surely more imbued with reality.

We have merely begun to understand the implications of this new, more inclusive history. I trust that we will do more than accept it with tolerance, for it challenges us to deeper thinking, more generous worldviews, and more holistic reconstructions of the past. The humanism of the Renaissance gave rise to the autonomous individual, the artist who was also a mechanic and a scientist. The end of the twentieth century was the period of the Renaissance for women and other groups who had been denied their history. The new history demands of historians not only rigorous analytic thought, but the creativity of the writer, the empathetic humanism that will lead to the creation of a truly representative universal history.

Notes

1. Both quotes from Carl L. Becker, "Everyman His Own Historian," *American Historical Review* 37 (Jan. 1932): 233–34.

2. *The Complete Writings of Thomas Paine*, Philip S. Foner (ed.), 2 vols. (New York: Citadel Press, 1945), 1:24.

3. The picture is Bruegel's *Die Kreuztragung Christi* (*The Road to Calvary*) in Gustav Glueck, *Bruegels Gemaelde* (Wien: Schroll & Co., 1932), plate 17. See also Max Dvorak, *Pieter Bruegel der Aeltere* (Wien: E. Hoelzel, 1921).

chapter ten

Holistic History

CHALLENGES AND POSSIBILITIES

In this essay I revisit a question that has occupied me since 1969: what is the significance of Women's History for the entire field of history? How will Women's History affect and change the practice of historians in the future? I wrote on this subject several times during the past decades and often addressed it in my public lectures. The longer I wrote and taught Women's History and the more I experienced the profound transformative effect it had on women students, the more I became convinced that the development of this new field of scholarship amounted to a major cultural breakthrough, a paradigm shift. Surveying the field in recent years I was struck not only by its astonishing growth, but also by the proliferation of different approaches and specializations that seemed to splinter the field and diffuse its message. Interest in the histories of various identity groups — African American, Latina, Native American, Jewish, Asian American, and women of other ethnic groups — added a new dimension to traditional knowledge about the American past. Lesbian/Gay/ Transgender and Sexualities Studies added several new categories of inquiry to the focus on socially constructed identities.

Gender Studies challenged and complicated the generalizations in Women's History. Theories, such as postmodernism and cultural studies, derived from literary theories, influenced much new research that focused on representation, images, performance, and popular culture, marking a sharp turn away from social history. While I saw the proliferation of interest groupings as a sign of strength, rather than of division, I was concerned at the lack of interest contemporary historians seemed to have in social movements and the actual lives and experiences of women in the past. I was alarmed at the fact that most current work was concerned with the recent past — a trend that was overwhelmingly obvious in the topics of dissertations — and that there seemed to be very little thought given to the larger, historical meaning of what historians of women's history are doing.

In the current essay I take a somewhat different view. I stress the far-reaching influence Women's History scholarship has had on transforming the general field. Rather than drawing conclusions from current trends, I decided for once simply to project my own ideas of where I think the field should be going. I end up with a call for a new holistic history and with several fairly utopian statements. Knowing full well that historians are not supposed to predict the future, I have taken this liberty on the basis of claiming the privilege of my age. Old women and men, at the end of life, are entitled to express their vision. And so I have done here.

The millennia-old omission of women from recorded history has resulted in a serious distortion of the record of civilization. It has presented a world to us in which seemingly all significant events were activated and executed by men, with women relegated to marginality and cultural insignificance. Men had agency; men built civilization and cultures; men devised theories and explanatory systems of thought; women took care of reproduction, the rearing of children, domestic production, and the maintenance of daily life. These false assertions led to the equally erroneous claim that women had no history, or at least no history worth recording.

With the growth of universities, which from their beginnings in the Middle Ages and well into the twentieth century excluded women from access to higher education, the male monopoly on formal knowledge became institutionalized. When the recording of history became a profession all scholarship was male-centered and male-defined. Man was the measure of all that is significant; male activities, like warfare and the control of land and resources, were deemed more significant than the rearing of children, the daily maintenance of life, and the building of communities. University-trained historians, all male, asked only androcentric questions of the past. The recorded history that resulted made it appear as though women had made only marginal contributions to the building of civilization. Such findings reinforced already existing biases against women and led both men and women to view women's subordinate place in society as though it were appropriate and acceptable. Although individual women resisted such definitions and asserted women's claims for equality, their voices were ignored, distorted, or defined as deviant.

By arrogating to themselves the representation of all of humanity, men have built a conceptual error of vast proportion into all of their thought. As long as men believed the earth to be flat and at the center of the universe, they could not understand its reality, its actual relationship to other bodies in the universe. As long as men believed that their experiences, their viewpoints, and their ideas represented all of human experience and all of human thought, they were not only unable to see the connections and complexities of human interaction, but they were unable to describe reality accurately.

Traditional history accustomed both men and women to a construction of the past based on narrow slices of reality and to an acceptance of a partial story for the entire narrative. The effect of this on women was that they internalized the myth of their inferiority, their passivity, their inability to think creatively and strive for originality. Believing themselves to be persons without a history of their own, they accepted the patriarchal gender characterization of being victims of history, at best, assistants to men in the building of civilization. That this has been damaging to women's development and to their ability to improve their position in society is in retrospect quite obvious. Less obvious is the damage this patriarchal fallacy has done and is doing to men.

The assumption of male innate superiority is obviously counterintuitive and contradicts the life experience of every male. Every man has known strong and capable women in his life, just as he has known weak and incapable men. In order to accept the dominant mental construct of male superiority men have had to suppress their own life experience. They have to be trained, and continue to train themselves, to live an intellectual lie. This damages not only their intellect, but their soul.

The androcentric fallacy has led to the acceptance of a record of the past that makes a false claim to universality. For traditional history has left out not only women, but the vast majority of men. Slaves, peasants, workers, colonials were made as invisible as were women. While exceptional women of elites, such as those substituting for missing male heirs as queens and rulers, were included in the historical account, traditional history has been, by and large, the history of male elites. It has been a history presented in slices of life, incapable of reviving and recreating the organic fullness and interconnectedness of human existence.

The male-centered historical framework was decisively challenged by the Women's History movement of the 1970s. That challenge led not only to the spread of Women's History as an established field in the profession, but to a decisive transformation in historians' thought and practice.

After forty years, what has Women's History added to historical knowledge and practice?

It brought a hitherto neglected and forgotten group into historical consciousness, thereby broadening the field of historical scholarship.

Because sources on women were scattered, often unidentified in archives, and since women were subsumed under their husbands' names, and generally underrepresented, historians of women had to find new approaches to research. They soon recognized that in order to find data about the past of women their approach had to be interdisciplinary. Women's History used the tools of social, economic, and demographic history to great advantage. Anthropology and psychology provided conceptual frameworks for interpreting the conditions under which women lived. Literary sources, such as diaries, memoirs, family correspondences, fiction, and poetry by women, offered information not only about the actual lives of women, but about societal strictures and gender role definitions that defined and constrained women's lives.

Church records and those of religious orders and church-affiliated groups provided rich sources on women's spiritual, religious, and welfare concerns. Testimonials of religious conversions became a valuable source for women's life histories. Many of these sources had already been in use to describe the activities of men. But for Women's History the emphasis and the interpretations were different.

As Women's History developed, its accomplishments enriched historical research and analysis as a whole. Five of its most significant accomplishments are worth highlighting here.

1. The methods used by historians of women to find documentation on women in sources that were not organized to make such searches accessible and the search for new and unusual sources influenced and helped other historians in dealing with hitherto neglected and silenced subjects. Historians dealing with the developing fields of various ethnicities, Gay and Lesbian History, Jewish Women's History, increasingly used interdisciplinary research, oral histories, and journalistic sources, such as letters to the editor.

2. The periodization of Women's History loomed early on as a major problem. It became clear the great "events" of world history—wars and revolutions—impacted differently on the lives of men and women. Further, economic, cultural, and technological changes that decisively altered the condition of men's lives did not similarly affect women. The conditions for women, in several aspects of their lives, showed great continuity over time, in contrast to discontinuities for men. For example, while the Industrial Revolution opened employment to a small number of women workers, they and all other women continued to be mainly engaged in housework and child rearing. The double burden of working women's longer hours of labor, combining paid work outside the home with unpaid work within the home, has continued for over 150 years and has shown

an amazing consistency and resistance to change, regardless of where it is being measured. It is as true for Western countries during early industrialization as it is for developing countries under twenty-first century globalization. Similarly, women have had access only to a gender-defined labor market, regardless of where they live. Throughout the nineteenth century in the United States, most working women were to be found in two occupations: domestic work and sex work. The same pattern shows up in today's developing countries, where sweatshop industrial work and sex work are the jobs in which most women work. Globalization has added another innovation: migratory domestic workers who leave their families, children, and home countries and work at substandard wages and often under deplorable conditions in foreign countries. Most of these are women. Recent scholarship has shown that, for women, access to education, the availability of safe contraception, and medical reforms guaranteeing a lowering of maternal and infant death rates represent more important historical turning points than do wars and revolutions.

Different periodization in regard to historical events and differences in economic access and mobility for women and men raise serious problems about generalizations and synthesis in historical writing.

3. Women's History, by uncovering the social construct of gender, has pointed the way to showing the social construction of other categories. African American scholars long ago uncovered the social construction of race. Ethnicity has similarly been destabilized as a natural concept and has been shown to be socially constructed. Biological sexuality has also been questioned under the impact of postmodernist theories. Lesbian, Gay, and Transgender History have become scholarly fields of specialization.

4. Women's History, prodded in the 1980s by challenges from African American historians of women, opened up to a more biracial and later a multiracial perspective. The discussion of "differences" among women inevitably led to the recognition that any number of categories by which people were separated one from the other were socially constructed, and that these socially constructed identities served as means of keeping elites in power. These discussions were broadened and enriched by the work of postcolonial historians and by postmodern theorists. A further extension of this critical inquiry focused on the long tradition of societies to socially create deviant out-groups, who, in times of crisis, become scapegoats for persecution, thereby shielding those truly responsible from public scrutiny. Some scholars have focused their work on exposing the interconnections

and interdependency of the categories race, gender, class, ethnicity, and sexuality. This work is ongoing and very promising. If we can at last go beyond two-dimensional descriptions to a rounded picture of how societies actually function, how power is constructed and sustained, how the subordination of large populations is organized and sustained, perhaps reform and social change could be speeded up and become more effective. Meanwhile, scholarship in a broad range of fields has been inspired and enriched by these developments.

5. Another accomplishment of Women's History is the wiping out, or at least the blurring, of distinctions between the public and private in human affairs. Since patriarchal gender definitions relegated women to the private, men to the public sphere, much of women's agency in history became hidden. By focusing on women's role, Women's History scholarship called attention to "influence" on the exercise of power, thereby gendering its inquiry. The role of petition campaigns, the unseen influences that created change in public opinion, the influence reform organizations exerted on political discourse—these and many similar themes became topics for analysis. The changed angle of vision provided by Women's History scholarship deeply affected such fields as Legal, Diplomatic, and Labor History. It also decisively transformed the writing of biography. The kind of biographies written until the 1980s, in which the public life of public figures is discussed as though their private lives had no impact on it, are today quite rare. The new biographies examine the connections between the public and the private and offer more complex, more lifelike representations than were possible with traditional history. They point a way to a future, holistic history.

IF THE PAST is a broad river flowing toward the ocean, it cannot be described in a single snapshot or in a series of snapshots taken at different spots along its way. The river has come into being out of tiny springs that at various points along the way became joined together. It has adjusted its shape; it has narrowed and deepened when the terrain demanded it; it has eroded its banks or been confined by them. The river has overcome obstacles by creating waterfalls; it has left side branches, stagnant and irrelevant, as it formed itself into a broad stream. It is not only made of water and earth, it constantly reforms itself in an interplay of gravity, rock hardness, wind, and moving energy. If photographs cannot adequately represent it, film can do better, but it will have to include a variety of standpoints and parameters—long shot, wide-angle lens, close-up.

The unseen aspects of the broad stream hide the obstacles overcome in its flow, hide the complex history of what made it as we see it at any given moment. The river's obstacles can be likened to the failed events in history, the unseen forces underlying public events, the resistances that shaped outcomes. Did the obstacles obstruct the flow of the river; did they restrain its breadth; did they deepen its channel and increase its strength? If the obstacles remain untold and uncharted, we cannot accurately describe what a river is—what made it and why it is as it is.

Each human action occurs within a network of forces; each is in organic connection to other forces; there is constant interplay, adjustment, and flow. It is probably impossible to adequately describe even a single event of the past in a way that encompasses all its complexity. But the historian must strive for more complexity, more awareness of the connections between the event and its surroundings—for a more holistic representation.

In real life, a person is constantly engaged in multiple activities, functioning on different levels of social organization. Dailyness and extraordinary moments of significance coexist, not impeding one another or obstructing the flow of events.

How do events interconnect? What precedes a visible event—what invisible forces, accidents, unplanned and bizarre coincidences? Conscious decisions lead to unforeseen consequences. How does the event connect to what happened before it? And after?

The play of power is never merely two-dimensional. It consists of overt power, and resistance to it, and of invisible powers—the constraints on the mighty rulers exerted by the nameless, the anonymous, the collectivities of the oppressed. Somehow, historians must be aware of these complexities and represent them.

THE COMPLEXITIES OF representing past reality are discussed by the great French historian Marc Bloch in his book *The Historian's Craft.*[1] The fact that he wrote this book while living underground as a member of the Resistance in France during the Nazi occupation attests to the urgency these questions concerning the practice of history held for him. He never finished the book; he was arrested and killed by the Germans in June 1944.

Here he contrasts the methods used by scientists to those of historians, whom he compares to artists:

> From the view which I have from my window, each savant/scientist selects his proper subject without troubling himself too much about the whole. The physicist explains the blue of the sky; the chemist the water of the brook; the botanist the plants. The task of reassembling the landscape as it appears to me and excites my imagination, they leave to art. . . . The fact is that the landscape as a unity exists only in my imagination. . . . For in the last analysis it is human consciousness which is the subject-matter of history. The interrelations, confusions, and infections of human consciousness are, for history, reality itself.[2]

The scientist can limit the scope of inquiry to a distinct field; the historian, like the artist, must reassemble the whole and encompass all the fields. Bloch makes the challenge even more complex by demanding that the historian include human consciousness with all its complexities in his description. Bloch asks for the writing of holistic history: "The knowledge of fragments, studied by turns, each for its own sake, will never produce the knowledge of the whole; it will not even produce that of the fragments themselves. But the work of reintegration can come only after analysis."[3]

Marc Bloch saw the need for historians to oscillate between related phenomena running over long periods and specific moments of direct experience. A holistic history, not bound by the old categories and "fields," must be true to the multicausal, multilayered, energy-flowing interplay of forces, the clash of contradictions that make up life. Each actor on the historical scene was once a living organism set within an environment, grounded in an interplay of cultures, belief systems, superstitions, customs, and trivialities. No event in life is two- or three-dimensional; no event occurs isolated in time and space. No slice of life can present reality.

How Has Women's History Affected Historical Studies?

The emergence of "gender" as a tool of analysis was an important and transformative development. Gender is the socially constructed definition of appropriate sex roles for men and women; it varies as to time and place and culture. Used early on as a cataloguing category to be added to other concepts, such as race, class, and ethnicity, in locating historical actors and explaining their decisions, it soon proved to have a far wider reach. Gender moved from being a descriptive device illuminating the social relation of the sexes to being seen as a critical factor in shaping power relations in society. As such it proved to have strong explanatory power extending from individual decision-making to public policy and law-making. Alice Kessler-Harris in her book *In Pursuit of Equity: Women, Men, and the Quest for Economic Citizenship in Twentieth-Century America* brilliantly demonstrates the transformative power of gender analysis.[4] In her study of the origins of supposedly gender-neutral New Deal legislation—social security, unemployment insurance, fair labor standards—she reveals how deeply ingrained beliefs about gender distorted the aims of these laws so as to reinforce women's economic dependency and diminish their economic citizenship rights. Government policy, based on the generally accepted idea that the primary role of women was maternal and subsuming all women under this stereotype, sought to protect women workers from exploitation by forbidding them night work and limiting their hours of employment even if that meant curtailing women's chances of gainful employment. Protective labor legislation, based on traditional ideas of social order—men in the workforce, women in the home—regulated and institutionalized a socially segmented labor force. Thus, gender became reified in the form of proscriptive laws. In a later work, *Gendering Labor History*, Kessler-Harris argues that the division between Labor History and Women's History perpetuates an outdated male-centered framework, obscures a true understanding of class, and marginalizes women.[5] Labor History, traditionally focused on men and institutions, must incorporate gender into its analysis, she argues. In order for Labor History to reflect accurately the changing conditions brought on by modernization and globalization, it is essential to understand how gender shapes class formation and how private and familial values determine decisions about labor migration and the sexual division of labor. Such a new Labor History, transformed by the integration of Women's History and gender analysis into the old Labor History, represents the vanguard of a future holistic history.

Other subfields of historical scholarship have already undergone transformation thanks to the impact of Women's History and gender analysis. The awareness, promoted by Women's History's contesting a strict division between the private and the public spheres, has led to transformative work in Diplomatic History. Scholars such as Ann Stoler and Chandra Talpade Mohanty have shown how institutionalized gender prescriptions were used by colonial powers to reinforce their rule over the colonized.[6] Regulation by the colonizers of the sexual practices of colonized men, proscription of racial intermarriage, and the pervasive myth of the need to protect white (colonizer) women from sexual attacks by native men served to strengthen colonial rule and to limit economic choices and possibilities for the upward mobility of colonized men. The same pattern of sexual and racial regulation has been abundantly documented in African American history, and it served similar aims of reinforcing dominant power. By now similar practices and patterns of empire-building have been shown at work in India, the Dutch East Indies, Algeria, and the Near East.

Diplomatic History can no longer be told as simply the contest of states by means of negotiations between diplomatic bureaucracies and political leaders. It also must consider the multiple ways in which gender definitions and the regulation of sexuality serve as instruments for gaining and consolidating power. The transformative force of questions and methods derived from Women's History have enriched historical scholarship and rendered it more complex and more interesting.

Similarly, the recent trend toward departing from a strictly Euro- or Western-centered historical narrative reflects the engagements of historians with questions derived from Women's History and Women's Studies. Transnational history is, by definition, comparative history; it contradicts hegemonic assumptions and decenters the narrative. Recognizing the complexities of periodic events, it is multicentered and manages to integrate the various brooks, rivulets, and streams that make up the river of history in its holistic narrative.

Legal and Political History have also been changed. New questions have been raised: What has been the effect of centuries of discriminatory treatment of women on the institutions of society? On its culture? How has the construction of deviant out-groups — witches, heretics, promiscuous females, homosexuals, welfare mothers — served the interests of state power? How have gendered definitions of citizenship affected social reality? The historian Linda Kerber in her most recent book, *No Constitutional Right to Be Ladies: Women and the Obligations of Citizenship*, examines the gendered obligations (rather than the rights) of citizenship, including taxation, the duty to work, eligibility for welfare, and the duties of serving on juries and in the military.[7] Offering a sophisticated and nuanced analysis of gender- and race-defined differences, Kerber rewrites legal history from a woman-centered point of view.

Where Does Women's History Need to Go?

In answering that question I will not attempt to predict where Women's History will go, but I will express where I would like it to go.

In the past forty years Women's History has not advanced far toward constructing a model for what a new egalitarian history of women and men might be like. Feminist theory has emerged from many other fields — sociology, literature, anthropology, psychology — all of which have influenced the work of women historians. The reverse has not been the case. Women's History has not influenced the theoretical foundations of the other disciplines.

I would like to see more theoretical work concerned with the question of how knowledge of women's actual historical past is necessary for moving women's issues forward in today's society and for gaining equality for women.

Women's History needs to continue the work of finding, reviving, and recording the missing history of half the U.S. population. This work is far from finished. There are still many periods, regions, and groups that remain undocumented and uninterpreted. The lives of rural women, of women of ethnic immigrant groups, and of working-class women (apart from those active in unions) have not been studied systematically. The stories and life cycles of women who combined traditional housewife and mothering roles with income-producing part-time work have been mentioned but not sufficiently documented. The multiple, often sequential child-rearing responsibilities of working-class women, who took care of their own, their relatives', and often their children's children, are cited in individual biographies but have eluded historians' research interest. While we have studied women in groups and organizations and have amply documented women in leadership roles, the majority of women have lived far different lives, with different constraints and challenges than those facing educated, middle- and upper-class women. The teachers trained by Emma Willard in her Troy, New York, Female Seminary and those trained by Catherine Beecher in her seminaries and through her American Woman's Educational Association (1852), who virtually staffed the emerging public school system before the Civil War, need to be studied individually and in groups. The women speakers who criss-crossed the country in the decade before the Civil War and for thirty years after, providing cultural, educational, and political challenges to their audiences, should similarly be subject to study. They lectured to vast and enthusiastic audiences; one can only assume that they exerted some influence on these audiences. The women active in the various minor parties and mass movements of the late nineteenth century—Greenbackers, Farmers Alliances, Populists—should be identified, studied, and evaluated in terms of their impact on reform and politics. In all of the cases mentioned above, primary records are extensive and available.

Sometimes historians have used easily available and voluminous records in limited and restricted ways that do not do justice to their potential. Although the vast network of women's clubs operating from 1892 on and their organizational records could provide material for dozens of dissertations and books, they have yielded only a few, which have provided merely a descriptive overview. Yet, if even a few of these dry, organizational reports of local clubs in all the states sent annually to their national headquarters were used in combination with deep and detailed research in the particular locality, a holistic and very rich description of the actual lives and activities of ordinary women would emerge. One example of the dynamic effect of women's initially moderate reform activities concerns a club of elite white women in Honolulu, Hawaii, who were active late in the twentieth century. Concerned with fostering community beautification in order to encourage tourism, the women undertook as a first step to remove all advertising billboards from the highway leading from the airport to the town center. The ladies were astonished when they suddenly found themselves in deep conflict with the city fathers, many of whom were their relatives or close friends. Shocked to discover that their high status and influence was of no avail against business interests, the women refused to yield. Instead they concluded that they must work to elect more civic-minded town leaders; they transformed their beautification club into an activist political organization. Several years later, having become a force in town politics, they succeeded. If the story of their club work were located in a deep analysis of the political, social, and economic forces in their community and were then compared with one or another case study of women's club work elsewhere, we might be able to discern long-range patterns and firmer generalizations about the meaning of women's community work than we have been able to do up to now.

Women's History should answer some basic questions relating to the meanings of the field. How did women's activities and ideas affect or change political, social, cultural trends? Some of this work has already been done in regard to reforms of the Progressive movement, women's struggle for higher education, and the temperance and women's suffrage movements. More needs to be done.

How have individual women's improvised care for the sick and elderly shaped the organizations of communities and of government policies? Thousands of women served on school boards and on library committees decades before women had the vote—what of their stories and their collective impact? Women, African American and white, were responsible for founding the first day care centers and kindergartens in the United States. Though it was through their labor that these educational innovations became part of the public school system, the significance of this work is yet to be studied. Women's cultural activities—the founding of reading circles, libraries, museums, orchestras, and centers for art and theater—need to be studied not in isolation, but as sex-specific activities spanning centuries. By linking and comparing various case studies we might understand how women (as a group) acted as agents in history differently from men.

Did women act just like men in the public realm? If not, how did they act differently and why? How did this affect outcomes? We already know that women organized differently from men in communities. We know that they went about the work of gathering antislavery petitions in ways different from their male relatives. We know that their priorities for communal betterment in the Progressive period were different from those of men.

Historian Charles M, Payne, in his important book, *I've Got the Light of Freedom: The Organizing Tradition and the Mississippi Freedom Struggle*, studied grassroots organizing modes in the civil rights movement from the 1940s to the present.[8] Rejecting the top-down version of history with its emphasis on the leadership of great men, Payne compared male and female patterns of organizing. He found that women were frequently the most numerous and effective force in the grassroots movement, both at the local and at the national level. Payne not only provided the reader with a powerful revisionist view of the civil rights movement, but also represented a growing and emergent trend in social history.[9]

Women's History needs to keep intellectually and institutionally separate from Gender Studies. Even though the use of gender as a tool for analysis has proven to be a useful and exciting new line of inquiry, it is no substitute for Women's History. If our long-range goal is to create a history that is organic, functional, and gender-neutral, then the restorative work of Women's History must be allowed to continue for a long period of time. After all, men have been defining history as a male enterprise for at least 2,000 years. In view of the overwhelmingly androcentric record of the past, the work of writing the missing history of women is a prerequisite for understanding what a truly holistic history might be like. I hesitate to ask for equal time, but certainly forty years is insufficient.

Our awareness of differences among women must permeate all our thinking. Women are at least half of every population we are studying. To do justice to this fact, we must recognize that women, like men, do not constitute an undifferentiated whole. The particulars of region, religion, ethnicity, race, and sexuality are the ground on which we must test every generalization. In so doing, we will be forced to do more comparative work, which might yield unexpected insights.

Linda Gordon's *The Great Arizona Orphan Abduction* is a masterly account of an obscure local incident that powerfully illuminates Mexican and Anglo race and gender relations, along with religious and family values, in a setting of sharp class conflict.[10] In 1904 several nuns brought forty Irish orphans from the New York Foundling Hospital to Clifton-Morenci, a small Western mining town, to be placed for adoption with Catholic Mexican families who had been carefully pre-screened as suitable parents. On their arrival, a waiting group of Anglo women observed the transfer of the white, blond children to the waiting Mexican parents and became highly agitated, considering these adoptions an outrage that violated taboos against interracial mixing. They incited their husbands and family members to form a vigilante group and kidnapped twenty of the children, nearly lynched the nuns and the town's priest, and forced them and the remaining children to leave town. The vigilantes coerced the Mexicans to turn the children over to them, and the Anglo women took twenty of them into their homes and later adopted them, firmly convinced they were "saving" them. When the New York Hospital sued for the return of the children, three judicial instances, from the local judge to the U.S. Supreme Court, ruled in favor of the Anglo adoptive parents on the grounds that since the original adoptive parents were Mexican Indians they were unfit to raise white children.

Linda Gordon deliberately used a wide-angle lens to tell this story. She interwove chapters that narrated the events with background sections giving a historical account of the major themes of the conflict. She traced the economic development of the copper mines, the importation of a Mexican workforce, the long history of struggle between management and labor culminating in a bitter strike that preceded the incident with the orphans. She explored the religious conflict between Protestants and Catholics, the differing notions of child and community welfare held by Anglo and Mexican mothers, and the conflicting cultural and family values determined by race and class. Her discussion of the history of vigilantism, Western expansionism, and racism provided yet another dimension that allows us to explore the construction of citizenship and law in a constant struggle of competing definitions. Using methods from several separate disciplines, Gordon endowed a local event with multilayered meanings and a rich texture that comes as close as possible to the lived experience.

Women's History must be women-focused and woman-centered, at least until the groundwork for a new holistic history is laid. Up to now we have been able mostly to tell how women lived under patriarchy and how they coped with its constraints and sometimes overcame them. We have made small beginnings into telling the stories of how women related to other women and how they supported one another. The stories and facts we know about this aspect of women's past are scattered among organizational histories, biographies, local stories. We need to assemble them so as to make the larger patterns visible. Women have worked for hundreds of years by building sustaining networks, some based on family affiliation, some on common interests, some on specific projects. Can we discern a distinct women's culture of organizing by networking?

Another area in which more scholarship is needed is the intellectual history of women. The centuries-old struggle of women for access to education at all its levels is well documented, but its meanings are insufficiently explored. How did their indoctrination to intellectual inferiority affect women's consciousness of self? What strategies did they devise for counteracting it? How did they formulate theories and plans for their own emancipation?

We might ask some transforming questions of our theoretical research: How has the tension between reality and image in women's lives affected women's consciousness? What is the relationship between changing gender definitions and changing economic and social conditions? What are the points of change in women's historic experience by which we might accurately periodize a history of women?

The truly transformative question remains: **If women were at the center of our analysis of any period or event, how would our account be changed?**

This seems to me the most urgent long-range question that needs to be explored. It is premature to expect to get a final answer at this moment, when the compensatory aspect of Women's History is not far enough advanced to make a large body of historical material about women available in adequate quantities to match information about men. But I think we can first of all begin to think about such a possibility and consider what steps might have to be taken to devise a model.

FINALLY, LOOKING BOTH backward and forward, I see the task of pursuing and maintaining Women's History as one of truly revolutionary significance. Not only are we restoring their history to contemporary women and those of the future, we are bringing the past of women of all kinds into the center of intellectual discourse, thereby disproving, once and for all, the distorted patriarchal version of the past that has been sold to both men and women as a true account.

I believe the work we have done in the past forty years illustrates that men and women have had a different relationship to history. They also have had a different experience of history. Even if they themselves belong to oppressed groups, men have lived with an intellectual construct called History that affirmed the agency and heroism of people like themselves, namely men. They have told and retold the story of male superiority, and many have believed it.

Women have experienced the past as a series of humiliations, defeats, and disasters. For them, living with the construct History has affirmed their inferiority, passivity, and lack of imitable heroines. I believe that the different experiences of history for men and women have created actual differences between the sexes that are more significant and determinative than are the obvious biological differences. If I am right and women and men have lived in different cultures, then the work of righting this false version of the past is more than educational and reformist, it is revolutionary and restorative. The Renaissance put Western white men in the center of history. The Enlightenment asserted the abstract rights of individuals and allowed the middle class access to political power. Now it is the turn of half of humankind, women, to understand that we have always been equal, always had a history, and always shared in the building of civilization and its mental products.

The new holistic history will at last come closer than anything that has been written up to now to presenting a rounded picture of past events, inclusive of the viewpoints and actions of those hitherto forgotten and left out. In so doing, it will ground women's claims for equality in the solid record of past achievements and make women realize their collective strength and their individual abilities. This new history, in which women and men will be at the center of power and agency will, for the first time, make equality more than an abstract goal. It will make equality a realistic possibility.

Notes

1. Marc Bloch, *The Historian's Craft: Reflections on the Nature and Uses of History and the Techniques and Methods of the Men Who Write It*, Peter Putnam (trans.) (New York: Alfred A.Knopf, 1953).

2. Ibid., 150, 151.

3. Ibid., 155.

4. Alice Kessler-Harris, *In Pursuit of Equity: Women, Men, and the Quest for Economic Citizenship in Twentieth-Century America* (New York: Oxford University Press, 2001).

5.Alice Kessler-Harris, *Gendering Labor History* (Urbana: University of Illinois Press, 2007).

6. Ann Laura Stoler, *Carnal Knowledge and Imperial Power: Race and the Intimate in Colonial Rule* (Berkeley: University of California Press, 2002); Chandra Talpade Mohanty, *Feminist Genealogies, Colonial Legacies, Democratic Futures* (London: Routledge, 1997).

7. Linda K. Kerber, *No Constitutional Right to Be Ladies: Women and the Obligations of Citizenship* (New York: Hill & Wang, 1998).

8. Charles M. Payne, *I've Got the Light of Freedom: The Organizing Tradition and the Mississippi Freedom Struggle* (Berkeley: University of California Press, 1995).

9. For another example of the new scholarship on the civil rights movement, see Barbara Ransby, *Ella Baker and the Black Freedom Movement: A Radical Democratic Vision* (Chapel Hill: University of North Carolina Press, 2003).

10. Linda Gordon, *The Great Arizona Orphan Abduction* (Cambridge: Harvard University Press, 1999).

chapter eleven

Transformational Feminism
(An Interview)

This interview took place in 1997 and appeared in a small journal with a specialized readership.* It did not reach my usual audiences of historians and feminist academics. I choose to include it in this volume because it states in a very personal voice, my own speaking voice, the essential themes of this book, which I have expressed in various forms in the preceding chapters. Unencumbered by proof and evidence, it is a straight opinion piece. As such, it sums up in a simple and forthright way what I have learned in life and practice, and what I have concluded from my work in the historical archival record.

It opens with a definition of feminism as a world philosophy for women and men. Feminism is generally considered a program—economic, political, social, and psychological—that advocates the equality of women in all of society's functions. It is based on the conviction that every kind of discrimination against and oppression of women is unacceptable and must be resisted. Women, just like men, must stand at the center of events, and share power and resources on a basis of equality with men. Insofar as feminism aims to change laws, customs, and oppressive practices, it is a reformist movement, in the mainstream democratic tradition. But feminism also has a much more radical dimension: it is a liberation movement, designed to alter society's culture and institutions and the relationships between men and women in such a way as to give women autonomy, self-definition, and freedom from the disadvantages imposed upon their sex by biology and custom. While the feminist reform movement has made important strides, the liberation movement has nowhere yet achieved its goals. Both definitions of feminism are programmatic and practical, yet utopian and philosophical.

When I speak of feminism as a worldview, I encompass both definitions and expand them to include a number of other major reform and liberation movements. In the twenty-first century violent overthrow and revolutions are counterproductive and cannot achieve their goals. Violence only induces more violence; wars no longer achieve long periods of relative stability, but instead only inspire the next cycle of violence and war. By their

*Gerda Lerner, "A Transformational Feminism," in *Woman of Power: A Magazine of Feminism, Spirituality, and Politics*, Issue 24 (Summer 1995): 42–45. Interview by Gail Hanlon.

past experience and by their demographic distribution, women are ideally situated to lead the kind of peacefully transformative movements necessary to save the ecology, reverse the maldistribution of resources, end poverty and hunger, and allow people to survive on planet earth. Women have, in the past, built formidable, nationwide coalition movements to achieve reforms; they can do so again. That is why I discuss feminism as a liberationist worldview for women and men.

Q: *What directions would you like to see feminists take in this decade in order to facilitate leadership within local and international movements?*

Gerda Lerner: First of all, I want to say that I consider feminism a practical, political program for the transformation of society, one that holds solutions for women and men. I consider it the most promising of the social programs now in existence. It is a program, a philosophy, and a political agenda. I believe that in order for the world to survive the twenty-first century with all the dangers that are now present—namely, nuclear power, rampant militarism, ecological dangers, and what I consider a ticking time bomb: the maldistribution of resources in the world—we must adopt feminist solutions to these problems.

And why feminism? Well, first of all, because the system of patriarchy that was built in the Bronze Age, in approximately the first millennium B.C. in Western civilization, arose out of a combination of militarism and the agricultural revolution. It created a system of hierarchical governments dominated by militarism, in which men hold the resources and distribute them to women who are either members of their family of birth or linked to them through a sexual relationship; they also share resources with subordinate men. As long as patriarchy exists, despite other changes we make in society—for example, efforts to fight racism, militarism, hatred of various minority groups—patriarchy will always reconstitute itself and create other hierarchical systems. The emancipation of women is essential to ending these hierarchical systems.

That's one reason. The second one is that because women are half the population and are represented in every group of the population, in every class, in every region, they cannot be put down like other groups have been. Other groups that have asked for transformational change or for revolutionary change have been defeated and wiped out. You cannot defeat half the human race. Therefore, women are the main instrument for making change.

Third, I believe that in the twenty-first century, violent overthrow and revolutions will no longer be possible. They only lead to increased violence and a cycle of violence, as we have seen in various places in the world today. So, instead of violent overthrow, there has to be a peaceful transition and transformation of society, and women are ideally located and ideally situated to lead that kind of movement.

And fourth, all of this can be accomplished only if feminism and women's leadership are used to build large coalitions with other movements, such as the ecology movement, the movement for racial justice, movements against various other oppressive systems like anti-Semitism, racial and ethnic hatred, homophobia, and movements for a more just redistribution of resources. If we can learn to build these coalitions, we can really transform society.

Q: Are there any changes that you would like to see the feminist movement make?
Lerner: I would like to see the feminist movement be much more concerned with the most oppressed groups in society. So, I would like to see as a firmly established priority our defense of poor women, of women on welfare, of women who are without health insurance, and of children (who are today one of the most oppressed groups in society). I would like to see that to be a central goal of our activities, rather than the promotion of the emancipation of middle-class women only. I am not saying that we have done only that, but I think that there has been a great deal of emphasis on the emancipation of middle-class women and that we have neglected the women that need help the most, so I would like to see the feminist movement make those issues central to its agenda in every area.

I would also like to see us conduct the fight against racism, sexism, nationalism, and anti-Semitism as if they were *connected* rather than separate issues. There is no way that we can abolish any of these evils unless we abolish them all. And unless we learn how to combine these issues, we are going to get nowhere. We are going to take one step forward, and six steps backwards, as we have until now.

Q: Are there other specific issues for which you would like to see feminists provide leadership?
Lerner: Yes, for example, very specifically right now with so-called welfare reform in the forefront of the political debate over the spectrum of society, from reactionary Republicans to liberal Democrats, I would like the women's movement to resist this formulation of the issue. I would like to

see us expose the phony nature of this attack and insist upon addressing the causes of the poverty and abuse now being experienced by poor people. As long as we treat as separate political issues the different forms in which hierarchy keeps the various groups subordinated, we attack symptoms rather than root causes. Hierarchical systems need various target groups that they can define as deviant. At the moment, black teenage mothers have been demonized as "welfare queens." We must show the linkage of their situation with that of white women on welfare and with that of the working poor, female and male, in order to show that the tactics of dividing victims from one another will not work. If we do not learn that by doing this we are defending ourselves, then I have very little hope that we are going to be able to make a valid social movement out of feminism in the twenty-first century.

What we have to keep in mind all the time is that we are not a movement of an "interest group," we are not a movement of a "minority"; we are a movement embracing half the human race, half the nation. We have to act that way.

Q: How do you think women can best support the leadership of activists and visionaries in the feminist movement?
Lerner: Well, first of all, I feel that the women's movement has not sufficiently used women's history as a tool for organizing. Our journals and our publications have paid very little attention to women's history. We have not analyzed the strategies and tactics of the women who came before us, nor have we fully understood their ideas so that we learn from them and do not have to repeat what they have already done. And so, in every women's organization, I would like to see specific attention paid to the goal of bringing in women's history as a tool for consciousness-raising, as a tool for learning, as a tool for giving perspective to women in their struggles.

One highly effective tool for raising community awareness on feminist issues has been the celebration of Women's History Month. The National Women's History Network has developed teaching tools, such as posters, games, and various instructional materials, for schools at all levels. In many communities, libraries, schools, and various organizations have worked together to celebrate women's achievements and leadership during Women's History Month. Another way that local organizations can use women's history is to use older women as resources. Meetings in which older women, representing various ethnic and racial groups in society, share their life experiences and talk about the organizational work they did in the past can be inspiring and educational for younger women.

Q: Is there considerable overlap with previous historical movements?
Lerner: Well, what I see is that we have not learned from history. For example, the nineteenth-century woman's movement built the largest coalition in American history around the issue of suffrage. We deal with it always as if we need to learn who were the true leaders, the high points, and so on, but there are many other lessons to be learned—about how you build such a coalition, and what happens to the various parts of the coalition, and how today we might advance over the position that they had.

For example, Florence Kelley (1859–1932), General Secretary of the National Consumers League, mobilized consumers to ensure that goods were manufactured under decent working conditions. She organized sixty Consumer Leagues in twenty states to boycott goods made under sweatshop conditions. Her vision, to make use of middle-class women's power as consumers to help working-class women, created a powerful instrument of pressure both for the passage of legislation regarding wages and hours and for an end to child labor. Incidentally, it also created an important feminist coalition that endured for several decades.

We desperately need such a movement today. Most people are totally unaware of it; they have no idea that this has been done before. There are many such examples.

If you look at reform, over the entire span of American history, you will see that in every reform movement in American history, the record of white women working with women of color has been better than the record of white men working with men of color. It hasn't been perfect, and it hasn't been as good as it should be, but it has been evident. There are things we could learn from that: How was it done? What was done wrong? And so on. I think that is a very important issue.

Q: How else do you think we can support women leaders?
Lerner: I think you are putting too much emphasis on leadership. Our job is to build grassroots struggle. Our job is to create leaders out of people who are not leaders according to the media definition of a leader, and to honor them, and to learn from them, and to allow them to go on with their lives in positions where they may have only local leadership. That was

the strength of the old women's movement. That was the way women have always worked. We have worked locally to affect national issues. Today, if there were less emphasis on leadership and more emphasis on grassroots organizing, I think we would get further.

A good example of how this has been done successfully has been in the struggle against violence against women, where feminists have organized locally in various forms. We hardly know the name of a single woman who has done this kind of work, but it has been a grassroots movement with tremendous impact on society as a whole. If we could transfer that kind of model to other political issues, paying less attention to advancing the careers of leaders than we do to building the grassroots organization that sustains leaders, we would be better off.

Q: You may have already addressed this issue in part, in the sense that you think "leadership" needs to be redefined; what, if any, obstacles to women's leadership are of concern to you?
Lerner: A "leader" in America in the twentieth century generally means somebody who makes a career out of the concerns, and issues, and political demands of other people; and who, as soon as she or he has attained a so-called position of leadership, is then a public figure who becomes corrupted to the point of no longer really leading anybody but her- or himself and the media. Now, not everybody does that. Gloria Steinem, at the beginning of the women's movement, coined a phrase that she herself has put into practice, but very few other women have, and that is: "Wherever you go, take another woman with you." That is leadership. But leadership is not a matter of being known, and being famous, and being interviewed, and being on TV programs, and being written up in the newspapers.

My concept of leadership is embodied by somebody like Ella Baker (1903–1986), who was the foremost organizer of the civil rights movement, yet, until recently, hardly anybody knew her name. Leader of the National Association for the Advancement of Colored People (NAACP) in the 1940s, Executive Secretary of the Southern Christian Leadership Conference (SCLC) in the 1950s, founder and chief source of inspiration for the Student Nonviolent Coordinating Committee (SNCC) in the 1960s, this African American woman was the guiding spirit and the organizing genius behind the civil rights movement. A leader of similar caliber was Kathryn Clarenbach (1921–1944), who, as chairperson of the National Committees on the Status of Women, was one of the founders of the National Organization for Women (NOW) and its first organizer. Later, as organizer of the First National Women's Conference in Houston, Texas, in 1977, she was at the center of the greatest network of women's organizations ever created. Like Ella Baker, she shunned publicity, but her leadership was inspiring and lasting. We need to model our ideal of leadership after women such as these.

To me, the woman who creates a local organization that continues to function after she is gone is exercising leadership. Leadership is creating something that lives on without you.

Q: So, when you define what you consider to be the essential facets of leadership, one of them would be to create something that lives beyond you?
Lerner: Absolutely, to create something that replaces and surpasses you, that has a life of its own because there are many people who will be drawn into it and who will give leadership to it as a group, even if you move on or go away. To me, that has always been the measure of leadership. If you can do that, you're a leader. If you can't do that, you're just a media personality.

Q: How have variables such as gender, ethnicity, religion, social class, and so on, shaped your ideas about your leadership role?
Lerner: I never thought about leadership. I still don't think about leadership. I think about a goal that I want to achieve. I wanted, for example, to make Women's History an accepted part of every academic curriculum from elementary school to the Ph.D.—that was my goal. I didn't give any thought to leadership. I thought about how that could be done. In other words, I analyzed where you would have to start, and what you would have to do, and then I tried to take whatever measures I could to interest other people—the main thing is to enlist other people to work on that goal with you. The point is that wherever we are as women, wherever we are situated in our lives, we can advance a feminist agenda if we stop thinking about how to be leaders and think rather about how to be doers, how to be agents.

How have race, gender, and so on affected me? Well, I'm a woman, right? And I'm a Jew, and I have suffered persecution at the hand of the Nazis. I have, therefore, understood very early that you can't win any kind of rights and freedoms if you tolerate measures for dividing people, such as racism and anti-Semitism. If you allow these systems to exist and do not resist them, then you can't attain any kind of emancipation. So that is something that I learned in my own life, and I have always tried to illustrate that to other people. When I came to America, I became very interested in the situation of people of color, because they are the primary victims of racism here in this country, whereas in Europe, Jews were the primary victims of racism. Because I understood that, I was interested from the start in struggling against racism and in linking the two issues.

If everybody goes just one or two steps forward, we can change the world. But if you are concerned about how to be a leader, all you are really concerned about is how you can fit into the patriarchal system in order to receive rewards, and that is not the way to go. That is not our problem. Our problem is to redefine organizational leadership, to figure out what it means and how to sustain it over a long period of time. The thing that hurts me the most is when I hear women saying, "Well, we've struggled so hard, and now feminism is in retreat and there's a backlash and I'm discouraged"—after only four or five years. That's ridiculous.

It took 72 years of unremitting organization and struggle for women to secure the rights of suffrage. It took over 100 years to eliminate child labor. It took over 130 years of organizing and political agitation for workers to win the right to unionize and to bargain collectively.

Another modern example of a successful coalition is the antilynching movement. It was begun in the 1890s by the African American journalist and club woman Ida Wells-Barnett and carried forward by the black women's club movement. It was not until 1920 that white club women hesitantly engaged in some joint efforts with black women to stop lynchings. They did not succeed until the 1930s, when the Association of Southern Women for the Prevention of Lynching (ASWPL) was organized. The tenuous and often conflict-ridden cooperation of black and white women finally, in the 1940s, changed public opinion nationwide without ever succeeding in getting Congress to pass an antilynching bill.

As history teaches us, any movement that cannot be sustained for fifty or a hundred years is not likely to accomplish its goal. For the future of feminism, we need grassroots organization. We need a long-range perspective. We need people with staying power.

chapter twelve

Reflections on Aging

In 2005 the editors of the German feminist journal L'Homme *queried me by email: would I be willing to be interviewed on the subject of aging for a special issue of their journal? I was unenthusiastic about the idea, since the subject was not within the areas of my competence, but I was intrigued enough by it to ask them to send me a list of the questions they wanted to ask me. The questions arrived and were both interesting and challenging. Suddenly, it occurred to me that I needed no academic competence to write about aging: like all old people, I was an expert, thinking and writing about my own experience. I agreed to do the interview.*

This happened at a time when I was struggling with serious health problems, considerable pain and some disabilities. I was considering whether to enter a retirement community that would guarantee me access to assisted living, when I needed it. I now live in such a community and am convinced I made a good choice. But at the time the decision was difficult for me. Agreeing to that interview was part of a slow process with which I needed to engage.

The interview was conducted by email and in German. I had not written anything in German in nearly fifty years and had only recently regained my ability to speak and read in German with the competence of a native speaker. There were a few editorial changes to make, then the interview was printed in the journal. After reading the printed text, I spontaneously decided to translate it into English. I had no particular purpose in mind for doing the translation, but as soon as I had done it, I decided to include it in this book. This is one of the few instances in my writer's existence in which the text led me to make decisions in life. Writing and life interacted almost outside of my volition.

> I'm quite well in myself. Nothing wrong with me. I can't see very well,
> I can't hear very well, and I can't walk very well, but I'm perfectly well.
> —VALENTINE VESTER, the "Grand Dame of Jerusalem"

Aging as a Natural Process

It is part of life, and yet it is more difficult than anything that came before it. It presents us daily with new challenges and demands. When one is younger, one goes through various life stages, all of which are culturally recognized and supported. Childhood, adolescence, adulthood, the stage of nurturing one's own family and children, maturity in work and social relations—these stages follow in predictable succession. Each stage presents us with new challenges and changing conditions; we adapt to them, always hoping for a good outcome, a stroke of luck, and better circumstances. If we fail to make good choices in one stage, there is always the next stage in which we can do better. But in old age there is only one next stage and that is death. Aging is the way to it, and it poses its own inexorable demands.

In old age we cannot take for granted that we will be able to enjoy the luxury of making good choices; we often have to choose the lesser of two evils. Our body, which we have always trusted as a reliable, familiar friend, now confronts us with its weaknesses and limitations. We have to develop a new relationship with it, adapting to its slow decline in capacity and strength. Pain and physical impairments become our steady companions. We have to get used to them, respect them and adjust to them, as best we can. Without pain and impairments nobody would ever be ready to die.

On the positive side, we can develop a new understanding of our body. We can listen to its needs, keep it as balanced and flexible as possible and refuse to coerce it with competitive and excessive demands. We can nurture it, look after its health with more care than we did when we were younger. We can exercise without stress, substitute for failing energy by steady effort, adopting relaxation techniques as our friendly helpers.

Aging forces us to give up activities, skills, and enjoyments we have long practiced. We have to learn to give up more and more of what we have accomplished, what we have gathered in and what we cherish. Getting old means giving up something forever at every stage of the process. The trick is to learn how to give up things gracefully and without despair.

Giving up more and more of what we have accomplished means learning to detach from whatever it was that made us successful and letting the work go to stand on its own merits. We can no longer demand of ourselves that we continue at our usual pace, nor can we, at this stage of life, make up for lost time. We must accept what is and prepare to let go of it.

Giving up more and more of what we have gathered in and what we cherish means simplifying our lives and letting go of clutter. It means choosing what is truly essential to our well-being and holding on to that, while giving up what is negative, destructive, and hurtful. It may mean

giving up old feuds and festering grievances; it may mean giving up things
we cherish, because we no longer have the energy or physical capacity for
pursuing them. Often, that is the most painful aspect of aging: the fine mu-
sician whose hearing deteriorates so that she can no longer enjoy music;
the passionate hiker who can no longer walk long distances or even short
ones; the passionate reader whose eyesight is failing. The losses of aging are
multiple and often cruel; they are more easily accepted if one accepts aging
as a natural process, an inevitable aspect of living and evolving. As long as
we are alive, we have the capacity to develop compensatory skills and seek
new insights. We must develop whatever we still can develop and learn
new ways of seeing, perceiving, and functioning. Learning to continue
living with diminished means has its own rewards.

One of these rewards is observing and treasuring the particular over
the general. Watching birds at the feeder and ducks in a pond can evoke
earlier sights of vast panoramas, eagles in flight, the search for daily sustenance and shelter of creatures in the wilderness. Leaves of grass can stand
for earth forces and for the persistent power of humble plants to renew the
earth. Mosses and lichen prepare the soil for mighty trees. We can learn to
observe more keenly and to think in metaphors, which is the great contribution of human beings to the evolution of life on earth. Even though
we are diminished in our physical capacities, we are still part of the greater
life cycle.

Aging is a process of purging, of purification: one lets go of unnecessary
expectations; one no longer agonizes over old quarrels and accusations;
one makes peace with one's life and one's way of living; and one learns to
treasure the gifts of each day. One enjoys old friendships and well-known,
comforting places, and yet one strives to make new relationships in order
to stay rooted in life. Living consciously through this process, one finds
a new kind of happiness, more serene, more peaceful than anything that
went before.

We can use the time of aging as an opportunity for developing a philosophy about living and dying. Our spiritual growth can continue, even
when our bodies fail us. Aging is a process preparing us for death. There is
strength and succor in acknowledging that fact, while continuing to take
part in life to the best of our abilities.

Aging as a Social Construction

While the natural process of aging presents each person with challenges and difficult adjustments, the social construction of aging often defines and complicates the problems of the individual. Cultures differ in how they construct and view old age; these cultural differences are expressed in attitudes, mores, laws, and political and economic policies.

During the twentieth century world populations underwent major demographic shifts at a historically unprecedented rate. Human longevity increased dramatically, and life expectancy rates went up worldwide, but especially in the industrially developed nations. My generation experienced a revolutionary change in regard to aging. In my childhood in Vienna, Austria, when an old lady friend of my grandmother died at the age of seventy-three, everyone could agree that she had experienced a ripe old age. One had a reasonable expectancy that one would die in the seventh decade of one's life. Demographics have changed in such a way that a woman in the United States has a life expectancy of eighty-six years. Since that is an average figure, this means that for many women old age has been prolonged by fifteen to twenty years. For men, the average life expectancy figure is eighty years. Thus, married women can expect to be widows for at least six years. Another change is that older people, due to advances in medical care, cannot only live twenty years longer, but they can expect to live those years in better health than did their forebears.

Society has not reacted to these new realities in a positive way. There is no model for "aging well" that is appropriate to the new reality. The media and advertisements show us white-haired people in vigorous health, usually in couples, enchanted over some new drug or medication. They never look older than seventy. At times we see them in ads embarking on a cruise or playing golf or potting plants in impeccable gardens. Nobody has knees that do not bend, joints that cannot flex, or insufficient strength to hold a trowel. The media's old women are slender, exquisite beauties in Chanel suits. Their inevitable aches and pains are immediately relieved by the advertised drug, which causes them to wear a perpetual smile.

Reality is considerably different. Although they are expected to retire at age sixty-five, tens of thousands of older people must continue to work out of economic necessity. The ranks of workers in their seventies and eighties are increasing, as promised pensions vanish or are severely cut.

Older employees usually cannot stay in the jobs they have had in their middle years and must compete for low-paying, low-status jobs.

For those with a secure pension and Social Security income, who still enjoy good health and would like to continue working, retirement can sometimes be postponed for five or ten years. Part-time jobs, although hard to find, offer a good solution. For professionals, such part-time retirement schemes have proven very beneficial. Unfortunately, flex-time and shared jobs are not widely available. If society recognized the changed demographic of aging, institutional adaptations could help to afford older people many more choices in regard to continuing employment. The benefit to employers in having experienced workers who enjoy the work they are doing and are reliable in their performance would be considerable.

In early centuries and even still before World War II older people could expect to find fulfilling roles as family helpers and members of extended families. But today American families live geographically far apart and the traditional role of family helper is not practical for families living in apartments and small houses. Families expect to see their grandparents on holidays and for special occasions, but for everyday life they expect the older generation to live independent lives. When bad health makes that impossible, the individual and his or her family are faced with a profound crisis.

For the individual, American cultural attitudes that favor youth, independence, and individual resourcefulness over communal solutions make it difficult for many older people to accept their need for dependence. They resist moving out of oversized homes and accepting community services, such as meals-on-wheels or the part-time assistance of social workers. They do not wish to be a burden on their children or their friends. Many withdraw into their homes or their apartments, hide their difficult condition from friends and neighbors, and wait until an accident forces them to seek outside help.

The choices open to sick and frail elderly persons vary with their economic resources. For the wealthy and those with adequate savings and financial resources, the preferred solution is to enter a retirement community. The quality of such communities varies greatly, ranging from excellent to substandard. Their availability depends on location; they are more readily available in urban centers than in rural areas. For many people, moving into such a community also means a major geographical relocation, since they often move away from the community in which they spent most of their lives to one that is closer to the location of one of their children. Still, society in general and the health profession favor that solution. Underlying it is the assumption that age segregation is beneficial and that it is normal that old people should live with other old people. Such an assumption is very much open to question. Many studies have shown that social integration is one of the most important factors in the well-being of old people. Yet at the very time when older people need the help of the younger generation the most, when interaction with younger adults and with children gives them new strength for living, American culture prefers that they be socially segregated.

In recent decades some affluent elders have tried to build alternatives to retirement homes by creating cooperative housing communities. These have sprung up in urban as well as rural communities, and quite a few of them seem to be successful. They can serve as models for offering more choices for the care of older people. These communities are often age-integrated, offering inducements to younger families to join them. They feature private living spaces, but one communal center for cooking and eating. Meals are shared, and people cooperate in shopping, repairs, and social activities. The downside is that it takes years and a sizeable investment of funds, energy, and know-how before such communities can be formed.

Retirement communities offer solutions to the problems of caring for old people only for the affluent. People with fewer resources try to service their needs with part- or full-time paid help. The problem with that is that even if the potential employer is able to afford such help, caregivers are hard to find. The fact that Medicare and other health plans do not offer adequate coverage and compensation for such care inevitably lessens the supply of available workers. In the United States, the lowest-paid, least-skilled jobs are reserved for those who care for children and care for the old. By definition, these are women's jobs, and expressive of the deformation of society through racism, they are jobs for minority women, often recent immigrants. Workers in inadequately paid positions that offer no job security or chances for advancement often cannot give the kind of reliable, supportive care that the frail elderly require. Thus, the absence of a well-functioning social network for supporting the needs of old people affects the care that even the most privileged retirees can receive.

Many people, regardless of income, prefer for cultural and religious reasons to share their homes with elderly parents or relatives. Again, depending on income, this can be a good or a very difficult solution for both generations. Small apartments and compact houses often offer no adequate living space for the elderly. Those who can afford it, build additions to their homes, but most people have to compromise with inadequate space that offers insufficient privacy. In the many families in which both spouses work, the live-in parent faces long days in isolation. For middle-class people, as well for the poor, such arrangements, even among loving family members, lead to considerable stress on both generations. Still, strong cultural, ethnic, and racial traditions and economic necessity make such arrangements the preferred form of elder care for millions of people.

Families caring for dependent family members have become endlessly inventive in creating voluntary networks for caring. Middle-aged siblings take turns living-in with a sick parent; neighbors and friends commit themselves to regular weekly visits, to donations of food, or to other caregiving chores. Social agencies and religious institutions send volunteers to share in the caring network. In the final stages, hospice and its pool of volunteers help families and the dying to cope.

The social construction of aging also varies from country to country. I noticed during my travels in Europe that older people have a far easier life there than they do in the United States. The welfare state and larger pensions make life more secure for the elderly, and many more families than in this country share their homes with their old folks. There are day care centers for seniors, and a variety of social services are available to help working families care for aging relatives. The fact that in most major European cities there is an adequate and affordable public transportation system of buses, streetcars, and underground trains makes it possible for older people to take part in public events and attend movies and theaters with ease. Old folks are everywhere visible in the street scene and in coffeehouses. That is not possible in the United States. Here, as long as one can drive a car, one has access to many public events; but when one no longer can drive, then one becomes truly isolated.

More than physical obstacles keep older people in enforced isolation. "Old age" has become a marker of social difference. Old people are depicted as having negative characteristics; collectively they are sorted into an inferior group. Aging is viewed as though it were a contagious illness. As a member of a group characterized negatively, the individual is lost to sight. In this regard there are sharp gender distinctions: old men are socially acceptable; they are welcome at social gatherings and defined as being "interesting." Old women are often regarded as socially unacceptable; they are considered "boring, needy, and depressing." It is easier for old men to make new social contacts than it is for old women. Widowers frequently find new marriage partners, often women much younger than themselves. For widows the chances of remarriage are statistically very poor. Men their own age are interested in younger women, and younger men shy away from older women. Of course there are exceptions, but the rule still stands. A number of widows have turned to other women and made successful lesbian relationships.

Marking old people as dependent and essentially useless is not an affirmation of life; it is an excess of hierarchical society, alienating people from nature and natural processes like aging and dying.

Personal and Societal Solutions for the Problems of Aging

How to personally survive in old age is a challenge. Dedicated activity for others or for the social good can help in making aging more tolerable, but this is not the only solution for aging. I see aging as a natural part of living, not as a catastrophe. There are as many ways of aging as there are people. In old age people become what they have always been, only more so. For some it means an intensive commitment to worthy causes and a purposeful engagement with other people. For others it means turning toward intellectual or creative pursuits. Some find contentment through new interests—gardening, handicrafts, whittling, spectator sports.

For those whose old age is marked by physical pain and increasing disabilities, the constant battle for competence and independence is an all-encompassing task. They have to strive for patience and inner peace in order to keep up their interest in life and to enjoy good days and good hours.

There are also many people who use their old age to turn more and more inward, to evaluate their own life and the lives of their family and to seek better understanding. Such people do not just want to be occupied; they also want to seek understanding and wisdom. They want to know what meaning this last phase of their life holds; they see aging as a challenge they must meet.

There is no single solution—aging is a dance on uneven ground, undertaken with weakened limbs. One tries out this or that step, and once in a while one gets back into the swing of it, finally experiencing dancing as it used to be and as it now is. Aging is soothed by learning to fully experience the present. We have come this far and what there is now is all there ever will be. And so we keep dancing, as best we can.

For myself, I now allow myself more time for quiet contemplation, for simple domestic pursuits, and for thinking. I have learned to live alone with great contentment, and I continue to enjoy a rich intellectual and social life. Although I was always physically strong, athletic and quick in mind and body, I am now excruciatingly slow, awkward, and more sedentary than I like to be. But I no longer make the kind of demands on myself I used to, and therefore I can appreciate doing what I still can do.

I am very fortunate to be a historian, able to continue my intellectual engagement with the past, which makes the present more tolerable. I'm also very fortunate in being a creative writer. Creativity and form-giving are the greatest gifts one can enjoy in old age.

The fact that I had an unconventional life with many disruptions and many enforced new beginnings was probably a good preparation for the necessary flexibility needed to adapt to old age. In old age one has constantly to adapt to major changes: when the body does not function as it used to function, when old friends die or move away, when one is forced to relocate to smaller quarters, when one has to give up forever occupations or pursuits one used to love. Much more than at any previous stage of life, the old person has to be flexible.

My lifelong commitment to social action as a political radical has greatly enriched my life and has helped me to be connected with many networks of colleagues and like-minded people. I look back on my years of political activism with satisfaction, even though there were many disappointments and defeats next to the successes. It was also a great advantage for me to have been active on two continents.

TO MAKE AGING EASIER and more constructive societies should invest more in aging: a good and cheap system of public transportation, so that old people have more access to the community; larger apartments or houses for young families, to enable them to shelter old family members; adequate pensions and health insurance, so that all old people can be assured of a minimum level of subsistence; no retirement centers or old people's homes without having a certain percentage of the units reserved for young families with children.

There are very few models of communal solutions for the needs of aging populations. Senior centers in many towns provide a good beginning, but their emphasis is on recreational occupations. At a time when many families need two wage earners to pay their way, it is difficult and expensive for such families to meet the needs of young children. Community cooperatives, in which older people could serve as volunteer "grandparents" for children after school hours, would help both the old and the young. Such arrangements could be made in stable neighborhoods that are not age-segregated. In my hometown there already exist groups that try to pair young people with small incomes and older folks who live in large, empty houses. The young people get cheap rentals and, in exchange, help the older folks continue to live in their house and garden by relieving them of the heavy physical labor. This kind of arrangement works quite well for both sides. It could be extended to meet the needs of children whose parents work long hours. In order to turn such model experiments into large-scale plans society and politicians would have to take the problems of aging populations seriously and understand that there is a new reality out there to which they have to adapt.

Above all, cultural attitudes toward aging need to be changed. Old age is not a catastrophe; old people are not problems and useless dependents. Old people can contribute much to society: through their knowledge and life experience, through volunteer work, through their patience and peacefulness. With some societal adjustments, some innovative programs, some respectful help, old people can continue to work part-time into very old age. Like all living persons, even the very old feel the need to be incorporated into community and social networks. Age segregation and isolation are much more frightening to old people than are pain and physical handicaps. Old people still are society's best link with the past, and their knowledge and experiences are desperately needed in a mechanized society that is more and more alienated from nature and natural processes. Even the very old and the handicapped can help younger people by modeling how to accept help. In our competitive society people are trained to be self-made and independent. But they also have to learn how to help others and how to accept help without feeling demeaned and diminished. Because modern society excludes or marginalizes old people and avoids dealing with death, the healthy and the living are full of fears and have no preparation for their own process of aging. The steady courage of older people, their patience, their optimism, and their childlike willingness to experience spontaneous joy could serve as models for the aging generation of their children.

Old age is not a contagious disease. It is the ripening of the fruit, the preparation for the harshness of winter, when the roots grow and strengthen, a time when leaf mold decays, making a seedbed for the new growth of mushrooms. It is the closing of the circle; the fulfillment of the contract of the generations. It needs to be treated with respect and honor.

appendix a

Biographies of Midwestern Feminist Leaders

Presented here are brief biographies of the women interviewed for the oral history project on leaders of the modern women's movement discussed in Chapter 5. They appear here in the same order in which these leaders are discussed in the chapter text.

Kathryn "Kay" (Frederick) Clarenbach (1920–94) was born in Sparta, Wisconsin, and died in Madison, Wisconsin. She attended local schools and earned B.A., M.A, and Ph.D. degrees in Political Science at the University of Wisconsin. She married Henry Clarenbach in 1946; they had three children. While rearing her children in the 1950s, she became active in the League of Women Voters. She taught one year at Edgewood College in Madison and then joined the faculty at the University of Wisconsin. She was Director of University Education of Women from 1962 to 1967 and University of Wisconsin Extension Specialist, Continuing Education for Women from 1967 to 1972. As Professor of Political Science she continued her work in Outreach until her retirement in 1988.

Due to her years of activism among faculty women and on behalf of women students, Clarenbach was at the center of a strong network of activists when she became Chair of the Wisconsin Governor's Commission on the Status of Women (csw) in 1964. A founder of the National Organization for Women (now) in 1966, she was elected as Chair of the first Board (1966–70), member of the Advisory Council, and President of the now Legal Defense and Education Fund (1982–83).

Clarenbach continued her central organizing role as Executive Director of the U.S. Commission for Observance of International Women's Year (1975–76) and deputy Coordinator of the Houston National Women's Conference (1977). Again, she acted as organizer, networker, and coalition-builder. She continued her leadership as founding chair of the National Women's Political Caucus (nwpc), the National Women's Conference Committee, and the Wisconsin Women's Network and as founder and Vice-President of the Wisconsin Congress of Labor Union Woman (cluw). As trustee and Chair of the Board of Trustees of Alverno College she continued her work on women's education.

Mildred "Millie" (McWilliams) Jeffrey (1911–2004) was born in Iowa, the oldest of seven children. Her grandmother ran the family farm after her husband's death and raised sixteen children. Her mother raised seven children and was Iowa's first female registered pharmacist. Her mother left her husband and moved to Minneapolis in order to give her children better educational opportunities. Millie earned a B.A. at the University of Minnesota and an M.A. in Social Research at Bryn Mawr in 1934. She married Newman Jeffrey in 1936; they had two children and the marriage ended in divorce.

Jeffrey was Education Director for the Pennsylvania Branch of the Amalgamated Clothing Workers and during World War II worked for the War Production Board in Washington, D.C. After the war she moved to Detroit and worked for the United Automobile Workers (UAW) union, serving in leading positions until 1976. She was the first director of the UAW Women's Department, 1945–49. She ran the union's radio station and then chaired its Community Relations Department. In 1974 she was elected to the Board of Governors of Wayne State University, an office she held for sixteen years.

Dorothy Haener (1917–2001) was the youngest girl in a family of seven children. She was the only one of her siblings to graduate from high school. Subsequently, she was self-taught or educated in work-sponsored training programs. In 1941 she entered the Ford Bomber plant in Detroit, where she worked until she was laid off after the war. She was rehired, when Kaiser-Frazier took over the plant, and worked there until 1952. She was active in the local UAW, helped to organize clerical workers, and in 1952 became International Representative. In 1960, she joined the UAW Women's Department, where she worked until her retirement.

As chair of the Women's Department Haener worked for passage of the Equal Pay Act and for adding the category "sex" to the Executive Order on Equal Employment Opportunities. She served on the President's Commission on the Status of Women. She was a founding member of NOW, and chaired the NOW Task Force on Poverty. As a member of the organizing committee for the 1977 International Women's Year Conference in Houston in 1977 she helped develop the plank on employment adopted by the conference.

Doris (Schumacher) Thom was born in 1920 and married Henry Thom shortly after her graduation from high school in 1937. She stayed home while her three children were young and started working in 1955 at General Motors in Janesville, Wisconsin. She became an active UAW member. In 1961 she became the first and only woman to serve on the union's Executive Board, a position she held for seven years, while also active on the regional Women's Committee. In 1965, as a result of her filing a complaint with the Equal Employment Opportunity Commission (EEOC), she became the first woman at the plant to move out of the wholly female Trim Line into a job category previously reserved for men only. She served two terms on the Wisconsin Governor's csw, was active in the leadership of the Democratic Party, and was a founding member of now.

Helen Hensler was born in Milwaukee in 1919 and graduated from public high school in 1939. From 1940 to 1977 she worked in the office of the Steelworkers Union at A. O. Smith Co. She was an active member in the Office and Professional Employees International Union, Local 9, serving in various leadership positions, including President of the local between 1975 and 1979. She attended various trade union schools for workers. She served on the County Labor Council and founded the Women's Committee of the Wisconsin AFL-CIO in 1970, serving as chair until 1986. She served on the Wisconsin Governor's csw and on the National Association of Commissions on the Status of Women. A founding member of the cluw and its Milwaukee chapter, she later became the chapter's President.

Clara Day was born in Alabama in 1924, the middle child of a farm family of twelve. She left high school when she married and later moved with her husband and one child to Chicago. There she earned her high school diploma. She began working at Montgomery Ward in 1947 and joined the International Brotherhood of Teamsters Local 743, after it organized her shop. She later worked full time for the union, in various functions, up to and including Executive Board Member and Trustee. She was a member of the Illinois csw from 1965 to 1980 and attended the Houston Conference as a delegate. A founding member of the cluw, she is the organization's Executive Vice President. She has been active in the civil rights movement, the National Association for the Advancement of Colored People (naacp), and the Chicago Urban League.

Nellie (Sweet) Wilson (1916–2008) was raised by her grandparents, former slaves, who then owned a farm in Texas. Her mother died when she was only three. After age twelve, she moved in with her father, who worked as an iron molder in Milwaukee. When he lost his job during the Depression, they had to go on welfare and she worked as a maid after high school. She married Alvin Wilson at age nineteen; they had two children, but the marriage ended in divorce and she took full responsibility for the children. In 1943 she got a war job at A. O. Smith. Laid off at the end of the war, she was rehired due to the union contract. She worked at the company at various manual jobs and became very active in the union. She became the first woman elected to office in the A. O. Smith local of the Steelworkers Union and won a seat on the union Executive Board (1963–69), where she worked to advance the status of women workers. Later she joined the staff of the AFL-CIO and worked with the Milwaukee Labor Council and the

Midwest Labor Leadership Project. She has been a leader in Milwaukee labor and community relations.

While raising her children as a single mother and working full time, Wilson earned a B.S. and later an M.A. degree in urban affairs. She organized the only minority chapter of American Association of Retired Persons (AARP).

Addie Wyatt, born in 1924 in Mississippi, moved to Chicago with her parents in 1930. She worked at Armour and Illinois Meat plants from the start of World War II. When she first ran for union office, for the position of Vice President, which had never before been held by a woman, she did not think she could win, because the majority of the members in the plant were white men. Not only did she win, but when the union President resigned a few months later for personal reasons, she was elected President of Illinois Meat Local 56 in 1952, the first woman and the first black person in union leadership. In 1954 Wyatt was appointed International Representative of the United Packinghouse Workers of America, and she continued on the staff of the union until her retirement in 1984. Much later, after decades of leadership, she served as adviser to the Reverend Martin Luther King Jr.

Martha (Wright) Griffiths (1912–2003) was born in Missouri. She struggled economically to attend college during the Depression. She married and moved with her husband to Ann Arbor, Michigan, where she became a lawyer. She entered Democratic Party politics and won a seat in the state legislature in 1949. She was elected in 1954 to the U.S. House of Representatives, where she served for twenty years and where she won many "firsts" as a woman. She was a leading force in the passage of the amendment against sex discrimination in the 1964 Civil Rights Act, helped to strengthen the EEOC, and in 1973 steered the Equal Rights Amendment (ERA) through Congress. Although she did not consider herself a feminist, she made crucial contributions to the struggle for women's rights.

Mary Eastwood was born in 1930 and raised in a farm community in Wisconsin. She earned her M.A. and law degrees from the University of Wisconsin. After a decade of activism in the NAACP, the Congress of Racial Equality (CORE), and various government jobs, she was assigned as a staff lawyer to the President's Commission on the Status of Women. Her research into the legal status of women led to her publication, co-authored with African American Pauli Murray, of the highly influential publication "Jane Crow and the Law: Sex Discrimination and Title VII." This work led Eastwood to become a strong supporter of the ERA and the EEOC and a founding member of NOW and of the Woman's Party. She helped define NOW's position on the ERA and abortion, but left the organization in 1968 and continued her legal feminist work as an Equal Opportunity Officer in the Justice Department, in various feminist organizations she founded, and finally as President of the National Woman's Party from 1989 to 1991.

Arvonne (Skelton) Fraser was born in 1925 in Lamberton, Minnesota. She grew up in a farm family in which Farmer-Labor Party activism was as much part of her upbringing as were daily chores. After graduating with a B.A. in American Studies from the University of Minnesota she worked for Hubert Humphrey's Senate campaign and then worked as secretary in the Democratic Farmer-Labor Party. In 1950 she married lawyer and activist Don Fraser and managed his election campaign for Minnesota State Senator. The couple had six children, but still Fraser advanced into Farmer-Labor Party leadership. When Don Fraser was elected to the U.S. Congress in 1962, the family moved to Washington, D.C. There, Arvonne continued work as Administrative Assistant in her husband's Congressional office.

Judith (Becker) Goldsmith was born in 1938 and raised in Wisconsin. During a brief marriage she lived in Buffalo, where she earned an M.A. in English and taught at the university level. In 1977 she divorced her husband and lived with her daughter in Manitowoc, Wisconsin. There she founded the local chapter of NOW and in quick succession became State Coordinator, National Executive Board member, and Vice President. She was National President of NOW from 1982 to 1985.

Her national leadership coincided with the unsuccessful campaign for ratification of the ERA and with the rise in violence against abortion clinics. Goldsmith, in what she defined as a midwestern style of organization, emphasized grassroots activities for NOW members, especially in abortion clinic defense, diversification of membership, and decentralization in decision-making. After her Washington work she served as Special Consultant to the Chancellor for Equity and Affirmative Action at the University of Wisconsin–Stevens Point.

Mary Jean Collins (Robson) was born in 1939 in Superior, Wisconsin. She grew up in Milwaukee, where she attended Catholic schools and earned her B.A. in history from Alverno College. She was active in the civil rights movement, as was the man she married in 1968, James Robson. In 1975 she divorced him and began to identify herself as a lesbian.

Collins became involved in the women's movement at Alverno College, through her teachers, Sisters Read and Doherty. She became active in the Milwaukee chapter of NOW and, after her move to Chicago, became President of that chapter. In 1970 she served as the first Midwest Regional Director of NOW. She advanced to membership on the National Board of NOW and ran for President, but was defeated by Karen Crow. From 1975 to 1980 she worked as organizer for the Illinois Nurses Association and won the first statewide union contract. She became Executive Director of Chicago NOW and directed the state campaign for ratification of the ERA until 1982. She moved to Washington, D.C., and served as Vice President of NOW, focusing on reproductive rights, lesbian rights, and issues of economic discrimination. She then continued her organizational work with Catholics for a Free Choice.

In Washington she formed several women's groups and worked closely with a network of powerful women in government positions. She was a founder of the Women's Equity Action League (WEAL) and served on its Board and as its President. In 1981 President Carter appointed her Coordinator of the Office of Women in Development at the United States Information Agency. Since then she has been active on the international scene and at the University of Minnesota's Center on Women Public Policy.

Sarah (Snell) Harder was born in 1937 in Chicago. She had two children in a first marriage that ended in divorce. In 1964 she married Harry Harder and later had two more children. The Harders accepted jobs at the University of Wisconsin–Eau Claire in 1968. There, she taught and held administrative positions concerned with affirmative action. Her political work centered on the American Association of University Women, whose President she became in 1985, continuing in that position until 1989. After attending the Houston Conference in 1977 she worked for the implementation of the women's agenda passed there, which led to the creation of the Wisconsin Women's Network in 1979.

Virginia (Bailey) Hart was born in Clifton Springs, New York, in 1914. Her organizational work dates back to the 1930s, mostly in the YWCA, then in unions. She fused her commitment to organizing and social action by teaching in the School for Workers in Madison, Wisconsin, and by activism in Democratic Party politics. When she was appointed Secretary of the Department of Labor and Regulations by Governor Patrick J. Lucey in 1973, she became the first woman to hold a cabinet position in Wisconsin. She continued in state government service until 1983.

Marjorie "Midge" (Cavins) Miller was born in Morgantown, West Virginia, in 1922. Like Virginia Hart, she started her organizational work in the YWCA, as program director in Ann Arbor and New Haven, and then continued that work, together with her husband Dean Leeper, as YMCA missionaries in postwar Japan. She was pregnant with her fourth child when her husband died in a typhoon in 1954. She continued her academic studies and in 1962 married Edward Miller, a physics professor and widower with five children.

Miller focused her work on Democratic politics, beginning with Eugene McCarthy's presidential campaign. She attended all but one Democratic National Convention and served on the party's National Committee from 1975 to 1984. From 1970 to 1984 she was a member of the Wisconsin State Assembly. She worked for sex equity in state employment, authored legislation against domestic abuse and for the advancement of displaced homemakers, and worked for the endorsement of the ERA by the legislature.

Mary Lou (Rogers) Munts was born in Chicago in 1924. She became a leader in the national student movement while she was at Swarthmore College. She married Ray Munts, a French educator, and they lived in Wilkes-Barre, Pennsylvania, and then four years in Madison, Wisconsin, while her children were young. In Madison, where Ray taught at the University, she worked as a volunteer in building the new liberal Wisconsin Democratic Party. During a ten-year period, while Ray worked for the AFL-CIO in Washington, she was active in the civil rights movement. In 1967 the Munts family moved back to Madison. Mary Lou worked as an organizer for several political campaigns and studied for a law degree, which she earned in 1976. She was elected to the state legislature in 1972 and over the course of six terms became known as the most productive legislator of her time. Her major accomplishments were divorce reform and marital property legislation and her leadership of the highly effective Wisconsin Women's Network. She was also active legislatively for human services, mental health, the environment, and good government issues. In 1982–84, when she served as Chair of the Joint Finance Committee, she was the most powerful woman in state government. She served on the Public Service Commission from 1984 to 1991.

Ruth Chickering Clusen was born in 1922 in Bruce, Wisconsin. Her parents moved frequently until they settled in Eau Claire, Wisconsin, in 1937. After doing war work in Washington, D.C., Ruth completed her B.A. in English in Eau Claire. She married Donald Clusen in 1945.

Her main organizational work was in the League of Women Voters (LWV). She was President of the Green Bay chapter of the LWV, then of the Wisconsin LWV, and then of the national organization from 1974 to 1978. In the latter capacity she organized the national presidential debates in 1976. She was also active on environmental issues, which resulted in her appointment as Secretary for the Environment in President Carter's cabinet. She worked on women's issues as a member of the Wisconsin Governor's csw and as delegate to the International Women's Year Conferences in Mexico City and Houston. She served on the University of Wisconsin's Board of Regents.

Sister Joel Read was born Janice Read in Chicago in 1925. She joined The School Sisters of Saint Francis in 1942, following graduation from Loretto Academy. She earned her B.A. from Alverno College and her M.A. in History from Fordham University, where she also pursued doctoral studies. She joined the Alverno College History faculty in 1955 and served as department chair before becoming College President in 1968, a position from which she recently retired. Together with Sister Austin Doherty, she initiated and supervised curriculum reform that was strongly influenced by their work with secular women's organization. Based on their understanding that effective education for women must take account of the social realities of women's lives, the two Sisters engaged in a long process of faculty re-education and curriculum reform. Alverno replaced grades with achievement assessment, involved students in self-assessment, and created a close connection with local businesses that enabled students to go from college to jobs by a graduated combination of academic learning and internships. Alverno's educational plan has proven spectacularly successful in helping racial minorities and economically deprived students to complete higher education. It has become a nationally acclaimed model. Sister Joel Read has been highly honored by awards and appointments, among them a presidential appointment to the National Endowment for the Humanities (1978–84).

Sister Austin Doherty, the daughter of Irish immigrants, entered her order in her mid-twenties and taught high school and college courses, while earning her M.A. in History from Marquette University and her Ph.D in Psychology at Loyola University in 1968. Her work within her religious order in transforming the role of women religious following Vatican II strengthened and inspired her educational pioneering.

She chaired the Psychology Department at Alverno College for seven years. As Assistant Dean for Curriculum Development from 1975 to 1978 she led the college's transformation from a standard liberal arts college to a model in competence-based learning. Since 1982 she has been Vice-President for Academic Affairs.

Gene (Cohen) Boyer (1925–2003) was born in Milwaukee, Wisconsin. She graduated from high school at age sixteen and held a number of jobs while attending college. She interrupted her study of journalism when she married Burt Boyer and followed him in his career as a baseball player in the military. In 1949 they returned to Wisconsin and settled in Beaver Dam, after their daughter was born. They purchased a furniture store, which they ran jointly. Gene Boyer was Jewish and became aware of sexism in her synagogue, where women were required to be seated upstairs only. She began her public activism when she was denied membership in the local Chamber of Commerce. She responded by organizing protests and finally founding a Women's Division of the Chamber. She helped to form a Wisconsin CSW. A founder and Board member of NOW, Boyer attended the Houston Conference in 1977 and was a leader in various women's organizations in Wisconsin. She has been widely recognized and honored.

Nancy (Farley) Wood (1903–2003) was born in Missouri. A high school math and physics teacher for several years after her graduation from Central Missouri Teachers College, she earned an M.A. in Education from the University of Chicago in 1927. She married John Wood and was a full-time homemaker and mother of five, while her husband held various jobs in Illinois. During World War II the family moved back to Chicago and Wood worked on the Manhattan Project of the University of Chicago, making radiation detectors. Unlike her male coworkers, she was not recruited by private industry after the war, so she founded her own company, producing radiation detectors.

She began working on women's issues in Zonta, an international organization for the advancement of women in business and the professions, in the 1950s and joined several women's advocacy groups. She was a member of the Illinois Committee on the Status of Women. A charter member of NOW, she served on the National Board from 1967 to 1975 and founded Chicago NOW.

Class Syllabus for Workshop on the Construction of Deviant Out-Groups (Chapter 7)

Class I. A New Conceptual Model for Dealing with "Differences"

1. Get acquainted.
2. Exercise I. What's Your Name? (see Appendix C).
3. Lecture: A General Model for the Creation of Deviant Groups.
   - Distribute copies of the model to each student. Go over model item by item, using illustrative material for each point.
4. Discussion of model.
   - Then discussion of "who benefits?" Answers: a) the dominant elite; b) individual members of the dominant group; c) members of other target groups.
   - A and b benefit by having better access to resources and property. All three, by self-definition—they are *better*; they are not the Other. Great group cohesiveness ("us" against "them"). Also, by scapegoating the out-group, societal problems are pushed aside and need not be dealt with, which feels comforting.
5. Discuss reading and research assignments.

Class II. Considering Patriarchy

Readings due for Class II:

Gerda Lerner, *The Creation of Patriarchy* (New York: Oxford University Press, 1986), chap. 4, "The Woman Slave."

Muriel Rukeyser "What do we see?" in *The Collected Poems of Muriel Rukeyser* (New York: McGraw Hill, 1978), 492–93.

1. Lecture: The Creation of Patriarchy.
2. Discussion of lecture.
3. Reading and discussion of Rukeyser poem.
4. Group formation: Assign people to groups of three. Each group will specialize in one or more of the topics below, and apply the model and the readings to their group topic.
   - Groups will prepare a short report (15 minutes) on their topic, which will be presented to the entire class later in the workshop.

• Topics for selection: Hispanics, Native Americans, Ethnics, Gays and Lesbians, Handicapped, physically different, fat, old.

Class III. Case Studies: Heretics and Jews

Readings due for Class III:

Leslea Newman, "A Letter to Harvey Milk," in Joyce Antler (ed.), *AMERICA AND I: Short Stories by American Jewish Women Writers* (Boston: Beacon Press, 1990), 324–39.

Evelyn T. Beck, "From 'Kike' to 'Jap': How Misogyny, Anti-Semitism, and Racism Construct the Jewish American Princess," in Margaret Andersen and Patricia Hill Collins (eds.), *Race, Class and Gender: An Anthology* (Belmont, Calif.: Wadsworth, 1992), 88–95.

1. Exercise II. Experience of "Difference" (see Appendix C).
2. Lecture: The History of Heretics and Medieval Jews.
3. Discussion of lecture.
4. Applying the model:
   • Heretics:
     a) They have different beliefs and religious practices.
     b) Mark them by their lifestyle—absence from regular churches. Also by their beliefs—set up inquiries, inquisitions, witchcraft tribunals.
     c) Outlawed by church and civil law. Death penalty in twelfth century, nearly universal in fifteenth century. Forced to go underground, which in turn is held against them. Accused of wild excesses, orgies, sexual perversions, blood guilt.
     d) No exceptions, except for those who convert or betray others.
     e) Scapegoats for plague (fourteenth century), defeats, and economic crisis. Albigensians are wiped out by end of fourteenth century. The suppressed ideas constantly resurface in new forms until the Reformation.
   • Medieval Jews:
     a) They do not accept Christ; they will not convert. Where assimilated, society marked them—hats and garments.
     b) Heathens; Christ killers; blood guilt; polluters.
     c) Forbidden from owning land, becoming artisans or craftsmen, attending universities; forced to live by peddling old clothes and rags; money-lending; pay higher taxes; forced to lend money to kings. As a result of these restrictions they are seen as exclusive, secretive, conspirators, stingy—Shylock; bankers and pawnshop owners.

d) Exception—Jews protected by kings and nobles.

e) Scapegoats for Black Plague; treated as heathens during Crusades; usury.

f) By 1400 Europe, except for Spain and Portugal, is free of Jews due to succeeding holocausts. Spain and Portugal expel all Jews by 1492.

5. Discussion of modern anti-Semitism.

6. Discussion of readings.

Class IV. The Deviant Majority: The Case of Women

Reading due for Class IV:

Lerner, *Creation of Patriarchy*, chap. 5, "The Wife and the Concubine."

1. Lecture: Women as a Group.
   - Their status, their definition as Other. Gender role indoctrination. Systematic discrimination against women in access to resources, in education, property rights and legal/civic rights. Historic overview of women's fights for emancipation. Where are we today?
2. Discussion: Applying the model to women:
   a) Difference visible and functional. Make it excuse for dominance. Women stay with children; need protection in warfare societies.
   b) Sexual division of labor, once functional, now becomes excuse for dominance. Women are weaker. Conquered women, forcibly removed from protective kin, become slaves and concubines.
   c) Laws to protect males' sexual and property rights in marriage. Double standard. Charges against them: women intrigue, are treacherous, less intelligent, more emotional, use their sexuality to secure privileges.
   d) The exception—one's own mother, wife, or sister.
   e) Control women to protect the state. Divide women into respectable and nonrespectable; give privileges to respectable, scapegoat the others. Prostitution and regulation.
   - Discussion points: Sexual deviance and distinctions; economic/legal discrimination; mothering and housework; educational disadvantaging; differences between women and other groups.

Class V. Race as Deviance

Readings due for Class V:

James Baldwin, "Stranger in the Village," in *Notes of a Native Son* (Boston: Beacon Press, 1955), 159–75.

Audre Lorde, "The Uses of Anger: Women Responding to Racism," in Audre Lorde, *Sister Outsider* (Trumansburg, N.Y.: The Crossing Press, 1984), 124–33.

Gerda Lerner (ed.), *Black Women in White America: A Documentary History* (New York City: Vintage Books, 1973), 172–93.

1. Lecture: Overview of African American History in the United States.
   - Emphasis on turning points in definition of "race," such as "who is a Negro?" Nat Turner rebellion and its aftermath; the right to bear arms; the failure of Reconstruction; *Brown vs. Board of Education*; the civil rights movement and its aftermath; black nationalism and separatism.
2. Applying the model to African Americans:
   a) Color and hair are used to define the difference. The Africans arrive as enslaved persons. Their status as slaves is used to reinforce their difference from the dominant. They are characterized and treated differently from white servants and immigrants.
   b) Visible racial characteristics are used as markings of inferiority. In absence of visible distinctions, slave status is used. U.S. law does not recognize mulattoes. The characteristics of inferiority are assigned to all members of the group. Lifelong inherited enslavement is institutionalized in 1650 Virginia law on definition of a slave: the child follows the mother.
   c) Slaves are severely restricted in access to resources, which come only through their masters. They are denied any kind of legal standing and family integrity. Black women are sexually available to white men. Black men and women have no rights over their children. Education, even reading and writing, is forbidden to them. In later generations, the resulting cultural differences are used to reinforce the stereotype of inferiority and to blame it on the enslaved group. After slavery ends, the same pattern of institutional discrimination persists.
   d) In slavery, exceptions were made for favored house servants, Mammies, and particularly skilled craftsmen among the enslaved. After slavery, the pattern of making personal exceptions persists and serves to uphold the system despite its contradictions.
   e) African Americans have served as scapegoats throughout their history in the United States, being blamed for fires, riots, the spread of diseases, criminality, and sexual aggressiveness. As late as the twentieth century, black soldiers returning from honorable service would face such accusations, some of them resulting in lynchings. Stereotyping the entire group as ignorant, improvident, irresponsible, and mentally inferior has been used as an excuse for scapegoating.
3. Discuss the readings in terms of the application to the model.

Class VI. Dominance and the Structure of Power

Reading due for Class VI:

June Jordan, "Report from the Bahamas (1982)," in *On Call: Political Essays* (Boston: South End Press, 1985), 39–49.

1. Lecture: Dominance and the Structure of Power.
   • Lecture deals with difference between personal and institutional discrimination. Show the structures of power and how they mutually reinforce one another. Follow Virginia Woolf's argument in *Three Guineas* to show this in regard to education, religion, political power, and military power.
2. Discuss how this impacts on groups we have studied. Include welfare mothers, gays and lesbians, AIDS victims, recent immigrants, Sierra Club in Alaska, Colonials, West Indian Blacks.
3. Exercise III A and B. Re-definition and Chair Exercise (see Appendix C).
   • Discuss this exercise and make connection to material already learned.
4. Discuss the reading.

Class VII. The Arbitrariness of the Target Groups

Readings due for Class VII:

Audre Lorde, "There is No Hierarchy of Oppressions," in *Council on Interracial Books for Children Bulletin*, vol. 14, nos. 3–4 (1983).

Peggy McIntosh, "White Privilege: Unpacking the Invisible Knapsack," *Peace and Freedom* (July/August 1989): 10–12.

Lori Punske and Alex Montoya, "Anytown," in *Teaching Tolerance*, vol. 1, no. 32 (Fall 1992): 50–61.

1. Exercise IV. Target Groups: Where Do I Fit In? (see Appendix C).
2. Discuss: Do we each belong to one group? What if we belong to more than one group?
3. Examine the categories used in this course. Discuss some of the terms: race, racial formation, historical experience, women, gender, Jew, Latino/a, Asiatic, Native-American, homosexual, welfare mothers. The point of the discussion is to illuminate the similarities in the social construction of deviant out-groups.
4. Groups that were formed in Class II report on their work.

Class VIII. How Systems of Dominance Work

Reading due for Class VIII:
Gerda Lerner, *Why History Matters: Life and Thought* (New York: Oxford University Press, 1997), chap. 11, "Re-Thinking the Paradigm: Class/Race."

1. Lecture: Systems of Dominance.
   - The system of hierarchical dominance depends on creating deviant out-groups. System works only by giving dominated enough benefits so they will cooperate with the system. This is done by giving each group some benefits over members of other groups. Privileges and obligations are carefully balanced so everyone seems to get something. Everyone has his/her own *Other*.
2. Detail how this works or does not work for some of the groups we have discussed. Let the class determine the list to be discussed.
3. Discussion of interdependent systems of dominance.
   - Eighteenth-century United States: White servants, severely oppressed, are free after their indenture. By outlawing white/black intermarriage, the state institutionalizes race discrimination. Black servants are fixed in life-long slavery.
   - Nineteenth century: Legal discrimination against African Americans continues. Compare integration of European immigrants, such as Irish, to persistent disadvantaging of Blacks.
   - Twentieth century: Discuss changes due to civil rights movement and backlash that claims "race" no longer is an issue.
4. Continue discussion of privileges of the dominant. Compare white privilege and male privilege. Use material in reading for illustration.

Class IX. Resisting "Deviance" and Its Effects

1. Lecture: How to Combat the Creation of Deviants and Their Scapegoating.
   a) Accept difference; cherish it. Give it space and expression. Don't assume or subsume or ignore.
   b) Avoid stigmatizing people—no single person represents the group; no person is responsible for anyone but him/herself.
   c) Be sensitive. Recognize the long history of pain for each group. Do not compare victimization of different groups or rank it.
   d) Allow for disagreements. No litmus test for politically correct positions. No guilt-tripping. Feeling guilty paralyzes; it solves no problems.

e) Remember that we are all potential members of different deviant groups: the aged, the handicapped, the outsider, the one who disagrees.

f) Interfere in institutional discrimination whenever possible.

Class X. Throwing Sand in the Gears of the Monster

Assignment for last session: Students bring examples from their own work dealing with discrimination, sexism, racism, homophobia—emphasis on how to combat it.

1. Discussion of personal examples given in the assignment. Can we add to the list?
2. Discuss differences between institutionalized discrimination and personal acts of discrimination. Why is it important to make that distinction? Human rights must be fought for and practiced at home. Discuss that proposition.
3. Evaluation of the course and suggestions for improvement.

A printable version of this syllabus can be found at www.uncpress.unc.edu.

Group Exercises for Workshop on the Construction of Deviant Out-Groups (Chapter 7)

Exercise I. What's Your Name?

Give each participant a piece of paper and ask him/her to fold it in half vertically. Each person puts his/her first name at the top of the page. Write on the left side whatever you can think of regarding your name. Don't re-read it. (2 minutes) Then read it over and comment on what you've written, using the right side of the page. (3 minutes)

Turn to the person on your left, who will be your partner. It is important that this be a person you do not already know. Adjust the seating if necessary in order to accomplish this.

Each twosome goes into a corner or separate space. The first person reads her/his comments from the left side of the page. The partner repeats what he/she heard. Then do the same for the right side of the page. Repeat this process for the other partner, then discuss what you have learned. (10 minutes)

Return to circle (whole group). Each person reports not on her/his own paper, but on that of the partner. The group discusses reactions. What is the basis for each identity? What is determined by the naming parents, what by the child? Does one's name determine one's self-regard? Why is naming so powerful?

Note: This exercise accomplishes two aims. It makes the group acquainted with each person and builds group cohesion. It also powerfully raises the matter of identity, name-calling, naming, and their consequences.

Exercise II. How Have I Experienced Being "Different" in a Way That Implies Inferiority?

Each participant tells an anecdote in response to this question. This is followed by taking three anecdotes at a time as a topic for class discussion.

Note: This exercise serves to provide the basis for emotional empathy with oppressed target groups by showing the ubiquity of oppressive experiences. It also helps to create trust in the group. Ground rules to be followed: Do not interpret another person's experience for him/her; no hurtful or critical comments; share, if you have had a similar experience; no competition in victimization; give people space to draw their own conclusions.

Exercise III. A) Re-Definition

Start out with an empty bottle. Ask each person to mime different ways the bottle can be used (examples: The bottle is a baby—rock it. The bottle is a gun—aim it). Other people find their own use of the bottle. No talking. Then move on to Chair exercise.

Exercise III. B) Chairs and the Structure of Power

Who is the Boss? Use five chairs, arrange them randomly in space. Ask one person to rearrange them so as to make one chair more powerful than the others. Other people improvise and improve on that arrangement.

Now put people with the chairs, one after the other, in such a way that each person becomes most powerful. After a person has chosen a position, he/she stays in it. Then the next person enters and makes himself the most powerful. No talking. Other people have to leave the arrangement as is, then find their own way of becoming the boss.

Discuss the redefining of objects. One can rewrite the script. One is not bound to follow the script. Ritual and placement can enhance power. Examples: the boss behind the big desk; having to stand, while another person sits; the teacher on an elevated platform in front of the students; the speaker at the lectern.

Note: This is a fun exercise with serious implications. It frees up creativity and illuminates the absurdity of some well-accepted rules and practices. It opens up the group to the need for re-definition.

Exercise IV. Target Groups: Where Do I Fit In?

DEFINING GROUPS	TARGET GROUPS
male	female
white, U.S., Christian	other races or ethnicities
middle-class or above	lower-middle-class or poor
healthy	ailing or disabled
traditional	radical
heterosexual	homosexual, transgendered
sober	alcoholic, now or earlier
normal weight	fat
never in trouble with law	ex-offender
legal immigrant	illegal immigrant
adult, below 70 years	above 70 years

The class can add categories. Then ask each participant to write down to which target group he or she now belongs or conceivably might belong in the future. It is possible to define oneself as having several identities.

Discuss your own definition with a partner. Then listen to your partner's story. Or else, if the group so decides, discuss the results in the group as a whole. It is important to create an atmosphere in which people do not feel their privacy is being invaded.

Note: This exercise may encounter considerable resistance. Some people say they cannot understand it; others think it does not apply to them. Once completed, it has a powerful effect. Participants begin to see ways in which they might become victims. It helps them to understand how arbitrary the divisive categories are and it helps them to focus not on the obvious "differences," but on the way in which the system of discrimination works to turn difference into dominance.

A printable version of these exercises can be found at www.uncpress.unc.edu.

Acknowledgments

I owe special thanks to my main readers, Linda Kerber and Alice Kessler-Harris. They offered more than several superb critical readings and many suggestions for improvements; they encouraged me throughout the process of revising and gave me new perspectives on how some of my arguments fit into the concerns of a younger generation of students and general readers. I feel honored by their faith in this book.

My daughter Stephanie Lerner Lapidus read the entire manuscript and offered many helpful suggestions. I especially benefited from her viewpoint as someone outside of the profession of history and her insistence that I strengthen the auto-biographical aspects of the book. Thank you, Stephanie, for what you did for this book, over and above what you do for me in giving support, encouragement, and love each day of my years of aging. The steady support and love of my son, Dan Lerner, of his wife Elizabeth, and of my grandchildren sustain and anchor me through sickness and health in my determination to continue my life as a writer.

I gratefully acknowledge the special contribution made to this book by my son-in-law, Todd Lapidus. The title of this book and the concept implicit in the title were the result of a long conversation I had with Todd, whose expertise as an educator in the field of business management enabled him to understand the connection between theory and practice, which is the core of this work, at a time when I could not see it as clearly. Thank you, Todd.

The chapter on Sarah Lawrence, Chapter 3, drew on the shared memories of several of the participants in the Graduate Program. I am greatly appreciative of the help provided by Amy Swerdlow, Eva Kollisch, Alice Kessler-Harris, and Carole Artigiani. In addition to sharing their memories, Amy Swerdlow and Eva Kollisch gave the chapter a critical reading that helped me improve it. My continuing contact and friendship with Sarah Lawrence students Pam Elam, Bonnie Johnson, Jan Simpson, Joy Jones, and Peggy Pascoe have kept memories alive and provided continuity that goes well beyond my actual time at the college.

I am also indebted to Natalie Rose, who shared her M.A. essay on the history of the Sarah Lawrence Graduate Program with me, providing me with an alternative view. The 2004 reunion on the twenty-fifth anniversary of our Summer Institute in Women's History for Leaders of Women's Organization provided me with new understanding of the transformative power of educating women in their history, as I saw the astonishing accomplishments of my former students that they credited to the intensive two weeks of training we had offered. Their accomplishments and enthusiasm inspired me to record my memories of the Sarah Lawrence Program in this chapter.

The oral history of Midwestern leaders of the modern women's movement described in Chapter 5 was based on the excellent research and interviewing skills of Jennifer Frost, Marie Laberge, and Joyce Follet. The latter has carried this project forward by creating a powerful video documentary, *Step by Step: Building a Feminist Movement, 1941–1977*, that tells the story of eight of the women leaders who were interviewed.

Several of the other chapters are grounded in the collective work of women of earlier generations and of twentieth-century feminist educators and students. It is impossible here to credit by name all who contributed by their work and spirit to what is recorded in this book, but I hope I have shown how much my own thought and practice have benefited from and been influenced by the work of others.

At the University of North Carolina Press, Kate Torrey patiently nurtured this book through several versions until it found its final form. Her sharp and insightful criticism and her painstaking insistence on formal elegance and unity of style made this a far better book than I alone could have produced. I deeply appreciate her contribution and her support of both the work and its author.

Lastly, I am grateful to Ron Maner for turning what could have been a pedestrian task into a cooperative endeavor by his tact and superb skill as a copyeditor.

Index